DIY COLOUR SERIES

HOME BUILDER

AURA EDITIONS

CONTENTS

Editor: Helen Davies
Art editor: Graham Beehag

Published by Aura Editions
2 Derby Road, Greenford, Middlesex

Produced by Marshall Cavendish Books Limited
58 Old Compton Street, London W1V 5PA

ISBN 0 86307 478 2

Typeset in Garamond by Quadraset Limited, Avon
Printed and bound in Italy by L.E.G.O. S.p.a.

CHAPTER 1

KITCHENS

Constructing a fashionable and well ordered brick-built kitchen from scratch is not as difficult as it may seem—and the style and layout can easily be adapted to your own specific needs. Cladding the walls is just as easy, using decorative wallboards which you glue or nail into place. To complete the constructional work you can erect your own custom-built oven and hob unit and open up a serving hatch between the kitchen and dining room.

EASY-BUILD KITCHEN

When it comes to kitchens, most people would rather add new life to what they've got than go to the trouble of rebuilding the units and worktops from scratch. But with Home Builder's ingenious system you can do both—at a budget price.

The kitchen on the right may look like an expensive designer's dream. But the system it's based on—using low-cost bricks, chipboard and wood—is actually cheaper to build than ready-made units looking half as good. It's easy to build too: there's no complicated jointing or special techniques to master. And it's versatile: once you've grasped the main constructional principles detailed overleaf you can build new units to fit around your existing appliances, plan a built-in hob or cooker unit, add new features like a breakfast bar, or replan the kitchen from scratch—the choice is yours.

How the system works

In planning the kitchen hard and fast rules are few, but there are some worth careful consideration before you start. One decisive factor is whether the floor is made from solid concrete or from wooden floorboards and joists. If it is solid, you can build the walls straight on to it.

If the floor is wooden—take up the floor covering to see—you may need to strengthen the floor to prevent it bending under the added weight. But if you don't want to go to this trouble, you can build the units to take wooden panels in place of the brick walls—veneered board edged with solid pine, melamine board or plain chipboard clad with imitation brick tiles are all possibilities. If you select one of these, weight should be no problem.

When planning the layout, bear in mind that the heart of the kitchen is the area between the refrigerator, sink and cooker—what is often referred to as the 'work triangle'. This should be small enough to minimize the need for movement, but with enough space to provide work surfaces for cooking and food preparation.

When you have decided on a general layout and what appliances and fittings—like a fridge, cupboard doors and wire baskets—to include, draw a detailed plan of where each item goes. Double-check positions and dimensions, making sure you take account of awkward shapes, like boxed-in service pipes or chimney breasts.

Once you have completed the plans, clear the relevant areas of the kitchen and mark each item's position on the wall and floor. You can then work to these marks.

First, mark the positions of the brick walls on the floor in chalk or pencil, then use a tape measure and spirit level to mark the height of the work surfaces all around the walls. If your floor is uneven, you will level it up automatically by working to the marks of the new work surfaces.

Before you begin building, remove the skirting board by prising it from the wall with a crowbar or claw hammer. Tap your lever between the two, then gently prise the skirting board from the wall at a number of points. Protect the wall surface by levering against a scrap of wood.

The unit walls

If your design includes them, build the brick walls first. Use ready-mixed mortar: a 40kg bag is enough for about 50 bricks.

Each course is made from three bricks. You must cut one of them to make the wall

1 *Build the new walls up to the marks you have made. When dry, paint them with emulsion*

2 *Work to a line drawn level with the top of the new brick walls*

match the width of the worktop. The design uses a worktop 610mm wide which complements the melamine-faced shelves and the dividing walls.

The front edges of the walls must at no point stand proud of the work surfaces, so make sure that the first course of bricks is correctly positioned.

As you build each wall, use a spirit level to ensure it stays upright. Keep a close check too on the finished height. The thickness of the mortar courses must be an even 10mm, so that for bricks with a nominal

thickness of 65mm the actual thickness of each course is 75mm. Twelve courses of brickwork takes the total height to 900mm—the ideal worktop height, and the right height to accept modern standard size under-counter appliances like fridges and dishwashers.

On alternate courses, you will need to cut a brick in half to make the front edge level with the course below. To keep the edge square, point the brick's broken edge away from the exposed outward edge of the wall.

If you are using wooden end panels instead of brick, cut these 900mm long from 610mm wide material. Stand them vertically with the aid of a spirit level and screw them to the walls and floor using 50mm steel angle brackets on the inside face.

Constructing the frames

Both the top and bottom frames of the units are made from the same material—50mm × 25mm PAR (Planed All Round) softwood. Where possible they are simply butt jointed, but you will have to cut notches for dividers and overlaps.

Each frame is made from two long pieces at front and back (rails), joined by shorter crosspieces (struts). Saw the rails to length, having first marked them with a try square.

Referring to your plan, mark out on the rails every point where you will want a divider to fit on the finished unit. You must make a notch at each of these points. The dividers are 15mm thick, so cut notches to accept them in the bottom of both rails.

Use an offcut of the board to mark the sides of the notches and make them approximately 25mm deep. Saw down the sides of each notch, then use a 15mm wide (or less) chisel to cut out the waste. Any roughness in the cutting will be concealed later.

To make the joint, notch the bottom edge of one rail and the top edge of the other at the point where they need to cross. Make the notch as wide as the wood is thick—lay

When the frame runs along both walls of a corner, or when it forms a right angle for the breakfast bar, make similar notches so that the rails can overlap each other. This makes a much firmer connection than simply butting one frame to another to join them together.

one on top of the other, and mark either side where you need to cut.

Finally, use a No. 8 twist drill to make screw holes in the back rail so it can be fixed to the wall. For a masonry wall, drill holes at approximately 500mm intervals. On a timber framed wall, work out and mark off where the rail will coincide with the wall studs and drill holes for the screws.

To assemble the frames, cut a series of struts. You will need one for each end of the frame, as well as one to fit above each notch. To make sure the finished frame will be the same size as the worktop, lay the rails together on the worktop. Put them on edge, flush with one side of the worktop, then mark the remaining width on to a piece of your frame timber to get the length of strut.

Assemble the frame again in a 'dry run' to re-check that it is the same size as the worktop. Lay it on top of the worktop and make any adjustments that are necessary to make it fit, then glue it together.

Fit the struts between the rails, using woodworking adhesive and two 50mm oval nails to secure each joint. Fit a strut over every divider position.

Where the frame rests on one of the new brick walls, site the strut level with the bottom edge of the rail—rather than the top

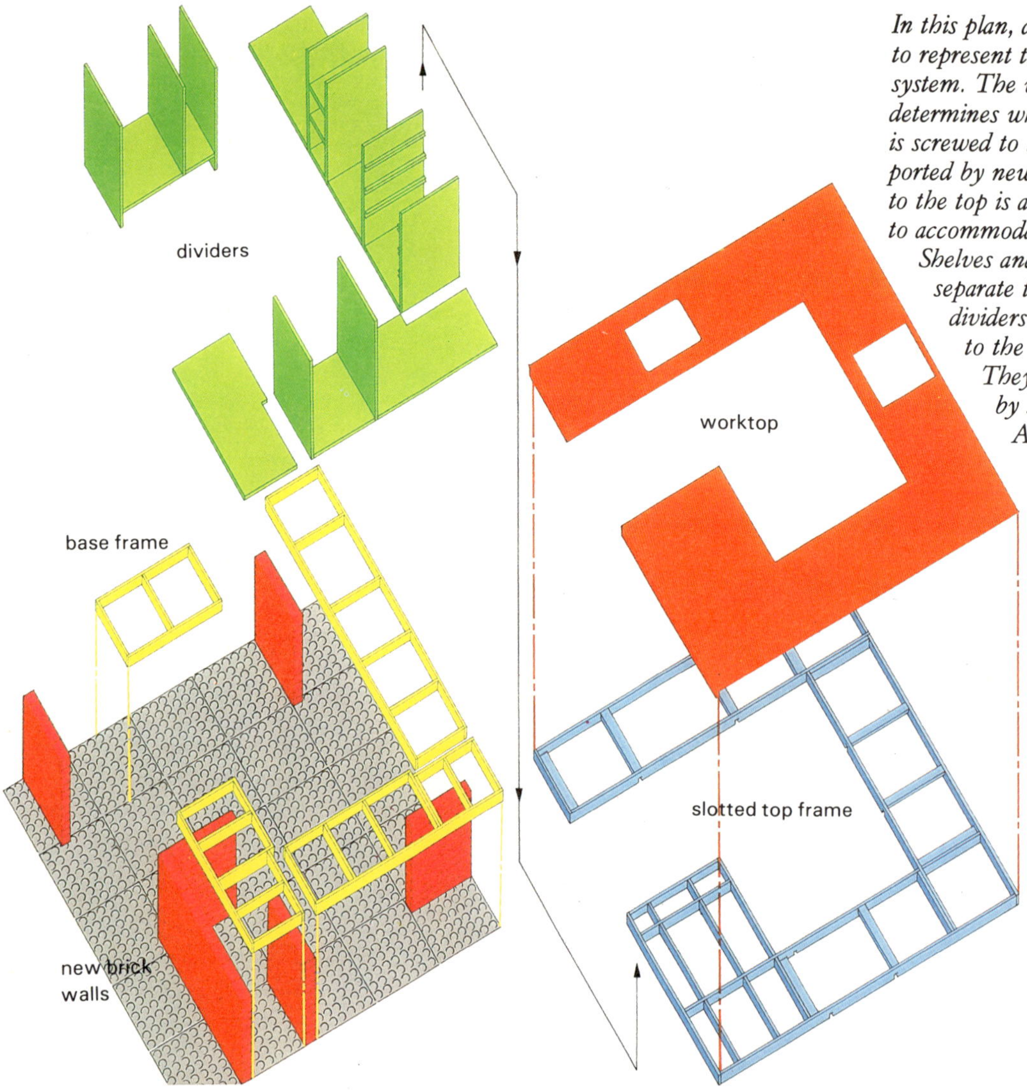

dividers

base frame

worktop

new brick
walls

slotted top frame

In this plan, different colours are used to represent the separate parts of the system. The wooden top frame (blue) determines where everything else goes. It is screwed to the kitchen walls and supported by new brick walls (red). Attached to the top is a work surface (orange), cut to accommodate the sink and cooker hob. Shelves and vertical dividers (green) separate the under-counter. The dividers run from the top frame to the base frame (yellow). They are held at the top by slots cut into the top frame. At the bottom they are 'trapped' in place by the lowest shelves which simply sit on the base frame. Similar panels can also be run down to the floor to form end walls. Make the distance between dividers as long or as short as you like. Fit shelves, appliances or kitchen fittings in between

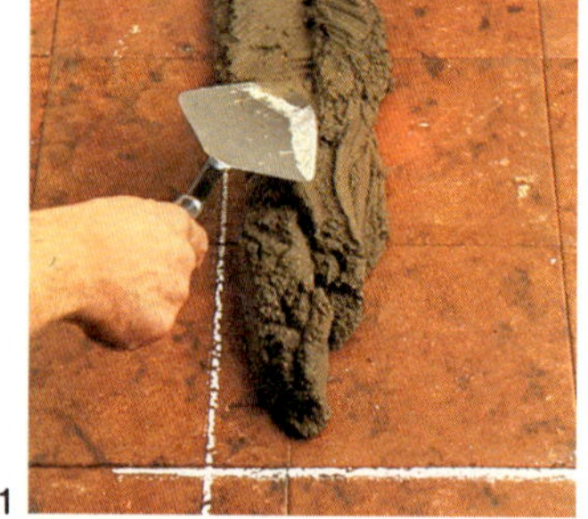

1 Use chalk to mark the floor. Scoop mortar into place, forming a V-shaped recess. 2 Scrape the mortar hard onto the end of the brick. Trim the edges to stop it falling off. 3 To cut a brick, first score marks on all sides. Then strike one side hard to cut. 4 Tap each brick down into the mortar. For long walls, use string to align the front edge. 5 Level across the top of each brick. Make the bubble lie exactly between the lines. 6 To finish the joints, use a rounded stick or 'point' with the edge of your trowel

3 *Cut notches in the top frame where you want dividers. Any roughness will be concealed later by the fascia*

4 *Where rails overlap, make similar notches on top of one and on the bottom of the other rail*

5 *Fix the struts to the rails with woodworking adhesive and nails*

6 *Add support struts to the ends and above each divider slot*

7 *Drill countersunk fixing holes in both the top and base frames. Mark the fixing positions*

8 *Insert wallplugs into the holes you have made and screw the top frame firmly in place*

9 *Screw through the edge of the base frame—use wallplugs for fixing to solid floors*

10 *Alternatively, fit steel angle brackets to the frame and the floor*

edge. You will then be able to drill through the strut, drill holes in the top of the wall, and screw the strut to the top of the wall.

Make the frames for the base, but bear in mind that they will be shorter than the top frames—they sit inside the brick walls rather than on top. Also, they do not require notching because the dividers simply sit on top of the frame.

If you have not built brick walls on both sides of free-standing appliances, like the refrigerator, you will have to let the divider on the other side run down to the floor. To do so, make the base frame shorter by 15mm than the notch above. This will allow you to fit a piece of the board as a 'wall' between the appliance and the unit.

When the frames are complete, prop or locate them in position and mark the places where you need to make fixing holes.

Remove the frames and drill holes to accept screws. For a solid wall or floor, use a No. 8 masonry drill to drill holes 25mm deep and then insert plastic wallplugs. Use 50mm No. 8 screws to secure the rails.

For a timber framed wall use a 2mm twist drill to bore pilot holes in the studs, then secure the rails with 50mm No. 8 screws.

In either case you will need to drill and plug the new brick walls so you can screw the ends of the frames to them. If, on the other hand, you are using wooden end panels you can screw the frames directly to them. Alternatively, it may be easier to use steel angle brackets to make the fixing.

Shelves and dividers

These are all made from melamine-faced chipboard (such as Handiboard or Conti-board) which is 15mm thick and comes in a variety of widths. If you use 610mm wide boards (the same as the worktops), there's less cutting to be done.

For the dividers, measure the height between the base frame and the top of the notches, then cut to these lengths.

If you need to make end walls to fit either side of a free-standing appliance, saw a divider so that it reaches from the notch to the floor. Slot in the divider, then drill and screw it to the base frame.

Cut the bases and shelves in the same way, after measuring the lengths needed between the divider notches.

With the dividers and shelves cut to length, drill holes in the dividers to accept the shelf supports. Use ordinary plastic shelf support plugs which simply tap into holes drilled in the dividers. Drill the holes with the recommended twist bit size and use a piece of tape as a depth gauge.

Slot the dividers into their notches in the top frame and slide them home. Drop the bottom shelves into position—you may need to screw end wall dividers into place.

Fit any fixed items into position as well. If you leave it until later, you may make more work for yourself. At this point, you can

To save time, cut a template from some old card or hardboard to fit your dividers. Measure the position at which you want to install shelves, then drill holes in the template as a marking guide. Note, though, that you cannot use this method if you want your shelves at random heights.

slide the dividers in and out with ease.

For the same reason, take care of any plumbing or wiring connections before the

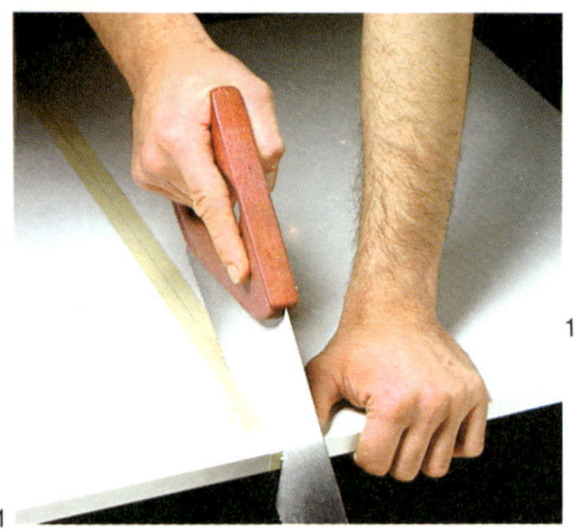

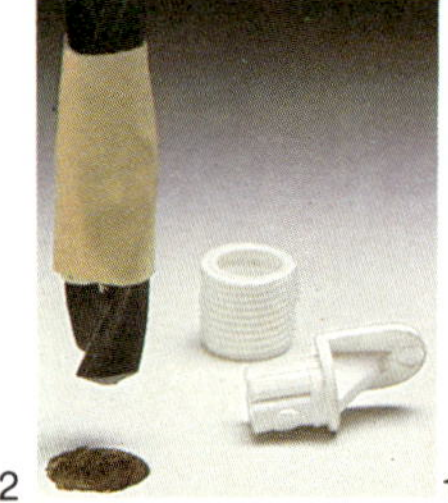

worktop is permanently fixed in place. It is best if fittings like the sink are positioned temporarily so you can work out the run of the connections. Cover any unsightly wires or pipework with panels of melamine board screwed between the dividers and shelves. Make sure when you do this that you can remove them for servicing.

Cutting melamine

For accurate marking, you need a try square, a ruler or other straight edge, a tape measure and a pencil. Use a panel saw or one of the power tools—a circular or a jig saw—for the actual cutting. Make sure your power saw is fitted with a blade suitable for cutting chipboard.

For hand sawing, measure and mark with care. Draw a line across one long side first, then down the two shorter edges, finally joining the marks together across the remaining long side of the board.

Choose a work surface that provides a comfortable and firm working height. A portable bench is ideal but a kitchen stool, raised door threshold, the top stair or one of the walls you have built will do. Any height

11 *Mark, tape over the line, then saw the melamine board for dividers*

12 *Drill holes for shelf plugs. Screw the sleeve into the hole, then tap the plug into the sleeve*

13 *Slot the dividers into the notches in the frame*

14 *Drop the bottom shelves onto the base frame to 'trap' the dividers*

★ WATCH POINT ★

Use a sheet of paper or card if you do not own a try square. Align one edge with the marked edge of the board, then carefully draw along the other without displacing it.

between your hip and your knee is generally comfortable—you can grip the board with knee and hand. You should be able to move your arm in a straight line from the shoulder so that you can use the full length of the handsaw or guide the power saw along the full length of the cut.

When hand sawing, periodically check below the board to see that the blade has not 'wandered'. If it has, twist the handle of the saw in towards the cutting line as you continue sawing. Use a planer file to remove the rough edge, always working inwards to stop further chipping, particularly when working on corners.

The worktops

The work surfaces are pre-finished square-edged kitchen worktops, 610mm wide.

Although these are not as commonly available as round-edged (post-formed) worktops, manufacturers will usually supply to special order. Many stockists will also cut large, standard size boards to the size you need.

Alternatively make your own worktop from a firm base of 19mm chipboard or blockboard. Get the supplier to cut it into 610mm widths, ready for use. Cover it with the decorative laminate of your choice, cut to size and glued with contact adhesive.

Mark out and cut the work surfaces to length to fit on to the top frame. Tape the cutting line and use a fine-toothed saw.

Whichever method you use, you may need to cut holes in the surface to accept a sink and—if you have one—a cooker hob. For both items, the cutting method is slightly different to that used for the shelves and dividers. The cutting line does not run from one side to the other. Instead, it begins and ends in the middle of the worktop. You

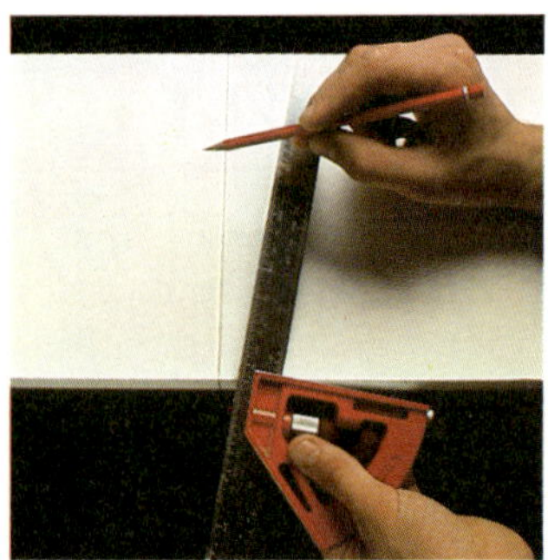

Mark off with a square. A combination square (above) is very useful—slide its blade out to use as a ruler or to extend the cutting line

Cover the marks with masking or adhesive tape to prevent the saw splitting the white surface. Tape around all four sides at once

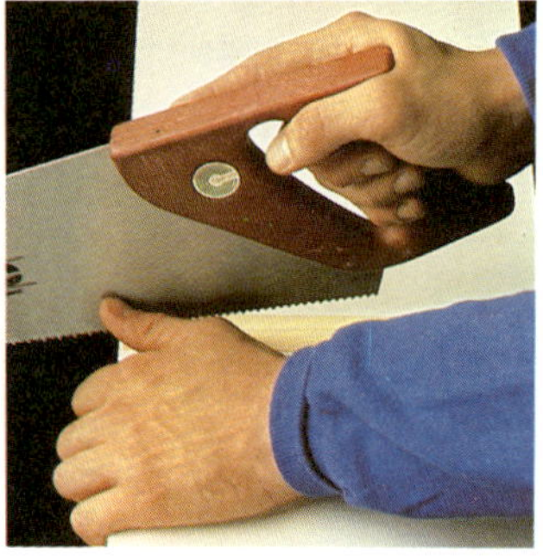

Draw the saw backwards at a low angle to begin the cut. Guide the blade with your thumb until a notch forms over the mark you have made

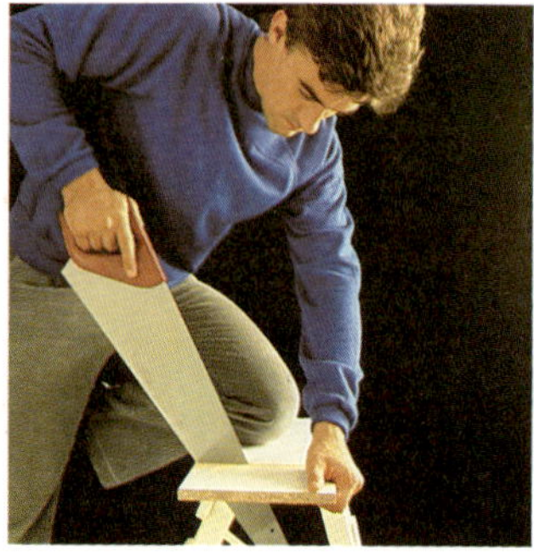

As you approach the end of the cut, support the offcut end of the board. Finish off with a few short, light strokes of the saw

15 *Use a drill, padsaw and panel saw to cut out holes for a sink or hob*

16 *Brackets and chipboard screws join the worktops to the frames*

will need to drill small holes in order to insert the saw and begin the saw cut.

Mark out the cutting lines in the normal way. Tape over the marks, then drill holes at the corners of your cutting line. At this stage, use a twist drill approximately 10mm in diameter.

Use these holes as a way to begin the saw cut. The ideal saw for this job is a power jig saw, fitted with a blade for cutting chipboard. Insert the blade into one of the holes, then cut along the taped cutting line to the next corner.

If you do not own a jig saw, make a series of holes at each corner. Join them as best you can with a padsaw, until you have a hole big enough to insert a panel saw. When this is possible, complete the cut. Any roughness around the edges of the hole does not matter—the sink, cooker or other appliance will conceal it.

If you need to shave any uneven edges, use a planer file. File in towards the centre of

the chipboard, first from one side then from the other, to avoid damaging the surface. Before you fit either the sink or the cooker, squeeze a flexible sealant around the edges of the hole.

To fasten the worktop, screw L-shaped brackets to its underside (use special chipboard screws here) and to the struts or rails. Begin the screw holes with a nail, small drill or bradawl—chipboard can be difficult to drive a screw into.

The final steps

With the top on, the basic skeleton will be complete and you can add the final touches.

If you are building a sink unit, cut to size and fix in place a narrow melamine board to hide the sink's waste trap and fittings. Drill and screw through the dividers and into the ends of the board to hold it in place, or use one of the many types of connector blocks.

The most prominent finishing touch is the stained wood fascia that covers the edge of the worktop and top frame. This should be at least 75mm wide—enough to cover both items and thus hold the dividers in their notches. You can use plain 75mm × 16mm softwood or one of the range of special mouldings—say, skirting or architrave—providing it is the right size.

Cut the wood longer than you need, allowing for an excess of about 50mm. Where the fascia will form an outside corner, cut mitres on the ends of the two adjoining sections so that you need not see the end grains of the wood. Do this with a mitre box or combination square. Simply butt the ends together at an internal corner.

Use any commercial wood stain to stain the fascia to the colour you wish before you fasten it to the edge of the worktop and frame. A wide range of colours is easily available at most DIY stores or department stores. Apply a number of coats, according to the manufacturer's instructions, then nail or screw the fascia to the edge of the kitchen units.

For the base, stain the wood of the frame rather than add a fascia. But make the colour darker as it is much more likely to get scuffed through wear and tear.

With the units complete, add doors if you want them. Use single-cranked hinges, which screw to the surface. Add magnetic catches and door pulls.

All that then remains is to seal the gap between the worktop and the wall with a clear sealant or a combination of this and decorative wood moulding. Fasten the moulding to the wall with wallplugs and screws. If necessary, use a wood filler to hide the screw heads before you apply a finish to the wood. Then fill any remaining gaps between the moulding and worktop with waterproof flexible sealant.

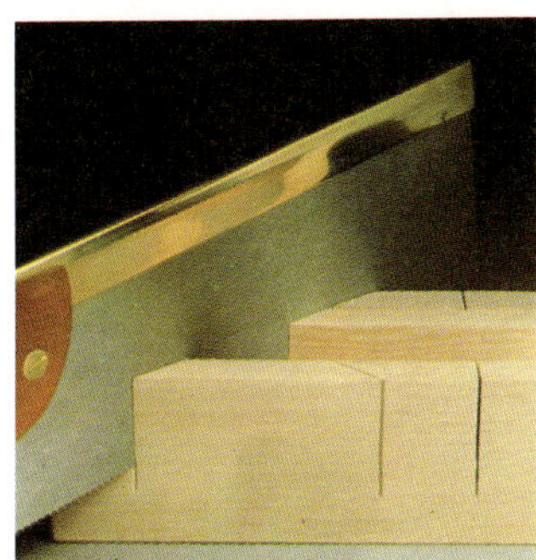

17 *Where the trim forms an external corner, cut mitres on each of the ends with the aid of a mitre box for accuracy*

18 *Squeeze a flexible sealant along the edge of the worktop before nailing the trim in place. Cover the heads with wood filler*

19 *For doors, use the same 15mm melamine board but with iron-on edging. Fit cranked hinges so you can open the door fully*

20 *Mask the work surface and walls to protect them. Then fill any holes with wood filler and sand down before finishing*

The shelves

Fixed to the wall above your work surfaces, shelves provide handy storage for decorative jars, containers and utensils. Easy to reach and easy to build, they make a bright and practical feature for any kitchen. And they also shed light on your cooking, because concealed lights illuminate the counter top.

The materials are all available in standard sizes—all you have to do is cut them to length. With templates to help with dimensions, there's little room for error here. And there's no complicated woodwork, like planing or difficult joints. The easy-fit components and bright wood stains of this system create a clean, modern look that fits in almost anywhere.

How the system fits together

Though it looks like one continuous unit, the shelving system is made in two distinct parts to make it adaptable and easy to install.

Wall-mounted frames are the rigid support for the whole system. These are made by screwing and gluing the sides (A) on to a top shelf (B) and bottom shelf (C). All the sides are notched to accept the light pelmet (D), then drilled for screw holes and shelf supports. The support batten (E) is glued and nailed to the underside of B.

White-faced hardboard is pinned to the back, then the whole frame is fixed to the wall through E. The continuous pelmet (D) is added later to conceal the light.

Loose-fit shelves (all the same length as B) are the other major part of the system. They are supported by push-fit shelf supports. Two fit inside each frame, the rest run from one fixed frame to another.

Every element of the fixed units—D, E and the hardboard backing—is carried over the loose shelves between them to give the unit its appearance of continuity.

If you want to alter the length of the unit to fit your space, adjust the length of the shelves and the support batten to a maximum of 700mm and a minimum of 400mm each. Divide the available space by the number of units you want, allow for the vertical sides, then estimate the common length of the shelves and the support batten.

Bright red-stained wood and wipe-clean white backing—shelves to suit any home. Hidden lights brighten the worktop too. Build the shelves separately, or as part of a complete kitchen re-design

What to buy

All the materials are inexpensive and readily available from timber dealers and DIY stores. Use standard planed-all-round (PAR) softwood sizes for all the woodwork.

With the exception of C, D and E, use 200mm × 25mm boards throughout. Buy eight 1.5m lengths for this design. You also need five 1.5m lengths of 175mm × 25mm board for C and 50mm × 25mm batten for E. D—the continuous pelmet—is made from 2.7m of 75mm × 25mm board.

For the backing material buy two full sheets (2440mm × 1220mm) of 4mm white-faced hardboard. To attach it to the frame you can use either 10mm panel pins or hardboard pins.

To join the fixed frames together, buy 50mm No. 6 countersunk screws and woodworking adhesive. Chipboard screws

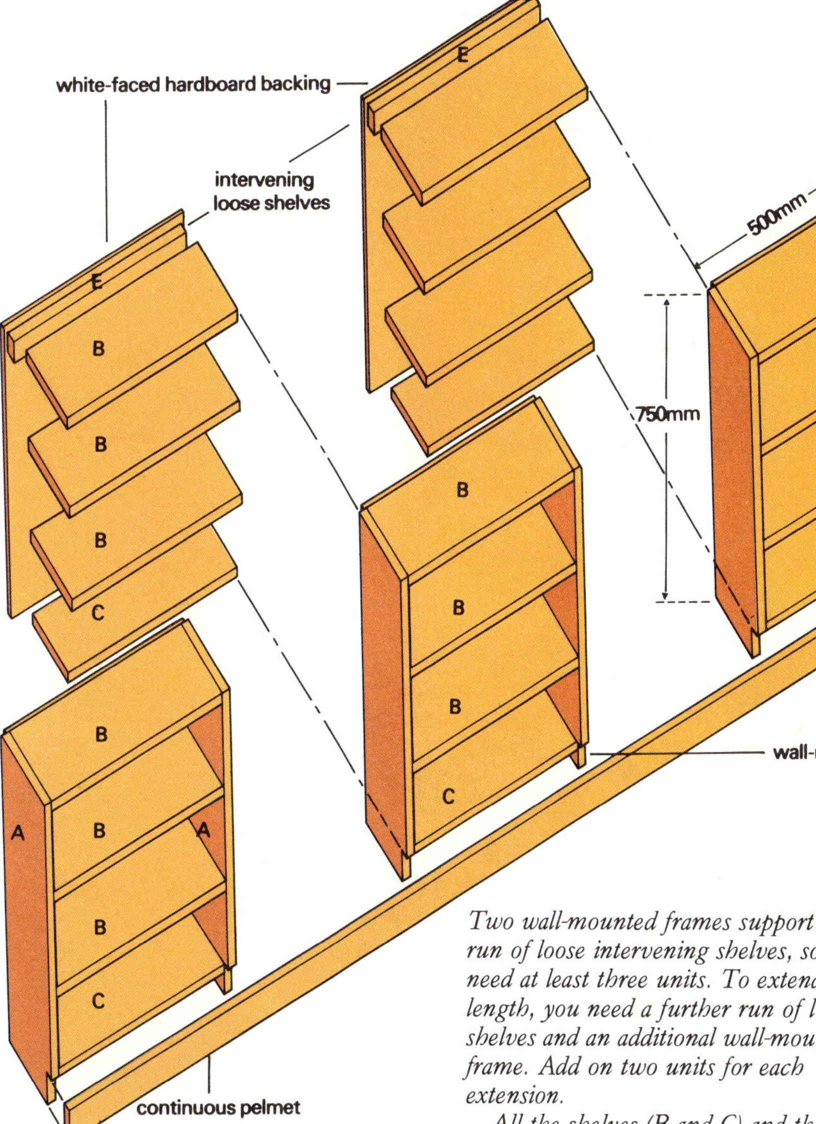

will hold better than conventional screws in the end grain of the boards. To nail D in place you need 50mm oval nails.

All you need to complete the units are the shelf supports. Use simple plastic push-fit supports here—the smaller, the better. To finish the surface, use any one of the wide range of wood stains and varnish obtainable from DIY shops. You'll also need a quantity of 63mm No. 8 screws and wallplugs for the wall fixings.

For the concealed lights, use two ordinary strip lights—those with a pull-cord switch are best. To wire them up, you'll need a plug, some lighting flex and a few cable clips to secure the flex.

Cutting the boards

Make a checklist of all the different parts you need. Mark each board after you have cut it to size.
•From a 200mm × 25mm board, cut one 500mm length for a shelf (B), and one 750mm length for a vertical side (A). Use a try square for accuracy, to ensure that the ends are completely square.

•Use B as a template to cut 14 more shelves. Lay it on top of the uncut board, align the ends and sides, then mark across the top. Lay the shelves on top of each other to check that they are all the same size.
•Cut five 500mm lengths of the 175mm × 25mm board to make the bottom shelves (C) and five 500mm lengths of the 50mm × 25mm batten to make the supports (E).
•Take a small offcut from the 75mm × 25mm timber. Hold this against a corner of A. Mark around it to make

Two wall-mounted frames support every run of loose intervening shelves, so you need at least three units. To extend the length, you need a further run of loose shelves and an additional wall-mounted frame. Add on two units for each extension.

All the shelves (B and C) and the 50mm × 25mm support batten (E) are the same length, but the white-faced hardboard backing is longer to overlap the edges of the vertical pieces (A).

The sizes shown can be altered to suit your space

cutting lines for the notch to accept E.
•Cut out the notch with a panel saw. Then use A as a template to cut three more identical vertical sides.

Making the wall-mounted frames

This part of the job is simplified by using templates as described below.
•Make a hardboard template for drilling the holes. Lay A against a small offcut of hardboard, mark round it, then cut the offcut to size with a panel saw.
•Mark shelf positions on the template. For

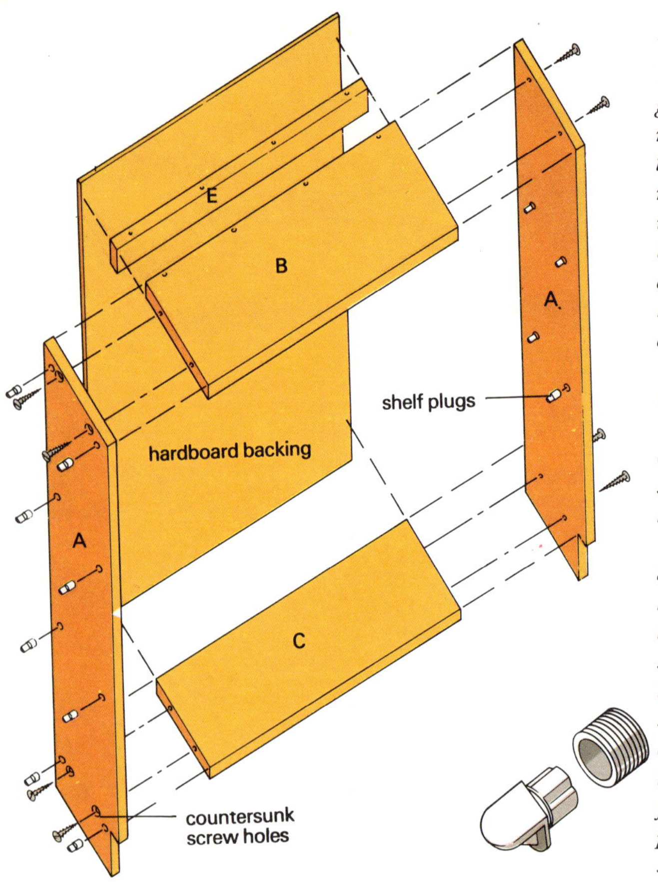

The wall-mounted frame (left). Two sides (A) are screwed and glued to the top (B) and the narrower bottom shelf (C). E, the support batten, is glued and nailed (or screwed) to the underside of B. The hardboard backing fits behind—it is glued and pinned to the frame, then holes are drilled through those already in E.

Shelf support plugs fit inside and outside the frame.

The four sides (two of A, one B and one C), must be square before you fit the hardboard backing

Shelf support plugs (bottom left). There are many suitable types, but choose the smallest—they must be less than half the depth of the wood so that you can fit one on either side. With this type the threaded sleeve fits the hole first, then the plug itself is pushed into the sleeve as the support.

ends, then screw the frame together. Check that the diagonal dimensions are the same to ensure that the frame is square.

• Apply woodworking adhesive to one side and the ends of E. Fit it onto the back of the frame, on the underside of B. Secure it with 50mm oval nails or No. 8 screws, driven through the sides of the frame. Make the other frames in the same way.

• When dry, lay a frame on top of the white-faced hardboard and mark round it for cutting. Using a panel saw, cut the sheet about 25mm narrower than the marked lines so that it does not overlap the sides of the frame. Cut four similar sections to fit behind the loose shelves and the two other frames.

• If you are putting the shelves up on a solid masonry wall, drill from the back and

the top and bottom shelves, mark the positions for two fixing screws 10mm from the end of the template and 50mm in from the sides. Site the intermediate shelves wherever you like. Draw their positions on the template, then mark the positions of the shelf supports 50mm in from each side of the template. They are generally sited immediately below the shelf, but examine the type you are using. Pierce the hardboard at all the hole positions.

• Align the template with each side of A in turn. Mark the wood beneath for reference with a coloured pen.

• Drill 4.0mm countersunk clearance holes for the screws. Then drill holes of the

correct size and depth for the supports. Manufacturers generally specify the size of the hole to make, but otherwise hold a drill bit against one to see. It should be fractionally smaller in diameter than the shelf support plug that you are going to fit.

• To ensure that the hole is the correct depth, set the depth stop on the drill, or mark the bit with tape. Screw in the sleeve, then push in the support.

• Lay two sides (A), a top shelf (B) and a bottom shelf (C) on edge—and in position—on a flat surface. Mark through the clearance holes onto the ends of the shelves. Drill 2.0mm pilot holes at these points, apply woodworking adhesive to the

countersink at the front two 4.5mm holes on the centre line of the support batten. Make holes 100mm from each end.

• If fixing to a hollow wall, make fixing holes where the screws will go straight into the timber framing of the wall. Timber studs are generally at 400mm or 450mm intervals. Tap the wall, or drill small exploratory holes where they will later be concealed by the units, to find them. Mark their positions and then hold the frames against the wall in the positions you want the units. Mark screw holes on each batten to coincide with the positions of the studs, then drill them from the back.

• Finish the frames before attaching the

1 *Use an offcut of the pelmet (D) to mark and cut notches in the sides*

2 *Make a template to fit A. Drill and mark holes for both screws and shelf supports*

3 *Use tape to mark the depth you need to drill for the sleeves of the shelf plugs*

4 *Cut the hardboard to fit the frame. Tape over the mark to prevent splintering*

backing boards. Rub down the wood lightly with fine glasspaper and a sanding block, to smooth it and remove any marks. Then paint it, or colour it with wood stain and apply at least two coats of varnish to seal it. Do the same to the remaining support batten and the loose shelves.

• Apply glue to the back edges of the frames and put the backing boards in place so that there is approximately a 12mm gap down each side. Fasten the boards securely with 10mm panel pins. Mark through the holes in the support battens with a bradawl, then drill through the backing boards.

• Apply glue to the remaining battens and position one on each of the remaining backing boards, the thickness of a shelf down from the top and with an equal gap at each end. Drill through E into the hardboard.

Fitting to the wall

Attach the frames and the intervening loose shelves to the walls through the holes in E.

Position one frame at a time. Place it against the wall, propped by stools or pieces of wood on the work surface. Using a spirit level, adjust the props until the unit is perfectly horizontal, then mark the fixing positions through the holes you have made in the support batten (E).

For solid walls, use a No. 8 masonry bit to drill the holes, then insert wallplugs. If the wall is particularly hard, a drill with a hammer action may be more effective.

For hollow walls, drill 2.0mm pilot holes into the wall studs and screw into these direct. Use at leat 63mm No. 8 screws and screw into all the studs you can find.

Attach the intervening backing board to the wall by screwing through E in the same manner, but slide the edge of the hardboard underneath the wall-mounted frame. If necessary, loosen the frame's screws to open a gap. Adjust the backing board's position until it is perfectly horizontal and tight against the frame, then tighten all the screws (see fig. 2, below). Attach the final unit in the same manner, then drop the loose shelves into place on top of their shelf support plugs.

Fitting the lights

Connect the wires of a lighting flex to the corresponding terminals inside the light. Attach a fused plug to the other end of the flex and connect it to the nearest socket to test that it functions properly. Remember to unplug before you start fitting the light.

Position the light under any one of the bottom shelves. The loose shelves are best. Just remove one to attach the light, then replace light and shelf together. Alternatively, wire cne light to another and fit one under one loose shelf and one under another to shed light along the full length of the worktop.

Secure the flex to the shelf with cable clips, available from any DIY shop or electrical store. Make sure you get the right size of clip to match your flex.

Trail the flex along the unit, and then in a straight line down the wall to the power outlet. If your light does not have its own built-in switch, you can add an in-line switch to the flex to make it more convenient for switching on and off.

Cut and nail the pelmet in place into the notches on the sides (A). Use a nail punch

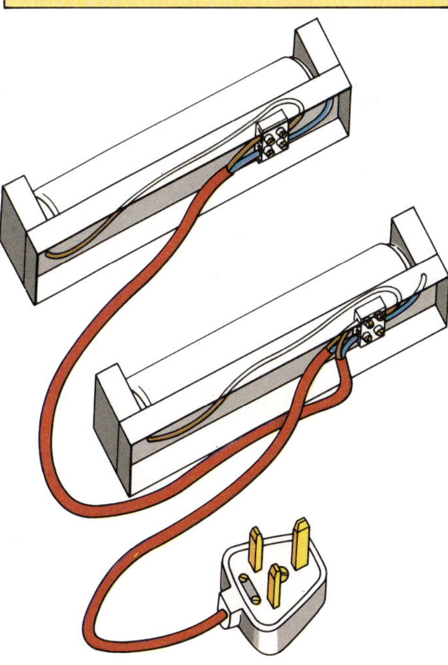

Wire two lights together to spread the light along the length of the worktop. Connect the wires of one length of flex to their terminals inside the light. Twist the wires at the other end to the corresponding ones in a second length of flex, then connect both to the terminals of the other light. Make sure all the connections are secure

to drive the heads below the surface (if you don't own one, use a large nail). Cover the small spots in the wood with wood filler, then stain and finish to match the units.

5 *Level the first frame, mark fixing positions, then attach with screws*

6 *Add the loose backing and batten. Tuck the backing under the last frame*

7 *Drop the loose shelves on to their shelf plugs inside and outside the fixed frames*

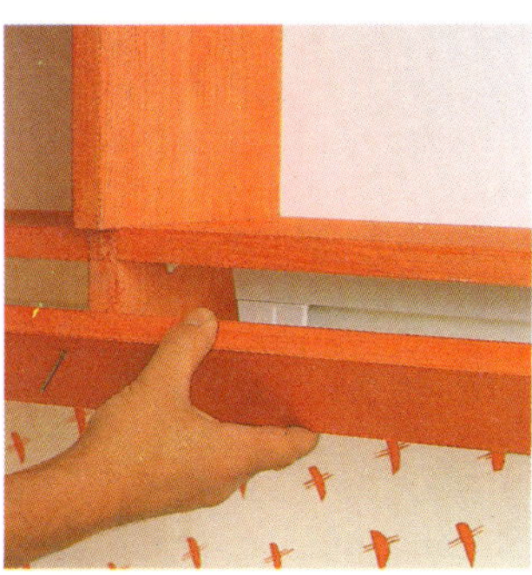

8 *Nail the pelmet to the notches in A and then punch the heads home*

WORKING WITH WALLBOARD

Panelling walls has recently become a popular alternative to wallpapering and painting. Apart from the decorative aspect, you can use wallboards to create a brand new surface—even if the existing walls appear to be in bad condition.

Wallboards (such as Laconite) are purpose made sheets of hardboard or sometimes plywood. One side is coated with a polyester finish which is coloured or moulded to create different effects: tiles, timber planks, hessian and a whole range of plain and textured patterns—there is a design for every sort of room. They are practical too; you can clean them with a damp cloth and they are resistant to most household stains and knocks, including

A good way to insulate a wall for either heat or sound is to fit battening and then sandwich insulating material—either polystyrene sheeting or glass fibre quilting—in the gap between the wallboard and the wall.

splashes of boiling water and spills from pots and pans.

If your walls are in good condition, you can simply stick them on with adhesive or, if you want to straighten up an old wall, fit them over a battening framework. However, if your walls are damp for any reason, don't be tempted to use wallboards to cover it up. The problem is certain to recur unless given specialist treatment.

Choosing wallboards

Decorative wallboards come in a variety of patterns and finishes; Laconite, for example, is made in a range of textured or plain woodgrain, tiles and decorative prints. Good DIY stores have sample swatches to help you make your choice. Tiles are always a good bet for bathrooms and kitchens, whereas simulated wood or hessian are ideal for living rooms or bedrooms.

When you buy your wallboards, check that all the panels are colour matched and, if they are patterned, that the patterns all line up when the boards are placed side by side. Checking the panels before purchase will help to ensure a satisfactory finish.

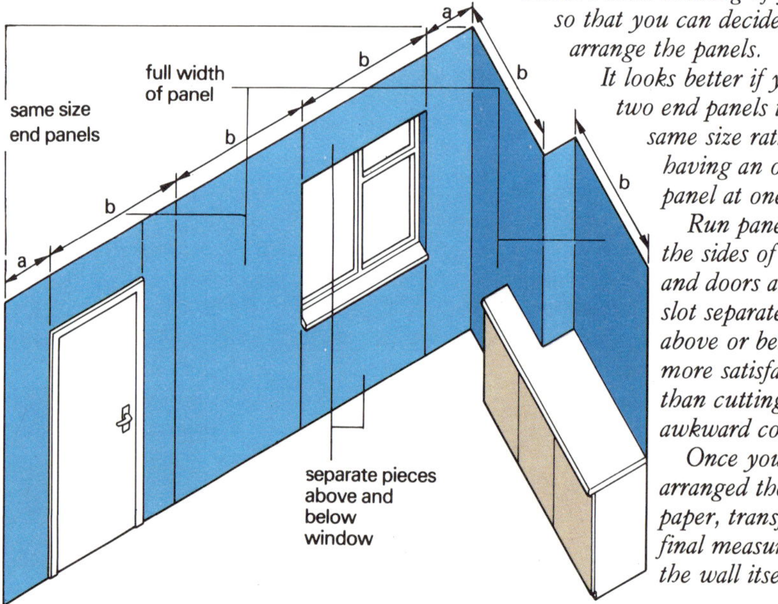

Make a scale drawing of your walls so that you can decide how to arrange the panels.

It looks better if you cut the two end panels to the same size rather than having an odd size panel at one end.

Run panels down the sides of windows and doors and then slot separate pieces above or below—it's more satisfactory than cutting out awkward corners.

Once you have arranged the panels on paper, transfer the final measurements to the wall itself

Planning

Have a good look at your walls and decide which method of fixing you are going to use. If your walls are flat and sound, you can stick the wallboards on with neoprene contact adhesive or flexible mastic based adhesive; if they are lumpy or out of plumb, you must use the battening method—basically you build a lightweight frame onto the wall and then fit the wallboard on top.

You can use either adhesive or panel pins to secure the boards to the battening. Pinning is cheaper and less messy but is only really successful on tiled or planked wallboards where the pins can be hidden in the grooves between the panels.

If you choose to batten your walls, check whether your walls are masonry or stud and plasterboard—it will make a difference to how you go about the job.

Wallboards normally come in 2240mm × 1220mm sheets so measure the height of your ceiling—the walls may be more than 2240mm high; if they are, don't worry as you will be able to make up small differences between the height of the panels and the ceiling with a skirting at the bottom or a cornice at the top.

Laconite also make boards in smaller sizes —1830mm × 610mm and 1220mm × 610mm which are useful for panelling above a worktop or around a bath.

> ## ★ WATCH POINT ★
>
> Don't be tempted to add bits on the end of a panel to make up the height of the wall—it's unlikely that you will be able to conceal the join. If you have a very high ceiling, panel up to a picture rail.

Wallboards are always put on vertically and, unless you are very lucky, you will have to cut panels to fit your walls. Decide how you want to arrange them by first drawing up a plan of your walls on paper.

> ## ★ WATCH POINT ★
>
> You can always use the architects' 'flashgap' technique: leave a space of 4–6mm between the edges of the board and paint the exposed backing wall or battening in a contrasting or matching colour.

Materials

Joints: Dealing with the joints in a planked or tiled board is easy—just fill them with a matching grout. To cover joints in plain boards, you can buy wooden strips or plastic extrusions—these are particularly useful for external corners (see page 17).
Adhesives: Unless you choose to nail on your wallboards, you will need an adhesive.

Manufacturers normally recommend a special adhesive—either mastic or contact —to be used with their brand of wallboard.
Battening: If you decide to use battening, buy planed all round (PAR) 50mm × 25mm softwood. While sawn timber is cheaper to buy, it is not so easy to line up accurately.

To fix the battening, use either 38mm masonry nails or 38mm No. 8 screws and the appropriate wallplugs—you won't need plugs for a stud wall as you can screw into the timber. The advantage with screws is that they can be loosened to get the battening plumb, but they are more expensive and fiddly to fit than nails.

Additional materials you may need

After planning how your wallboards are going to fit along the walls, decide how to treat skirtings, cornices and picture rails.
Skirtings: Providing they are in good condition, re-use your original skirtings. If needs be, you can always buy lengths of skirting from your local timber yard.
Cornices: You can get strips of coving (for cornices) from your DIY shop. Fix to the wall with adhesive or plasterboard nails.
Picture rails: Picture rail moulding is sold by the metre priced according to the design. You need panel pins to fix the rails; their length depends on the wood's thickness.

Estimating

Calculate the number of wallboards you need with a length of batten cut to the width of a sheet. Go around the walls counting off the number. If you are using battens, to calculate the length you need for a masonry wall, multiply the number of wallboards by three and add one for each corner, door and window. Multiply this number by the height of the room. Add to this the distance round the room multiplied by three.

For a stud wall divide 400mm into the height of the room multiplied by its length. Note that you need one screw or nail per 400mm length of battening.

One cartridge of mastic adhesive will fix two 2240mm × 1220mm panels; a litre can of contact adhesive, one panel. Always play safe by buying a little more adhesive than you calculate.

It is impossible to give a precise estimate for the number of 15mm panel pins needed to fix one sheet of wallboard—it will be something between 30–40 on average.

Coving strips, skirting, and picture rail moulding is sold by length, so buy them according to the size of your walls. Fix them in place with either plasterboard nails or panel pins spaced 1m apart.

Tools for the job

To cut the wallboard use a fine toothed panel saw; for fixing, a spirit level, plumbline, square, tape measure and hammer. Other useful things to have around will be a nail punch, plane or rasp, sandpaper, hard roller, a straightedge, stepladder or hop-up, drill and bits, and a padsaw. You may also want to use a mastic gun, an adhesive spreader, a stripping knife and a filling knife.

Preparing the walls and boards

Two days before you intend to start hanging the wallboards, stack them loosely in the room so they get conditioned to the temperature in which they will be hanging.

How you go about the next stage of preparation depends on whether you are fixing the boards with adhesive or on battens.
Preparing for fixing with adhesive: The surface of the walls must be sound, so strip off wallpaper and old paint and fill any hollows. Then sand down the walls.

Mark off the spacings of the boards across the walls. The first board to be fixed will be the one in the middle—use a chalked plumbline to mark its position. You won't have much leeway to reposition the panels once they are glued, so have accurate and clear guidelines from the start.
Preparing for fixing on battens: first, remove architraves and skirtings—you will be able to re-use them later on.

The sort of framework you fix up will depend on the nature of the wall: on masonry walls the battens run vertically; on stud walls they are horizontal (see page 16).

For a masonry wall, start by cutting lengths of batten to the height of the ceiling or picture rail—one for each corner and one for the sides of each door and window. Fix them with either masonry nails or 38mm screws and wallplugs every 600mm. If you use screws, drill clearance holes and mark through them the positions of the wallplugs. Check with a spirit level that the battens are vertical—if not insert packing pieces. Next cut and fit the top and bottom battens.

1 *Fill any holes and then smooth down*

2 *Mark the position of the first board with chalk*

3 *Lever skirtings off carefully to avoid damage*

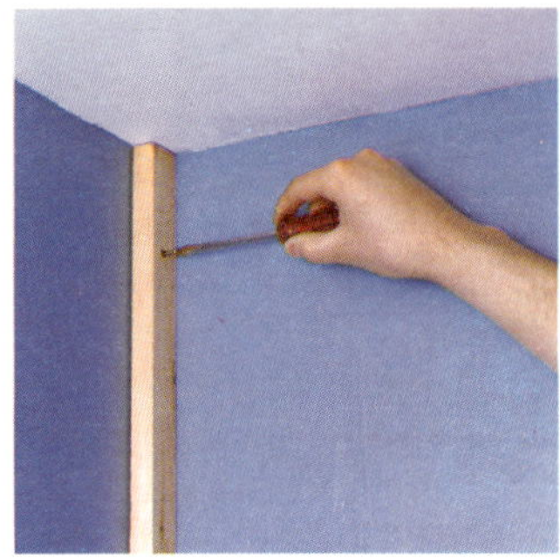

4 *Screw the end battens to the wall first*

5 *Insert packing pieces to get the battens vertical*

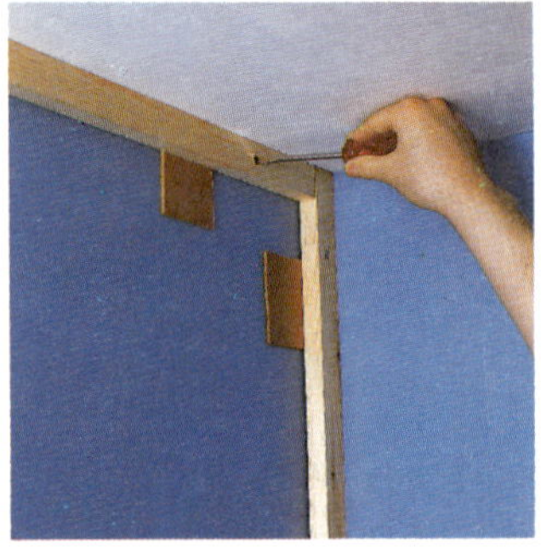

6 *Next, secure the top and bottom battens in place*

7 *Fix intermediate battens about 400mm apart*

8 *Use a cartridge gun to apply mastic adhesive*

The rest of the vertical battens are spaced so that each sheet is supported along its edges with two intermediate battens in between—every third batten must be positioned to straddle the joints; the intermediate battens are added at roughly 400mm intervals. Cut these battens so that they fit tightly between the ceiling and floor battens and screw or nail them into place. Stretch a piece of string between the two outside battens to make sure that the frame is in line. For extra support, skew nail horizontal battens halfway up the vertical ones, using 38mm oval nails.

If you have a stud wall, all the battens are horizontal and spaced at 400mm intervals up the wall (see illustration). Make sure that you fix them into the studs and not into the plasterboard which will not be strong enough to take the weight of the boards.

On stud walls, run the battens horizontally (left); on masonry walls set them vertically (below right)

Hanging the wallboards

Start fixing panels in the middle of a wall and work outwards to each side, cutting the end panels and any tricky bits last.

How you treat joints in the panels will vary according to the finish: wood effect panels can simply butt together while tiled boards can be caulked later. Plain boards will need cover strips which are either pinned or glued into position.

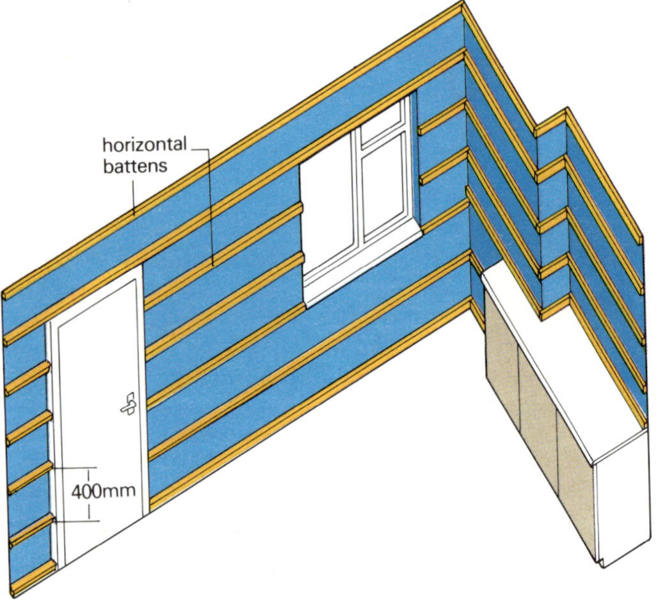

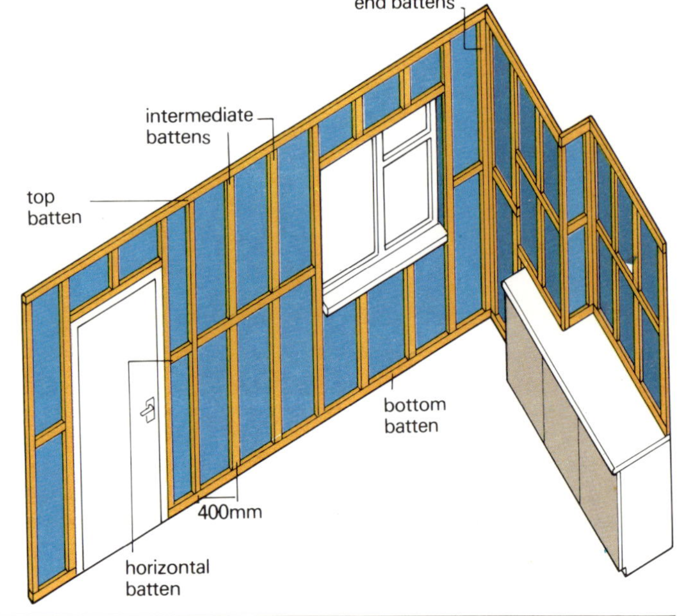

If you decide not to use cover strips at internal corners, arrange the junction of the boards so that the open joint is least obvious from the most used part of the room.

External corners need corner mouldings; it is difficult to mitre the boards accurately and corners need protection from knocks.

Adhesive fixing: Apply *mastic adhesive* from a cartridge gun; form a continuous strip or 'worm' right around the perimeter of a board, followed by a series of blobs—the size of a marble in parallel lines 400mm apart.

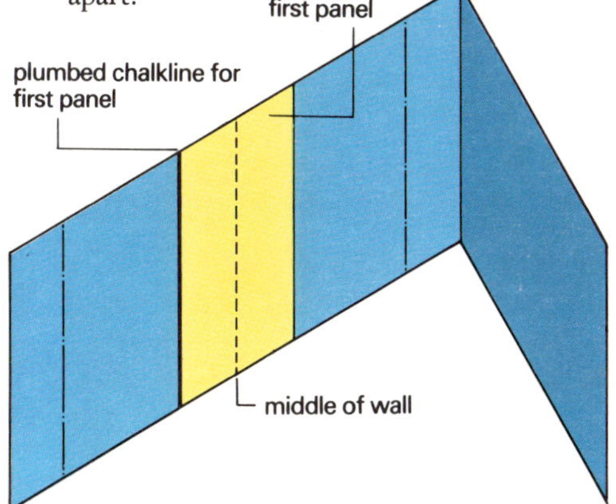

Fix your first panel starting in the middle of the wall

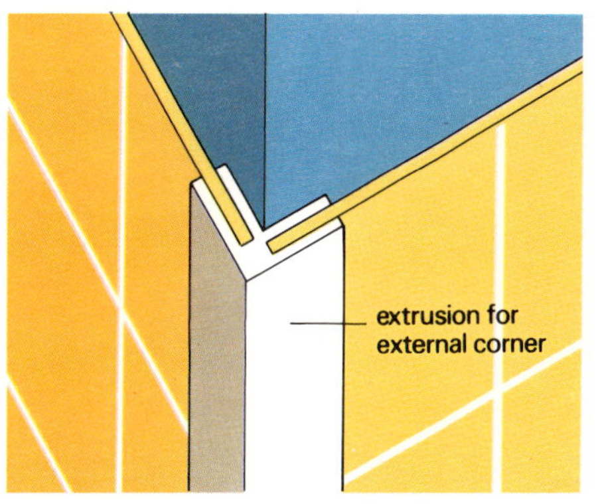

External corners are dealt with by fitting special mouldings made for the job

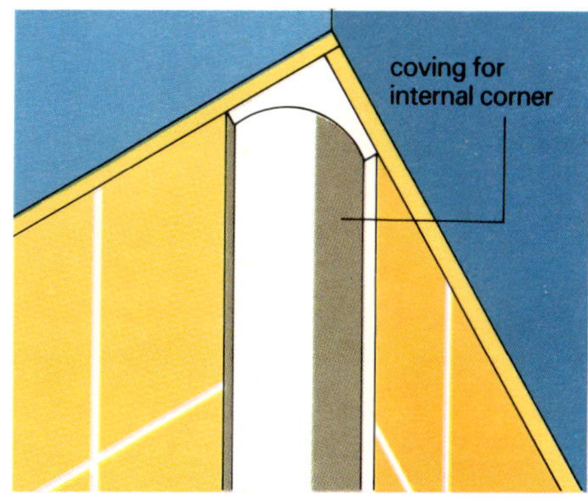

Internal corners can be finished off with a coving strip to cover the joints

this is not easy to do in practice.

Fixing to battens: If you are using mastic adhesive to fix panels to battens, apply a strip from the cartridge gun to the battens and then offer the panel up.

If you have decided on contact adhesive, an easy way to work out where the battens line up on a panel is to coat the battens first and to hold the wallboard up against them to get a transfer of glue. After removing the panel, apply contact adhesive to the back following the pattern of the battens.

If you want to nail on your panels, start by holding one in position against the battens—a wooden wedge placed on the floor will help you balance the sheet. Using 15mm panel pins, nail the middle of one edge to the batten behind. Then working fanwise, nail the rest of the panel to the battens—pins should be spaced about 150mm apart on the edge and 300mm apart on the intermediate battens. Always pin through the grooves of timber planking or tiling-style board.

9 *When gluing follow the lay of the battens*

10 *Pin the panels in place through the grooves*

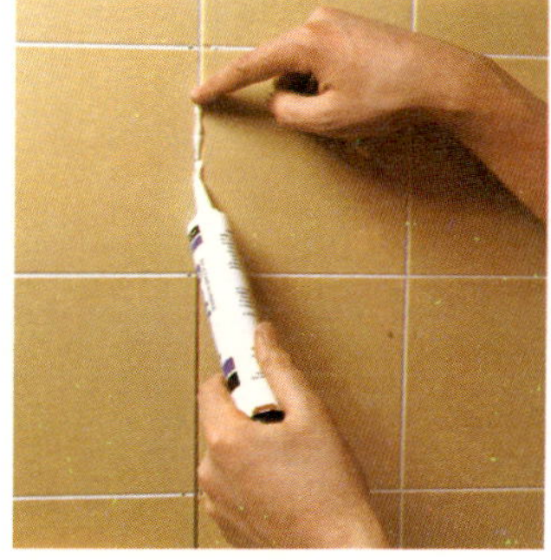

11 *Use a grout or sealer to fill tiled boards*

12 *Pin on scrap pieces before the skirting*

Press the panel up to its mark with the top edge tight against the ceiling. Smooth it over and then immediately take it off; half the adhesive will be stuck to the wall in the same pattern. Leave the adhesive to dry for about 20 minutes and then replace the panel to its mark and smooth it over with a hard roller. The adhesive works immediately so make sure you get the positioning right first time.

Spread *contact adhesive* over the whole of the back of the wallboard, and the wall, and then leave it to dry for 15–20 minutes. When the adhesive is touch dry, position the panel against its mark and firmly roll over it. Some contact adhesives allow you to make small adjustments but with big panels

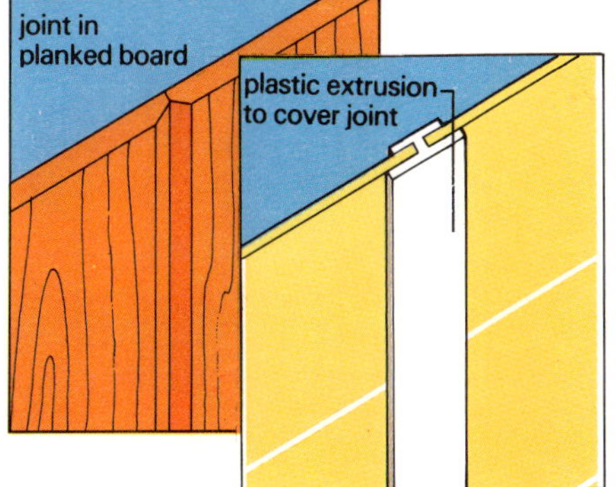

Wood effect boards are simply butted together (left)
Flush joints can be bridged very effectively with plastic strips (right)

Finish off by punching the pin heads home and filling in the holes—use a waterproof filler in a bathroom or kitchen.

Skirtings, architraves and trouble spots

At some stage you will encounter problem areas like light switches and, when you have finished, refitting the skirting.

The most complicated situation is where you have to cut a hole in the centre of a panel—as when fitting over electrical outlets and switches. In other cases you can generally refix fittings over the top of the panelling.

Switches and sockets: If you are sticking your wallboard directly onto the wall, you won't have much trouble; you simply cut out a rectangle that fits over the switch. To mark up where to cut the rectangle, align the panel to be cut next to the switch. Against a straightedge, draw two parallel lines across from the top and bottom of the switch plate. Then measure the distance from the preceding panel to the sides of the switch plate and mark off the two measurements on your parallel lines. Join up the points where the lines cross and cut out the rectangle. For the neatest result, cut the hole fractionally undersize. Switch off the mains and remove the faceplate before boarding the wall. Then refix the plate over the board.

With a battened wall, the problem is more elaborate. The best way to solve it is to bring the switch forward so that it is flush with the surface of the wallboard.

Turn off the electricity at the mains and remove the switch plate. Then unscrew the mounting box and pull it out. Construct a simple frame of battening around the opening and secure the switch box to a batten offcut. Measure up and cut out a rectangle from the panel and then fit it over the switch box before replacing the plate.

Radiators: The only satisfactory way of dealing with radiators is to remove them before hanging the panels and then to refit them when you have finished. If you are using the battening method, provide extra battens to support the radiator brackets; wallboard is not a structural material.

Windows and doors: Run full length panels down the sides of windows and doors and fill in with cut panels below and above, giving them adequate support if you are using battens.

Skirtings: When you come to refix these, nail or glue scrap pieces of wallboard across the wall or the battens below the bottom of the panels. Make chalk marks on the floor in front of the battens if you have used them, and then nail on the skirting.

Architraves: Like skirtings, architraves are simply nailed on. If you have used battening, sandwich a piece of packing—the thickness of the batten plus the thickness of the wallboard—between the architrave moulding and the door frame (see below). You can use hardboard as a packing material—simply pin or glue it in place and then paint over it in a matching colour.

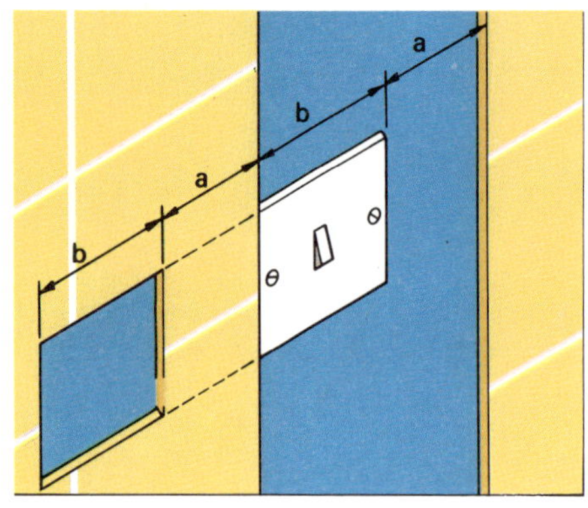

Mark off the measurements (a) and (b) and cut out a hole for the switch plate

Fill the gap between the architrave and the door frame with a strip of hardboard

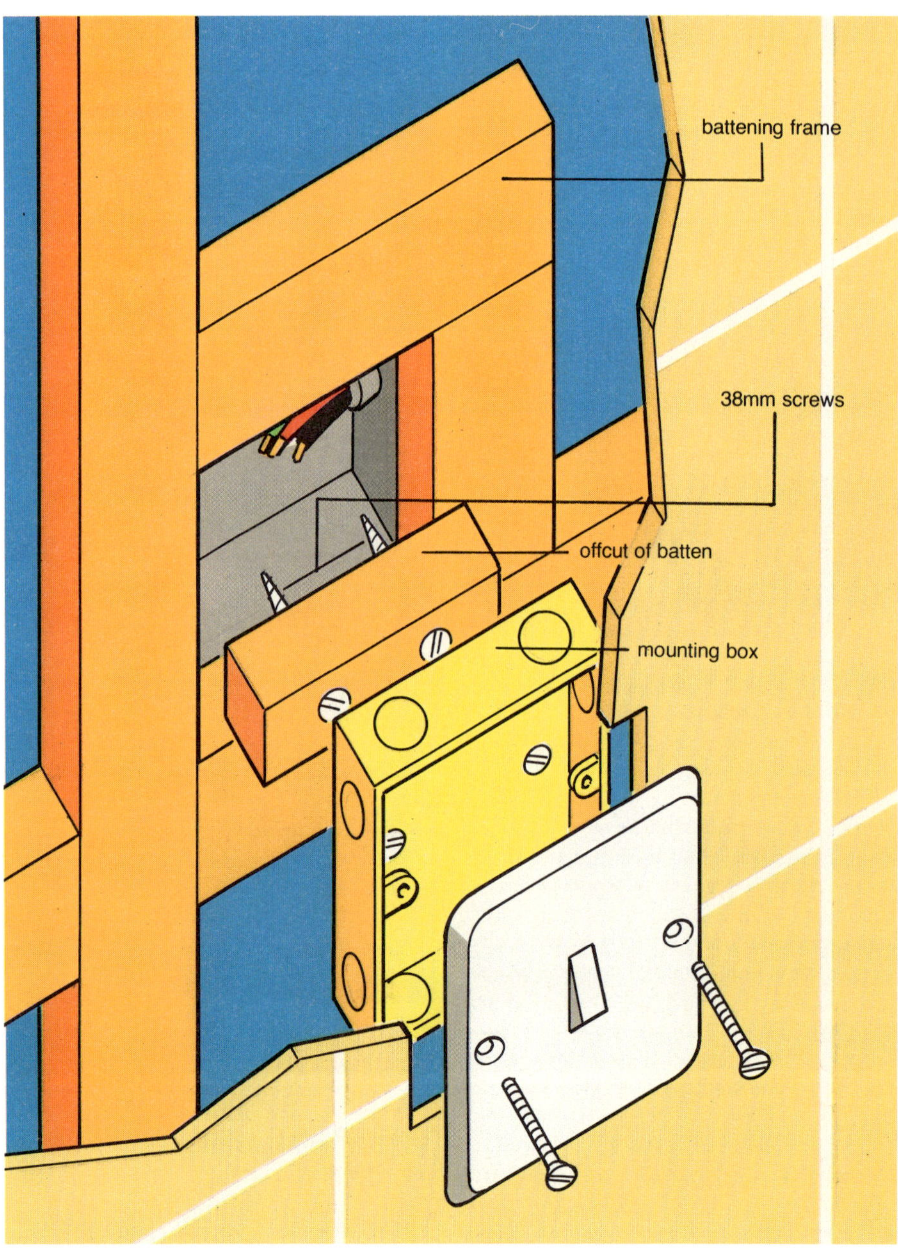

Re-fix the mounting box to an offcut of batten set back into the recess. Construct a simple frame to secure the box in place before fitting on the panel

Installing a hob and wall oven is a job that many people leave to the manufacturer's franchised engineers. Yet even when gas is involved most of the work still comes down to basic carpentry which is well within the capabilities of the average do-it-yourselfer. What this means in practice is that if you plan and build the units and install the hardware ready for connection, you can save a lot of money. In the UK, wiring up all-electric units yourself is legal.

Planning considerations

Before you even look at a manufacturer's brochure, you must work out where your wall oven and hob can go. Don't be too restricted by the position of your present cooker: connections are easily extended or re-routed, though in the case of gas appliances the work must be left to a qualified fitter. These are the points to consider:
• Try to keep the classic kitchen 'work triangle' of sink/cooker and worktop/fridge. A round trip between the three areas should measure no more than 7m.
• The oven and hob should be no more than 2m apart. If they're reasonably close, the connections will be simpler and less disruptive to make. But bear in mind that you need worktop space for both—including heat resistant surfaces on which to lay hot pans and trays.
• Many kitchen unit manufacturers include units for wall ovens and hobs in their ranges. These are a boon if you're doing a large-scale kitchen overhaul, but they don't fit all models and may restrict your choice. If you're fitting the oven and hob into an existing layout, it's almost always easier—and cheaper—to adapt or build on to what you've already got.
• Give priority to the hob's position rather than the oven's—you'll use the hob more. If your existing worktops are neither spacious enough or strong enough to take such an appliance, consider replacing the run with a ready made post-formed worktop at the same time.

What you can do yourself

How much of the installation work you can do yourself depends very much on whether

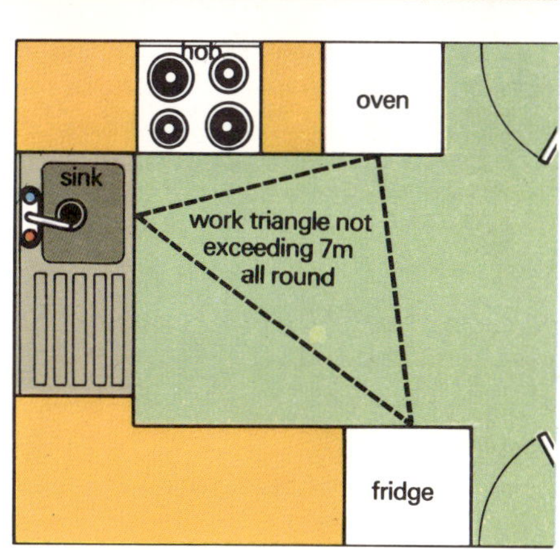

The ideal kitchen layout keeps the distances between the oven/hob, fridge and sink as short as possible. If you have two doors into your kitchen, arrange the layout so that the walkway in between doesn't cut across your 'work triangle'

the appliances are gas, electric, or a combination of both. In all cases you can cut the hole for the hob and construct an eye level cabinet for the oven. Where gas or part-gas appliances are concerned, you then fit the hob and the oven cabinet making sure that there is enough access for the gas fitter to run in and connect supply pipes.

Buying considerations

Choosing a hob and wall oven is largely a matter of studying brochures and picking out the models whose features most appeal to you. Even so, some types require more involved installation procedures than others and it's as well to be aware of these before you make a final choice.

•If you don't have an existing gas supply, running one in could be more trouble than it's worth. You may, for example, have to take out several kitchen units to give the fitter access. If you do have gas, you may need to run in an electricity supply as well. This must come direct from the fuse board or consumer unit, and may again prove to be a disruptive procedure.

•Where electrical appliances are concerned, current rating is the critical factor. Most hobs and single wall ovens are jointly rated at 30 amps, which means that you can use an existing 30 amp cooker circuit for the connections. On the other hand, if you opt for a double oven, you may find that the makers rate this and the hob at 45 amps. If your existing cooker circuit is the 45 amp sort, there's no problem. But if it's only 30 amp—even if the cooker point itself is rated at 45 amps—you have two choices: either you connect the hob to this and run a separate 30 amp circuit for the oven; or you replace the existing 30 amp circuit with a 45 amp one, using larger cable. Unfortunately, both options land you with more work than simply connecting to an existing power point.

Order of work

When the appliances arrive, sit down and work out a strict order of events to minimize the amount of time your cooking facilities are out of action. If you need the services of a fitter, plan for this in the same way so that he's with you for the shortest possible time. In the 'run-up' to installation you can take the following steps:

•Pre-build the oven cabinet in another room. Test-fit both the oven and the cabinet; make any adjustments at this stage so that on installation day you can simply disconnect the old cooker, fit the cabinet to the wall, then connect to the electricity and slide in the new appliance.

•Where appropriate, arrange the new electrical connections. If you are fitting a

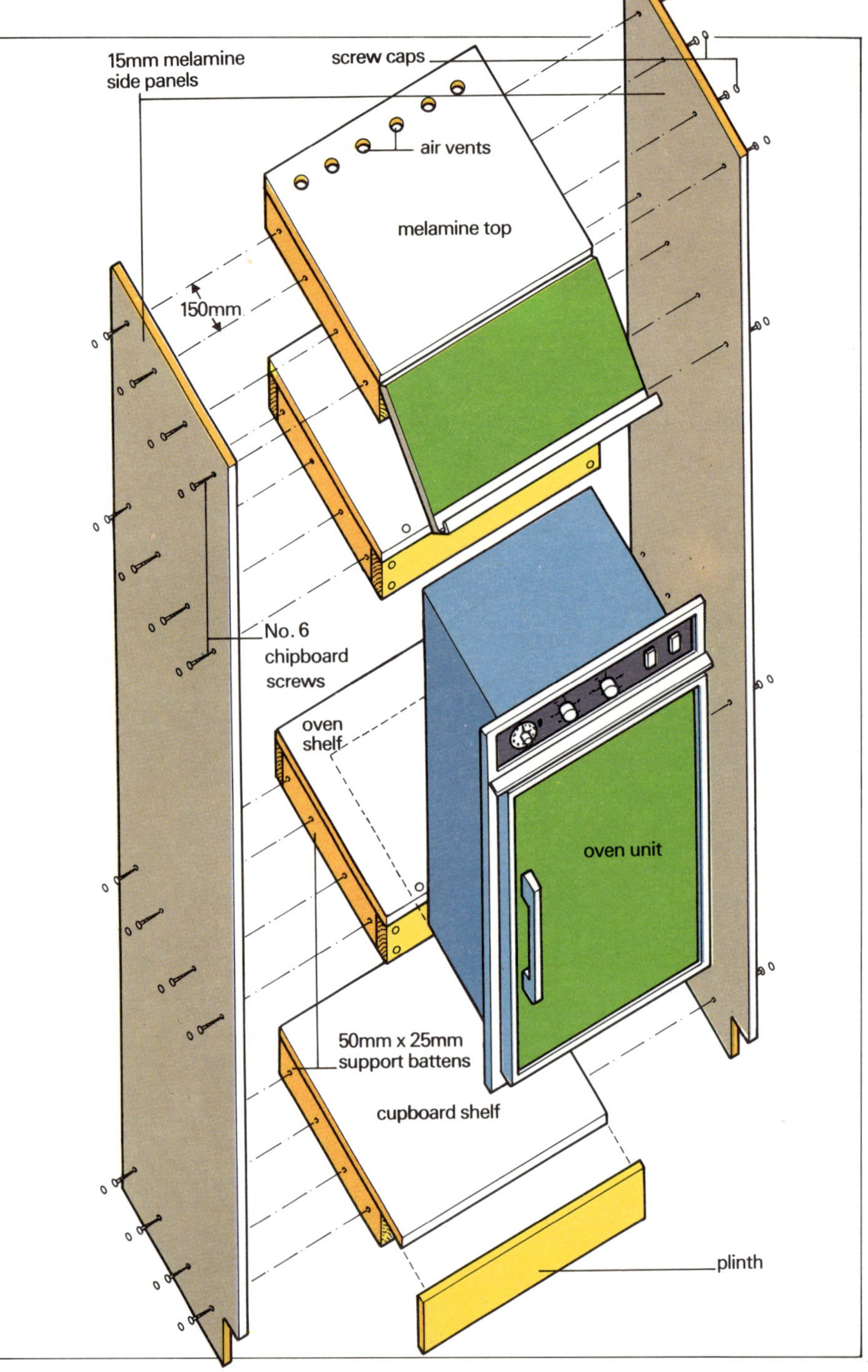

How the cabinet is made: the tops of the side panels are designed to line up with the tops of existing wall cupboards; you could extend them to the ceiling but this would involve scribing a fascia.

The feet of the side panels are cut away at the front to align with your existing unit plinths. When you measure the cutouts, don't forget to allow for the thickness of the hardboard or thin plywood strip that will run between them.

The oven compartment is formed by two melamine shelves resting on a framework of battens screwed to the side
panels. The shelves don't extend all the way back: there is a slight gap to allow air to circulate freely.

The top panel is drilled along the back edge with at least six 30mm holes which act as vents for the fumes from the oven.

The whole construction is held in place with at least eight metal angle brackets screwed to the side panels and wall. The best and least obtrusive position for the brackets is underneath each of the shelves.

During installation, the cabinet is temporarily braced by off-cuts of batten nailed across the top and bottom corners

new cooker point in place of an existing one, wire your cooker up to this so that you can keep it running until installation day.

• Cut the recess for the hob.

• Choose an 'installation day' on which you can fit both appliances, get gas supplies run in and make any final electrical connections that are necessary.

Qualified gas fitters are much in demand, so book one to come and make the connections well in advance of your installation day. While he's with you, get him to check the hob and oven for flame failure—gas appliances are easily damaged during installation and gas leaks are dangerous.

Oven cabinet

The oven cabinet design featured here is simplicity itself—a box construction in melamine faced chipboard strengthened with 50mm × 25mm softwood battens.

Plan out the size of the cabinet once you know the dimensions of the oven and have fixed on a location. Make a sketch plan, noting the main dimensions, and take this

determined by the oven, the fascia of which must obscure the softwood framing completely and just lip over the edges of the chipboard (see diagram, left).

• **Oven compartment height:** Obviously the oven should be at a comfortable working height, but it's also a good idea to align it visually with something else in the room— the foot of a wall cupboard, say. Most people find that having the foot of the oven at elbow height is ideal.

Once you've determined the height of the oven, you can work out the height of the compartment as you did its width.

• **Cabinet depth:** This is determined by the depth of your existing units rather than by the oven. Most units are 600mm deep and this will give you plenty of room for manoeuvre with the majority of ovens.

Make the depth of the shelves 50mm less than the side panel depth to give you your ventilation gap.

• **Top panel:** This will be as deep as the side panels and as wide as the shelves plus an additional 30mm.

There are plenty of variations on the basic design. The space below the oven can be turned into an extra cupboard by fitting a lay-on door with recessed hinges to match your existing units. In this case any gap between the top of the cupboard and the foot of the oven compartment can be taken up by a fascia of melamine board.

The area above the oven can also be en-

A good way to check the width is to mock up the front of the compartment using offcuts of softwood and melamine board. Adjust the offcuts for optimum position, then measure the distance between them. A piece of batten cut to length can be used as a template for all the other shelves.

countersunk woodscrews to fix the shelves to the battens. Other requirements include iron-on edging strip for finishing the edges and an offcut of plywood or hardboard for the kickboard on the false plinth.

Construction

Start by marking up and making the cut-outs for the false plinth to be positioned at the feet of the side panels.

Now lay the panels exactly on top of one another and mark off on the front edges where you want shelves to be. Transfer these marks to the inside faces of the side panels using a try square extended with the help of a steel rule.

Use the marks as position guides for the shelf support battens. Cut the battens to length—the width of the side panels minus

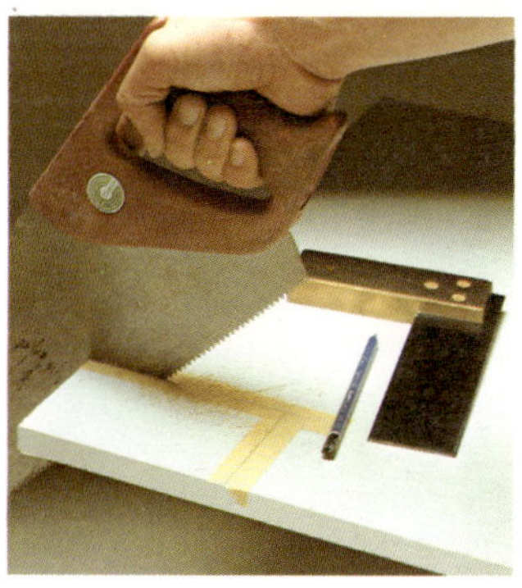

1 *Mark plinth cut-outs and tape lines before sawing*

2 *Screw through the melamine to fix the supports*

3 *Drill clearance holes for the kickboard screws*

4 *Scribe the side panels with a pencil taped to a block*

to your timber supplier who will hopefully cut the chipboard panels for you.

Refer to the diagram on page 20 to see how the cabinet is constructed. When you work out your design, bear in mind the following critical dimensions:

• **Side panel height:** This is the same as the tops of your wall cupboards. If you haven't got wall cupboards, aim for a height of around 2.5m.

• **Shelf (compartment) width:** This is

closed—this time by an upward-hinging door held by stays. Alternatively you could leave both areas open and fill in the spaces with extra shelves.

Having finalized the basic box design and decided how many lengths of board you need, make a generous estimate of your softwood requirements. You'll need a supply of 32mm No. 6 chipboard screws to fix the battens to the melamine boards, and a roughly equal number of 38mm No. 6

the thickness of the battening that goes across the front—and drill the panels for No. 6 chipboard screws at 150mm centres.

Lay each side panel on top of the support battens, making sure that they are lined up against their marks. Drill pilot holes into the battens before fixing them in place and then cover the screw heads with plastic caps for protection.

With all the shelf supports in place, lay the side panels on edge and support them a shelf width apart. Drill the side edges of the shelf panels (and the front edges of those either side of the oven compartment) to take No. 6 woodscrews. Fit the shelf panels between the side panels, drill holes through into the shelf supports, and screw them in position. Now fit the front battens, first by screwing into the end of the shelf supports (a little glue on the screws will help them grip), then by screwing into them from the shelves above and below.

To complete the basic cabinet, drill and screw on the top using chipboard screws. Follow by cutting and fixing a piece of hardboard or 4mm plywood to act as the false plinth kickboard. Add any other refinements—doors, extra shelves, upstands at the back of the shelves—at this stage too.

The final job is to brace the cabinet at the back so that it doesn't crack and break when you move it into the kitchen. Do this by nailing thin battens diagonally across the side panels.

Insulation: You can if you wish insulate the inside of the oven compartment by tacking in pieces of insulating board. Research has shown that even the best wall ovens still give off heat, so this is probably a good idea, particularly if you want to use the space above for storage.

Fitting the cabinet

Although you leave fitting the oven until installation day, it's as well to make sure that the cabinet fits at this stage.

Manoeuvre it more or less into position and remove the braces temporarily. Start by checking for obstructions on the wall such as a skirting, pipes and cable. Then mark off against the backs of the side panels where they would strike them and cut suitable clearance notches.

Now try the cabinet hard against the wall. If the resulting gap with the cabinet standing freely on the floor is excessive, the back edges of the side panels must be scribed to the profile of the wall. Do this by running down them with a pencil and a thin block of wood held hard against the wall, then trim back to the scribed lines with a planer file or a plane.

When the cabinet is a perfect fit, screw on the angle brackets.

Arranging the electrics

You have several options when arranging the electrical work, depending on whether or not you have an existing cooker circuit.

Even if you do, you must make sure that it is the correct rating for the new appliances—safety is the overriding factor.

If you have an existing cooker circuit, check its rating by examining the appropriate fuse in the fuse board or consumer unit. If the fuse is colour-coded red, it's a 30 amp circuit; if the fuse is green, it's 45 amps. (Note that if you have a shower, this will also be on a 30 amp or 45 amp circuit. To avoid confusion, switch off the main switch and remove the fuses in turn to find out which serves which.)

If the circuit rating isn't high enough, you must isolate the circuit and install a new one. As the existing cables are almost certainly buried in the wall, the easiest way to do this is by running new cable in plastic conduit (mini-trunking) to a new double switch cooker point located in the best position (see the diagram, right).

If your existing circuit's current rating is satisfactory, turn your attention to the cooker control point. To be of use, it must be no more than 2m from either the hob or the oven; it must also be of the correct current rating. Check the latter point by turning off the main switch and removing the cooker point faceplate—the rating will be given on the back.

Most manufacturers recommend that you connect the hob and oven together and then connect whichever of them is nearer to the cooker point. All the connections must be made in cable of the appropriate rating for the circuit—6mm² twin and earth for 30 amp, 10mm² twin and earth for a 45 amp circuit.

Connections at the appliances must be made strictly in accordance with the manufacturer's instructions, but you can leave these and the connection at the cooker point until final installation (see page 24). Make sure that the point—and its terminal plate—is screwed firmly to the wall before turning the electricity back on.

Adding a new 45 amp circuit

For this you'll need a new 45 amp fuse and fuseholder to match a spare fuseway in your board or consumer unit, plus a surface mounted double switched cooker point. You will also require enough 10mm² twin and earth PVC sheathed cable and plastic conduit to stretch between the two. The conduit is available with angle joints, allowing you to run it unobtrusively along skirting boards.

It may be that you can run the cable

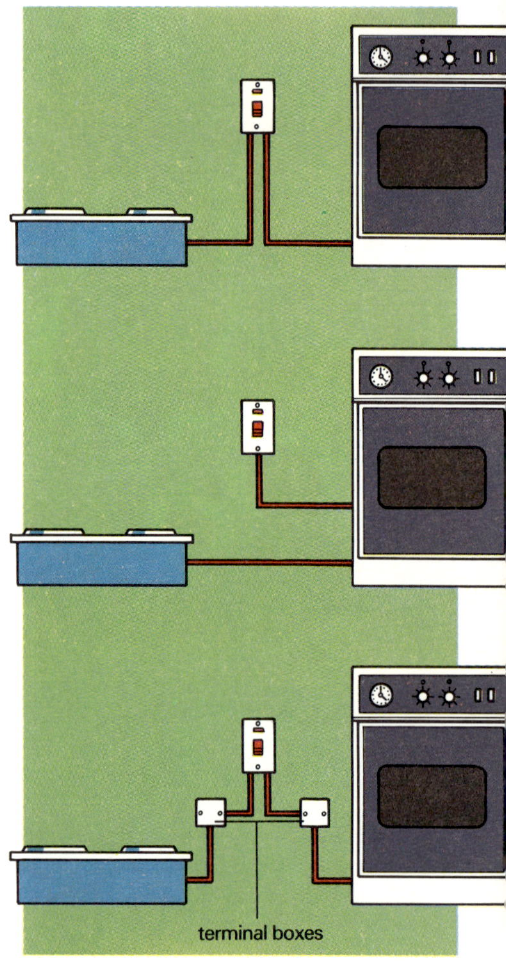

Consult the manufacturer's instructions on how to wire up your hob and oven to the mains. There are three possible options (above) depending on the type: they can be wired independently (top); the hob can be wired to a junction in the oven which is then connected to the cooker point (middle); or they can be wired up independently via wall mounted terminal boxes (bottom)

under the floor—ground or first floor—so that you only need conduit where it runs up or down walls. This is certainly a neater option, but you'll have to lift quite a few floorboards so bear in mind the disruption entailed. If the cable has to cross joists, feed it through holes drilled one third of the way down—simply notching them could result in the cable being punctured when you relay the floor.

Fasten the backing plate of the cooker point to the wall using screws and wallplugs or cavity fixings as appropriate. Fix the backing part of the conduit along your chosen route using screws, nails or even a strong adhesive adhesive.

Strip back enough outer sheathing on the

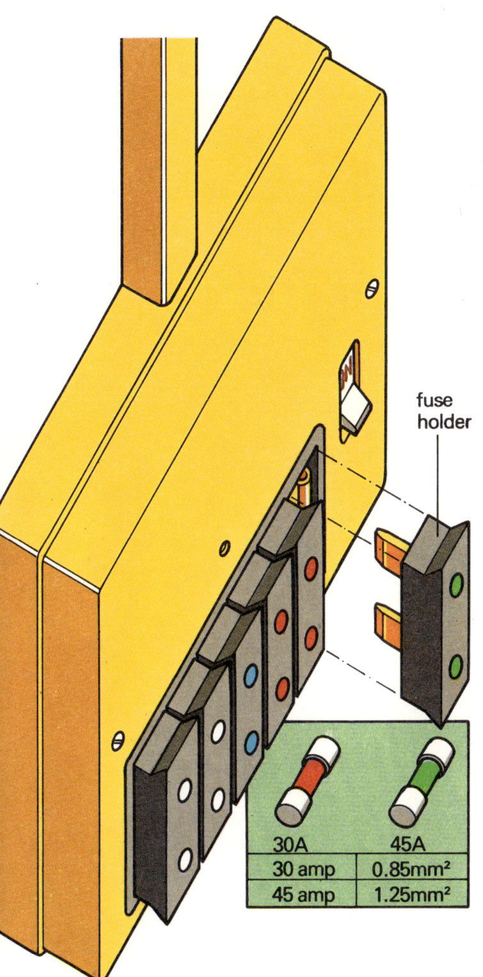

If you are adding a new 45 amp circuit, buy a colour coded fuse holder to match your consumer unit (above) and check the colour of the cartridge or the diameter of the fuse wire

the bare earth core with a length of green and yellow PVC sleeving. Finally, connect the cores to their appropriate terminals on the cooker point faceplate: red to L, black to N and earth to E.

Now feed the cable back along your chosen route to the consumer unit. Where it passes through conduit, simply lay it in the back part and then snap on the cover. 10mm² cable is very thick and stiff but you should nevertheless ensure that it is straight and there are no kinks.

Cutting the hob recess

Cutting a hole for the hob in your worktop is a job that sounds simple in theory, but in practice it's hard work.

If your worktop is the usual thickness—25mm—and you don't own a jig saw, it's worth hiring one. The alternative is a pad-saw, but it really is too small for this job.

Take the dimensions for the cut-out from the manufacturer's instructions and follow any specific advice given on positioning. Mark cutting lines on the worktop surface in felt-tipped pen, checking with a rule and try square that the corners are square and that the entire hole is square to the worktop.

If the worktop is laminated, score around the cutting lines with a laminate cutter (you could use a tungsten-tipped tile cutter) held against a steel rule: this will stop the laminate from chipping when you cut it.

Now put pieces of masking tape over the four corners and mark drill holes just inside the lines. The holes you make must be large enough to insert your jig saw blade, so you may have to drill two or even three over each other to achieve the desired result.

Take each cutting line in turn, starting from a corner. Hold the saw firmly but don't try to force it along—concentrate in-

stead on keeping it in a straight line and let the blade find its own way through. If you do try to force the blade through the work-top, it is more than likely to bend away from the cutting line and possibly break. Another symptom of pushing too hard is a very hot blade. Remember, too, that the jig saw will create a lot of dust, so clear away any food

cable to allow you to connect it to the cooker point faceplate. Bare the ends of the live (red) and neutral (black) cores by stripping about 20mm of the insulation; sheath

5 *Remove the terminal plate before screwing the back of the cooker point to the wall*

6 *Remove the base of the hob and use it as a template to mark your cutting lines on the wall*

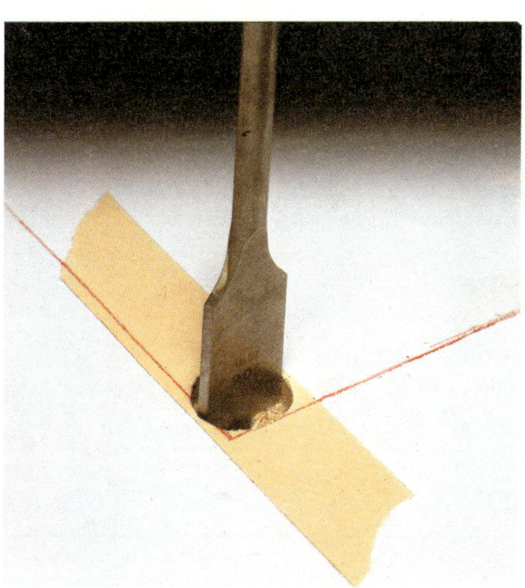

7 *Drill holes in the corners large enough to take the blade of the jigsaw, before you begin sawing*

8 *Score along your lines to prevent chipping and then cut out the recess with a jigsaw*

9 *Square up the corners of the recess with a rasp or padsaw. Test fit the hob or hob base and adjust*

10 *Connect the wires to the appropriate terminals in the hob and oven; ensure the cable is locked in place*

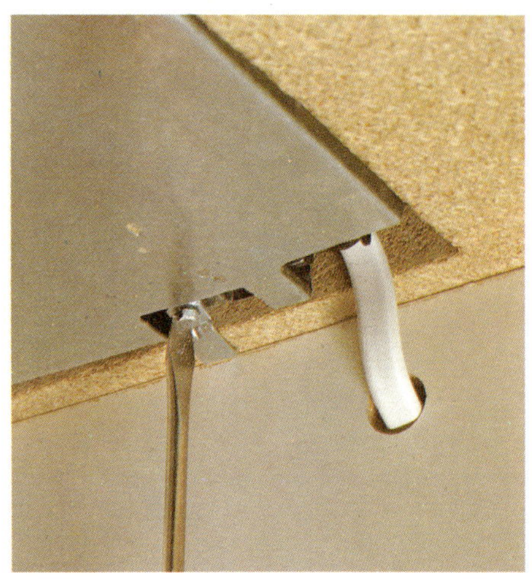

11 *Feed the cable out through a hole in the back of the unit and tighten the hob securing clips underneath*

and cover up the kitchen surfaces.

After the hole has been cut, cut back into the corners using a rasp or padsaw. Test-fit the hob or hob base and make any adjustments at this stage. Don't worry if the cut lines are a little ragged: they'll be concealed later by the hob's sealing lip.

Final installation

It's impossible to be specific about what you do on installation day, because so much depends on the nature of the appliances you're installing. But you have one clear priority: to make the changeover from old to new cookers as quickly as possible.

Start with the hob, which may be in two parts or a complete unit, depending on the model. Most simply drop into the recess you have cut and are secured by clips or screws—the instructions will show you how. But check first whether or not you have to prepare the base with an all-round bead of silicone sealant.

Before you actually drop in the hob, connect the linking cable (either direct to the oven, direct to the cooker point, or to both) in accordance with the instructions. Make sure that there's a hole in the back of the kitchen unit for you to feed the cable through to its connection point.

Now fit the oven cabinet. Remove the temporary braces, offer it up to the wall, and mark off the angle bracket fixing holes. Slide the cabinet out of the way and drill the wall to take wallplugs (solid wall) or heavy duty cavity fixings (stud wall). Afterwards, refit the cabinet and secure the brackets with 38mm No. 8 screws.

As with the hob, follow the manu-

12 *When you have secured all the wires in the cooker point, screw the plate back on followed by the cover*

facturer's instructions on how to fit the oven inside the cabinet. Make any cable connections before you slide the oven in and feed the cable out through the back of the cabinet to its connection point.

Connecting the electricity: First of all, turn the electricity off at the main switch on the fuseboard or consumer unit.

Cooker point end: If you are connecting to your old cooker's point, unscrew the faceplate, loosen the terminals and remove the old cable. Replace it with the new cable from the hob or oven, remembering to sleeve the bare earth core with a length of green and yellow sleeving. Follow exactly the same procedure if you are connecting to a brand new cooker point.

Consumer unit end: If you are connecting new cable here, feed it in through the top of

13 *Double check that you have used the proper fuses in your consumer unit: green for 45 amps, red for 30 amps*

the unit and strip off enough outer sheathing for you to be able to connect the cores to their relevant blocks. Sleeve the earth core with more green and yellow sleeving.

The earth core goes to the common earth block; the black core goes to the common neutral block; the red core goes to the circuit's fuseholder. But before you connect the live red core, double check that the fuseholder (and the fuse which goes in it) in the fuseway is the correct rating for the circuit.

Check all the terminal connections, make sure that the cooker point cover is firmly screwed back on, replace the consumer unit cover and switch on to test.

Connecting the gas: Connections to fixed gas supplies will be made by flexible pipe, so the gas fitter will want access to your new appliances.

BUILDING A SERVING HATCH

There is nothing like a serving hatch for convenience, especially if there's no doorway linking the kitchen with the dining area. Making your own is inexpensive, and requires only a few tools and materials.

The real work involves making a hole in the wall in the right place and at the right height, and—in a masonry wall—providing support for the brickwork above the opening. This means adding a lintel. It's not difficult work but it is messy, and it's important to choose a height and size to match your walls and kitchen. In this respect, it's a matter of measurement and alignment.

Once you've made the hole, you just fit a simple timber frame into the opening to line the hatch—make sure that the wood is as wide as the wall is thick. Then add doors and trimmings to match your decor.

You can use one of the wide range of ready-made doors available or make your own, so you can match any decor—from modern to traditional.

Planning considerations

There are several considerations when planning where to put a serving hatch. First you must determine whether your wall is load-bearing and arrange the work accordingly—you'll need suitable supports, both temporary and permanent. But if the wall is a hollow timber framed type, it's more straightforward.

The position of the serving hatch is your second consideration. The centre of the wall is ideal from a structural point of view, but it's not essential. What's important is that the bottom of the finished hatch is level (or nearly level) with your kitchen worktop and that the top is lower than any kitchen fittings—cupboards or shelves, for example.

On the dining room side, try to avoid having to rearrange all the furniture to suit the location of the serving hatch. Accessability is essential so, although the hatch should be close to the dining table, it should not be directly above it.

Buying and hiring

For a serving hatch in a masonry wall, you only need basic tools—a power drill and assorted bits, a long masonry bit, club hammer, brick bolster, spirit level and wood working tools. But you'll need to hire two expandable steel props—commonly known as Acrows—plus about 2m of 100mm × 100mm timber and some sturdy planks. Get these from a tool hire shop. You need them for temporary support.

You'll need safety goggles and gloves to protect you as you work and plenty of builder's bags to remove the rubble. Dust sheets will also save a lot of clearing up.

You can use a timber lintel, but if the wall carries a heavy load and you're in any doubt, use a pre-stressed concrete lintel instead. There are two types: those for single brick thickness walls, and those for double brick thickness walls. They're both pre-stressed and available from builder's merchants in a variety of lengths. For holes of this size (less than 1.5m) a steel lintel is not necessary.

The amount of timber you need for the lining depends on the thickness of your walls. For the threshold use timber that is about 50mm wider to provide a small sill. Use wood that is 25mm thick.

You also need enough decorative moulding for both sides of the wall. Look

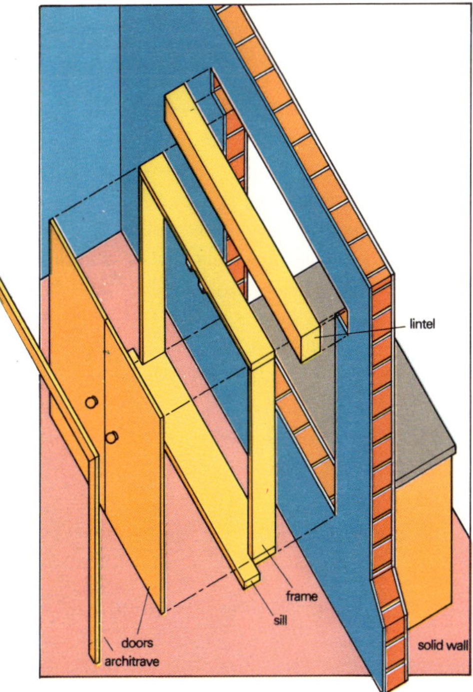

Fit the lintel to support the load above, then insert the 25mm frame and sill. Hang the doors and architrave

carefully before purchasing, and buy some that matches your existing woodwork.

One 20kg bag of ready mixed bricklaying mortar is all you need for the masonry work, but make sure that you've also got enough interior filler to cover any mistakes or small cracks in the walls.

Clearing the plaster

Before you begin the job, prepare yourself and your house for the work that lies ahead. This mainly involves checking and measuring but it also involves making a mess, so begin by folding back carpets and laying dust sheets in the affected areas.

To determine what type of wall you have,

check that the wall is clear of power sockets or light switches. If it's not, turn off the main supply and leave it off. Unscrew the cover plate of the switch or socket and examine the direction of the cables—normally they go up or down, rarely straight across the wall. If you can't tell, carefully chisel away plaster from a small area around the socket until you can see which way they go. If the cables are routed across your proposed opening, they must be re-routed first. Unless you are absolutely certain of the procedure involved, leave this job to a professional electrician.

Score the upper line with a sharp trimming knife to prevent both the plaster from crumbling and the wallpaper tearing beyond this line.

If this line happens to fall directly over the ends of the bricks and mortar joints between them then the position of the vertical line on this side requires no adjustment. If it does not, adjust it to coincide with the end of the nearest brick. Move the right-hand boundary by the same amount, score it and erase the original line.

Work towards the right, removing the plaster to the end of the brick nearest to the

1 *Mark out the proposed outline of the serving hatch. Score along the top line with a sharp knife*

2 *Using a brick bolster and club hammer clear away the plaster from around one whole brick*

3 *Clear away the plaster from the whole area within the new lines. Work in one direction moving across the opening*

tap it with your knuckles. If it sounds hollow it will be a timber frame wall.

If, on the other hand, it sounds solid, then it is most likely to be a masonry wall. It will be brick or blockwork covered by a thick layer of plaster. In this case, drill a hole with a masonry bit about 1.4m from the floor and roughly in the centre of the proposed hatch. If your drill bit is long enough, drill through from one side to the other.

Using this hole as the centre, mark out an area 760mm long by 610m high—use a spirit level and pencil. Before starting work,

Using a brick bolster and club hammer, start chipping away the plaster in the upper third of the marked area, working towards the scored line. Don't worry about clearing the plaster back to the vertical boundaries.

Should the upper scored line fall directly over a mortar course, then the horizontal position of the hatch needs no adjustment. But it is most likely that you will have to raise or lower this top line to take advantage of the nearest mortar course.

After adjusting and re-scoring the top line, adjust the lower line by the same amount. Erase the original line and score the new one to avoid confusion.

Working downwards from the exposed area, remove the plaster to the nearest mortar course of the lower scored line. When you have reached this line the distance between the top and bottom should be between 570mm and 650mm apart.

For the vertical boundaries, first score the left-hand line and start working in the direction of this line.

scored line. The two sides should be between 700mm and 820mm apart.

Clear away any remaining plaster and measure the exact area. Find the centre by drawing the two diagonals and marking where they cross. Precisely in the middle, drill a hole completely through the masonry wall to the other side. Using this hole as a centre point, mark out and score an area with exactly the same dimensions as the other side. Then proceed to remove the plaster from this side. The edges of this side should also fall directly on mortar joints.

Inserting the lintel

It's very important to ensure that the wall—and any load that it carries—is properly supported until the lintel is in place. Once the lintel is installed, the rest of the brickwork can be safely removed.

A brick wall is exceptionally stable— even with a hole in it—but if the wall carries any load at all you must be as cautious as possible. You must insert a 'needle' of timber through the wall above your intended opening and prop it up on either side with adjustable steel props. These will support the load until the lintel can permanently take their place.

Begin by inserting the needle—use 100mm × 100mm timber about 2m long. At a point about 750mm above the top of the proposed opening, remove the plaster from a small area on both sides of the wall. Remove enough to expose at least one whole brick. Using a masonry drill and wearing goggles, drill into the mortar on all sides of the brick. Remove as much mortar as possible by this method, then tap the brick lightly to dislodge it. If it won't budge, drive a bolster into the joint until it will.

Repeat this process on one of the staggered bricks above the first one. If the wall is more than one brick thick—it's unlikely to be a cavity wall though—repeat this process on the other side.

Insert the needle through the hole and support it on either side with adjustable steel props. Lay stout planks underneath the base of the props to spread the load.

Adjust the props and tighten them until the needle is stressed against the top of the hole. Make sure the props are plumb and that the needle is level. If they are, the needle is now ready to carry the load that was taken by the wall.

Mark out and score an area one brick course higher and extending 100mm beyond either side of the proposed hatch.

If you can't remove the brick intact, break it up. Drill into the brick itself, insert a narrow cold chisel and give it a series of heavy blows with a hammer.

Clear the plaster from this area and repeat the procedure on the other side of the wall.

Start to remove the bricks from this course, one by one. Use the method described earlier to remove the first brick and the others should follow with ease. Clean an opening that is large enought to accommodate the lintel but no bigger.

Mix up some ready mixed bricklaying mortar and lay a small bed on either side of the proposed hatch. Insert the lintel and pack under its ends—use more mortar and slivers of wood or slate—until it is perfectly level. Fill any gaps between the surrounding

4 *Remove a couple of bricks to create a hole for the needle. Locate it about 750mm above the top line of the hatch*

5 *Insert the needle and tighten up the props on both sides until the needle is stressed against the top of the hole*

6 *Lay the lintel on a bed of mortar. Fill the gaps with mortar and allow to cure for at least one day before removing props*

masonry and the lintel with the rest of the mortar. Leave it to cure for at least one day before you move on to the next stage.

Making the hole

Once the mortar has set around the lintel you can remove the temporary supports and fill the holes you have made. From now on the lintel itself will support the wall and any load that it carries.

Remove the bricks below the lintel and back to your scored lines. Start on a central brick and drill out as before. Now that the masonry is supported, you can use the bolster and hammer more freely. If you encounter a stubborn brick it is wiser to return to the method of drilling out the mortar rather than using force.

On alternate courses at either side of the opening, use a bolster and hammer to cut the bricks in half, leaving them flush with the ends of the uncut bricks.

Use one (or more) of the bricks you remove to fill the hole you made for the needle. Lay a bed of mortar in the hole and squeeze in the brick. Fill any gaps with the

7 *Remove the bricks for the hatch opening starting from the centre. Cut the side bricks in half with a bolster*

8 *Fill the rough edges of the opening with mortar using two battens temporarily nailed to the wall as your guide*

remaining mortar. If rough edges extend back more than 50mm from the edge of the opening itself, trowel mortar onto the surface of the bricks to a point about 3mm below the surrounding surface.

Don't worry about the finish around the opening at this stage—most of the rough edges will be either plastered or covered by the wood moulding.

★ WATCH POINT ★

It may be easier to remove the whole brick and chop it in half on a solid surface. Lay a bed of mortar in the hole the brick came from and re-insert the half brick.

Making the frame

You must line the opening with timber of a suitable width. Measure the thickness of the wall—it will determine the width of the timber you use. For the lower surface, add an extra 100mm to the width so that it will overhang into the dining room. Measure the opening from side to side and top to bottom for the lengths you need. Buy twice as much wood moulding for the architrave, as you need it on both sides of the wall.

Cut the wider board 200mm longer than the width of the opening. Cut a notch at each end that is 100mm deep and the same width as the thickness of the wall. This allows it to fit into the hole leaving an overhang on each side. Test fit the threshold into the opening, with the ledge protruding on the dining room side.

For the top of the opening, cut a piece of the narrower board to the same length as the threshold (between the notches). Plane this board to the same width as the wall.

Place the board and threshold together across the bottom of the opening. Hold a further length of the narrower board up to them and mark where it meets the bottom of the lintel. Cut two pieces to this dimension and plane them to the width of the wall. Check to make sure that the ends are perfectly level and square.

Join all four sides using 50mm oval nails and wood glue, driving the nails through the longer horizontals into the ends of the shorter pieces. You should check that all the corners are square.

In each of the vertical sides, drill 4.5mm countersunk clearance holes. Drill two 50mm from the top and two 50mm from the bottom. Drill two similar holes in each

9 *Cut the bottom board 200mm wider then the opening. Cut notches in the ends and test fit the sill into the opening*

11 *Align the frame in the hole using small wooden wedges. Check that the frame is square and level*

end of the two horizontal pieces.

Place the frame in the opening. Level it and make it flush with the wall by tapping small wooden wedges between the frame and the sides of the opening.

Mark through the clearance holes onto the wall beneath—use a long masonry nail—then remove the frame to drill the holes. Use a No. 8 masonry drill and plug the holes with wallplugs. Replace the frame, level it and screw it in place with 63mm No. 8 screws. Check that the frame is level and square as you tighten the screws.

Fitting the doors and finishing

Fit ready made doors—planed to fit exactly—or make your own from blockboard. All you need to do then is to fit two 50mm flush hinges, door knobs and magnetic catches.

Cut the blockboard to fit the opening, then saw it in half to make two doors—the slight gap will allow opening clearance.

Test fit the doors and mark both doors

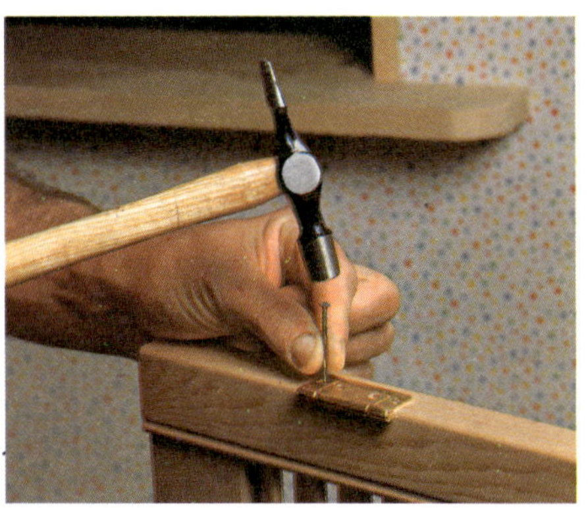

10 *Mark both the doors and the frame for the position of the hinges.*

12 *Cut and fix the architrave for the sides of the opening first followed by the top. Mitre the corners*

13 *Punch the nail holes and fill them with wood filler before finishing*

and frame for the hinges. Mark points 75mm from top and bottom. Make sure that the doors open into the dining room.

Fit the inner leaves of the hinges to the doors first then to the frame. Fit doorknobs.

Add the magnetic catches to the top of the frame so that each door closes against one catch—hold the door closed and flush with the frame front to mark the catch position. Screw the catches to the frame then fix the striking plates to the doors.

CHAPTER 2

BATHROOMS

Help overcome the problem of limited storage space in the bathroom by building an underbasin vanity unit—or make use of wasted space at the end of the bath for storing towels or other items. You could also build a bath bar—an adaptable shelving system fitted above the bath to keep essential items close at hand.

UNDERBASIN UNIT

Until a few years ago at least, architects and builders seem never to have spared a thought for the countless odds and ends that accumulate around a washbasin. Cupboard space is always at a premium in bathrooms and bedrooms, and medicine cabinets are usually too full of medicines to cope with such items as shampoo bottles, shaving tackle, talcum power and perfumes.

This project is designed to solve the problem by converting the area underneath a basin—space which normally goes to waste—into a practical cupboard unit, ideal for storing bathroom odds and ends. And at the same time it streamlines the basin area by hiding unsightly brackets and plumbing fittings beneath the basin.

The unit can be fitted around almost any type of pedestal or wall-mounted basin, although with the latter you get more useful shelving space. Height and width don't matter, because the bowl is fully enclosed. In fact, about the only restriction is that you have enough free space below the basin to make the job worthwhile.

You may find one major problem, however: a basin with a complex or compound curve down the front and sides. This makes the job of scribing the cut-outs a little more difficult, but if you follow the directions given you should get a good fit. The same applies to pedestals—you must scribe the shape of the pedestal onto the shelves and cut this out to make them fit; again, by following the instructions you will be able to do it accurately with the minimum of aggravation and waste.

There are plenty of variations on the basin design. The unit shown incorporates a built-in towel rail, made by extending the nosing moulding which is ingeniously used to edge the top and side boards. And it would be a simple job to make a narrower unit with matching mirror—ideal for a vanity basin in a small room.

The main construction material is 19mm man-made board faced with 3mm plywood or plastic laminate. Naturally if you opt for a painted or laminated finish to go with a modern, practical style of decor it makes sense to use one of the cheaper materials—blockboard or chipboard. But for a more homely stained or varnished look, you should always choose a high quality faced plywood.

Planning the job

Assuming that you have the room and that the project is a practical proposition, your first job is to fix the height of the unit: it is this which governs the sizes of most of the parts, and consequently the amount of wood and materials you will need.

Inspect the rim of the bowl closely and decide how much to leave above the worktop surface. The ideal worktop level is

PART	MATERIAL	SIZE	QUANTITY
A (top)	19mm board	990mm × 430mm	1
A1 (facing)	3mm ply or 1.5mm laminate	990mm × 430mm	1 (2 for laminate)
B (sides)	19mm board	740mm × 380mm	2
B1 (facings)	3mm ply or 1.5mm laminate	750mm × 380mm	2 (4 for laminate)
C (front edge trim)	38mm × 25mm softwood nosing moulding	4m total length	—
D (rear edge trim)	38mm × 25mm PAR softwood	4m total length	—
E (towel rail)	25mm dia. softwood		1
F,H,J (fixing battens)	50mm × 25mm PAR softwood	2.6m total length	—
G (lower shelf)	19mm board	716mm × 415mm	1
I (kickboard)	19mm board	716mm × 50mm	1
K (doors)	19mm board	698mm × 357mm	2
L (shelves)	19mm board	716mm × 415mm	2

generally about 25mm down, at the point where the front of the bowl starts to curve away towards the trap. Because the actual contact area of the worktop is only 1.5mm–3mm thick (the thickness of the laminate or plywood facing), you should have little difficulty in achieving a close fit at this height.

Use a spirit level and felt-tip pen to mark a 'height line' around the bowl and then measure to the floor at several points; the measurements should all be the same, but it's worth checking at this stage.

Now study the diagram on page 32 to see what parts go where and work out a cutting list based on your chosen height. The sample cutting list given with the diagram assumes a standard basin height of 800mm, a width of 560mm and a depth of 400mm. In all probability one or both of these dimensions will be the same on your basin, in which case you can simplify things by using the widths and depths which are quoted in the cutting list.

Tools and materials

Make sure that you have a clear idea of what materials you're using and a full cutting list before you go shopping. For a unit of the size shown you'll need a full sheet (2440mm × 1220mm) of 19mm board; work out the total area of 3mm ply or plastic laminate according to which parts you intend to face.

Apart from the boards and timber other items you need are:
• Two pairs of 55mm butt hinges for the doors.
• Two pairs of small magnetic catches.
• 9mm dowels for the towel rail.
• Four pairs of screw-in shelf studs.
• Iron-on edging strip or laminate strip for the doors, shelves and kickboard.
• A large supply of PVA woodworking glue and 50mm panel pins.
• Contact adhesive and 38mm No. 6 screws (laminate facing only).
• Twelve 62mm No. 8 screws and wallplugs for the wall fixing.
• Paint, stain or polyurethane varnish as required for finishing.

Tools for the job are perfectly straightforward and should be found in any well equipped carpentry toolkit. The cut-outs for the bowl (and pedestal, if fitted) can be made with either a power jig saw or a coping saw, although the latter will give you more control. If you choose laminate facings, make sure you have a proper cutter and a metal straightedge to run it against.

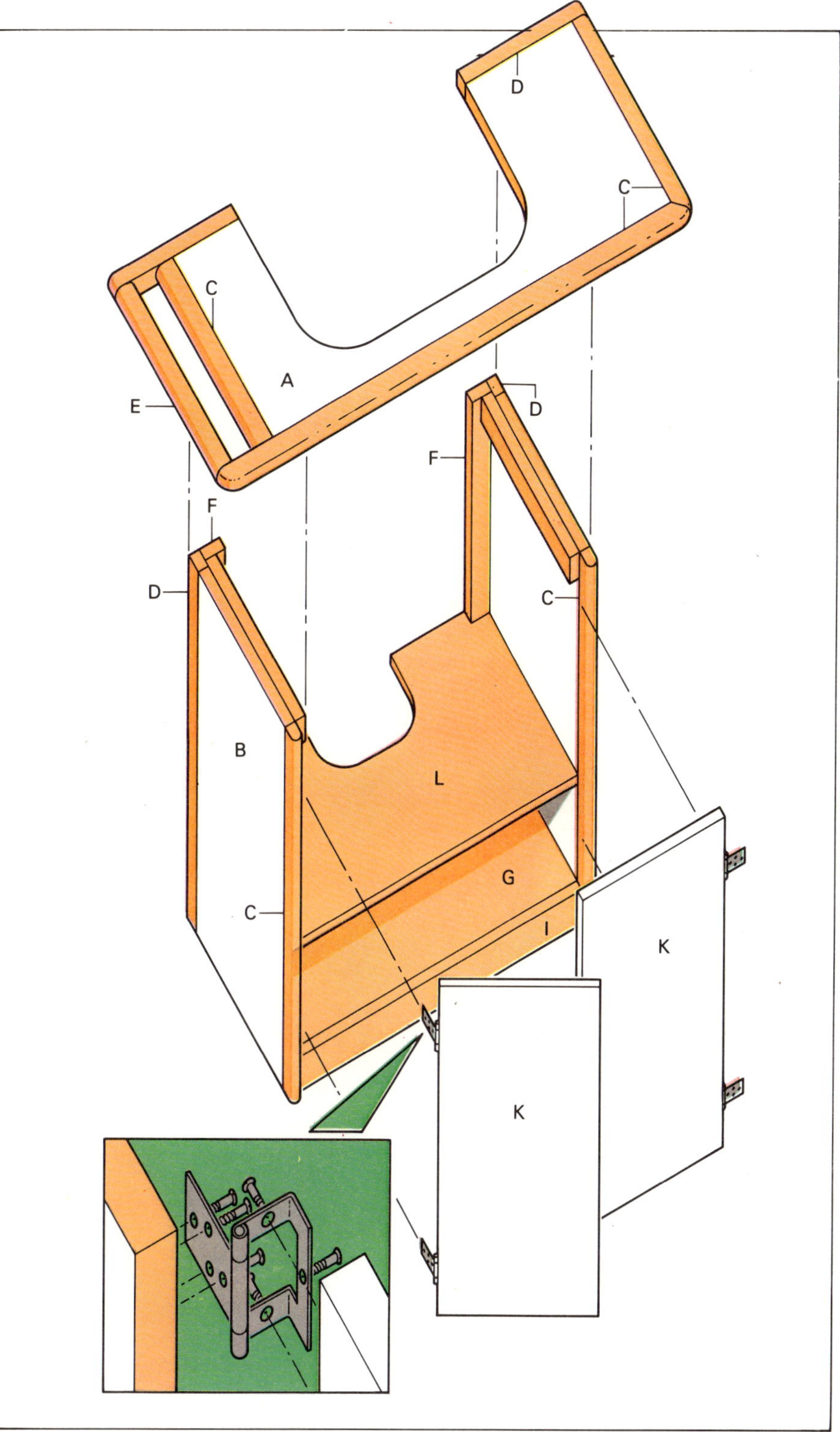

How the unit fits together

The top (A) and sides (B) of the unit are 19mm thick board faced with plywood or laminate (A1, B1) glued in place. Both sides of the board must be faced if laminate is used to prevent warping. Each board is finished with 38mm × 25mm twice rounded softwood moulding (C) on the exposed edges and with ordinary 38mm × 25mm PAR (Planed All Round) softwood (D) on those that are concealed; the wood is glued and pinned in place.

The optional towel rail (which can go on either side of the unit) is made by extending the edge trim outwards and fitting a piece of 25mm diameter softwood round (broomstick) between them.

The sides are screwed to the wall via

The base unit is simple to make, especially if your basin is wall-hung rather than a pedestal type. Remember that you must apply laminate to both sides of the side panels: this prevents them warping, as well as helping to improve the view when the cupboard doors are opened. The bottom shelf is structurally important

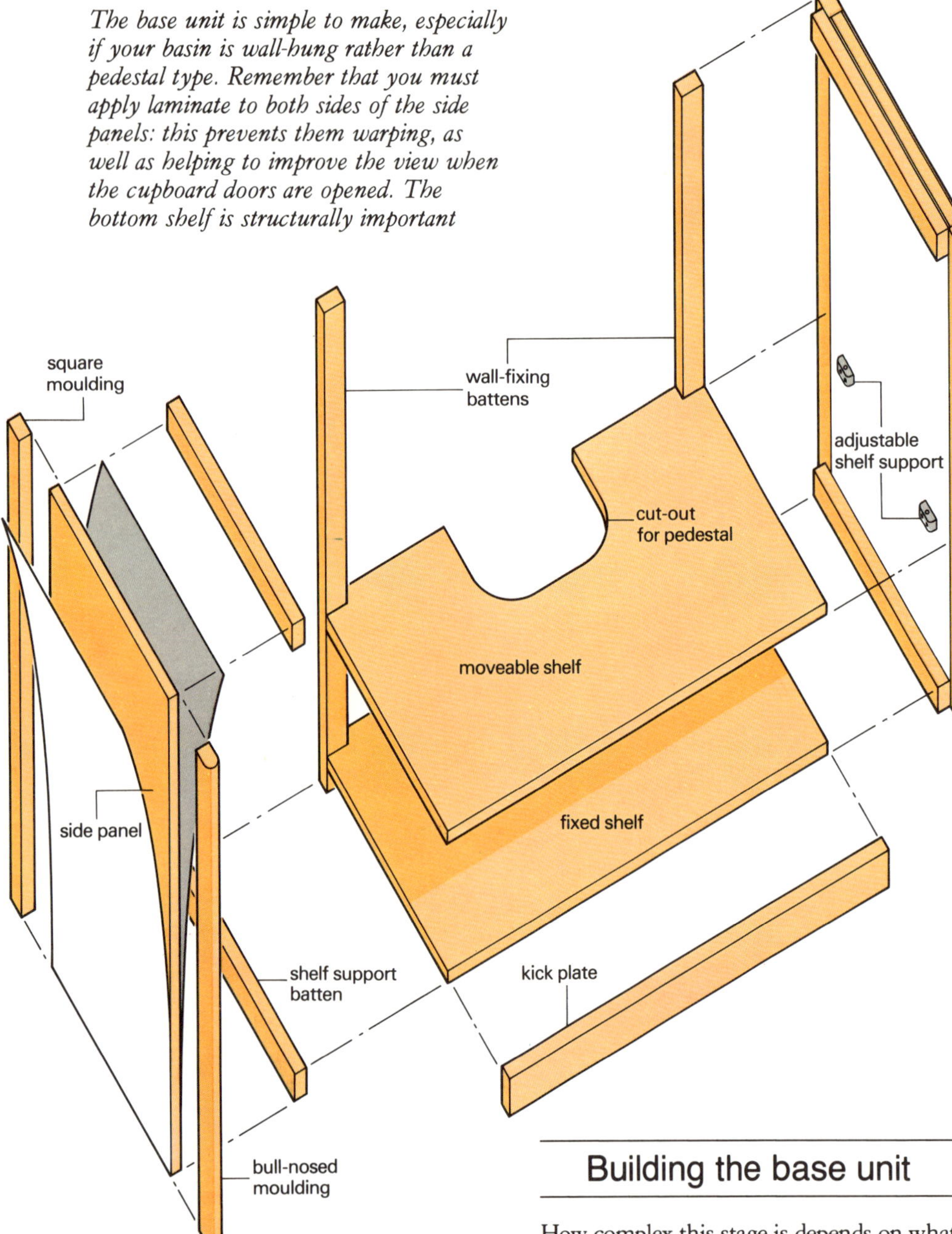

vertical battens (F) pinned and glued to the rear trim. A fixed lower shelf (G) stiffens the construction; this is supported on battens (H) pinned and glued to the sides and is concealed by a kickboard panel (I).

The top is glued and pinned down into the sides before applying the facing (which then conceals the pin holes).

The double doors (K) are hung on butt hinges let in to the sides.

Adjustable shelves (L) are supported on screw-in shelf support plugs. They can go at any height, but with a pedestal basin you'll need to saw cut-outs to clear the pedestal itself. The same applies to the fixed lower shelf (G). You will probably have to try the cut-out for the pedestal a number of times until it fits.

Building the base unit

How complex this stage is depends on what sort of finish you want to give the boards. If you plan to use laminate, apply this as and when you cut the boards to size. The same applies to stain, which will be much easier to brush on before assembly.

Start with the side panels of 19mm board. Cut these to your chosen worktop height, minus the thickness of the top itself. Use the panels as templates to mark the facings for cutting—with a marking knife if they're plywood, or in felt-tip pen for laminate.

Cut laminate by running down the cutting line a few times with the cutter held against a steel rule, then snapping off the waste over a metal straightedge. In the case of thin ply, using a marking knife will break the surface and minimize the risk of splintering when you saw it. Even so, make

sure the board is well supported either side of the cutting line.

When cutting thin ply by hand, use a sharp panel saw rather than a rip or cross-cut saw as these, by their very nature, will create splinters and tear the wood.

Assembling the parts

Glue the facings to the side panels using whichever adhesive is most appropriate, spreading it thinly with a notched spreader. Clamp the assemblies using G-clamps and offcuts of wood until all the components are completely dry.

Use the panels again as templates to cut the front (nosing) and rear (softwood) edging to size, and also the two vertical wall fixing battens. Glue the edging strips to the panels (make sure they're the right way round), then reinforce the fixings by pinning them at 100mm centres; punch the pin heads until they are well below the surface of the wood.

Drill clearance holes in the wall fixing battens to take the No. 8 screws. The holes should be at roughly 100mm centres, but it's worth checking beforehand that their positions don't coincide with obstructions below that could make this impossible.

When the panel edgings are dry, pin and glue the battens flush with the rear ones by pinning through from the outside. To do this without weakening the edging fixings, you'll need to support underneath the panels with offcuts of the same batten materials. Take great care to keep the battens flush as you pin them, by holding the assemblies against a wall, or a board clamped to your bench.

Cut the shelf support battens to size. These extend from the rear battens to the front nosing minus 19mm (the thickness of the kickboard). If the insides of the side panels are laminated, drill and screw the battens in place; otherwise pin and glue them. Don't forget to check that support battens are level, by measuring from the bottom at both ends.

Now cut the fixed shelf to size, according to the width and depth of your unit, and glue on laminate facings if required. Use a tenon saw to cut notches in the two rear corners of the shelf, so that it clears the fixing battens and lies flush with the rear edging. If you are dealing with a pedestal basin, make a cardboard template of the pedestal and use this to saw a cut-out in the board. Make the cut-out rather small and test-fit the shelf, enlarging it progressively for a good fit.

1 *Check that the corners of the plywood sheet are square before you start work. Use a try square*

Stop the unit from going out of square at this stage by pinning a length of batten across the top, near the front edge. Check as you do so that the sides remain plumb by holding a spirit level against them.

Drill the wall to take plugs or cavity fixings as appropriate, reposition the unit and screw it firmly to the wall.

Making the top

Because the top of the unit has a laminate facing, you don't need to get the cut-out in

2 *Drill the fixing batten screw holes before you fix them to the side panels —not once they're in place*

3 *Cut the mitred joints in the side and rear nosing of the top panel and offer the two pieces up to check their fit*

4 *Make the cut-out in the top panel using a power jigsaw. Don't force the saw through the timber*

5 *Before cutting the other mitred joints at the same end of the top panel, offer up the two nosing pieces; mark them off*

Stand the two side panels upright and lay the shelf between them, on its support battens. Get an assistant to hold the assembly in this position while you pin and glue the shelf in place.

Complete the base unit by cutting the kickboard panel size and pinning and gluing it against the shelf front edge.

Now slide the unit into position underneath the basin and mark the locations of any obstructions that are stopping it sitting flush against the back wall. Make cut-outs for these in the side panels where necessary.

Try the unit again, this time checking that it is level with the battens hard against the wall. Make adjustments by trimming the bottom edges of the side panels with a plane or planer file. When all is well, mark the positions of the fixing screws through the battens onto the back wall.

the 19mm board absolutely perfect. Use a template to cut the facing accurately.

Start by sawing the 19mm board to size then refer to Making the template, for how to transfer the profile of the basin to the board. Cut out the waste and try the top.

Use the template next to mark the cut-out onto your facing material. Make sure that you cut the facing to the waste side of the line so that you still allow yourself enough room for final trimming. Remember, if you are using laminate, to face the underside of the board too.

Try the facings and board together in a final dry run, but don't glue them yet.

Edging the top must be done in strict order if the parts are to join accurately:
• Cut the front nosing roughly to length and mitre the end furthest from the towel rail.
• Cut the longer side moulding approxi-

6 *At the opposite end of the top panel, clamp the nosing in place and use it to mark the cut lines on the towel rail itself*

The top panel is easily made. Only the basin cut-out presents problems. Remember the laminate panels sit flush with the edge nosing

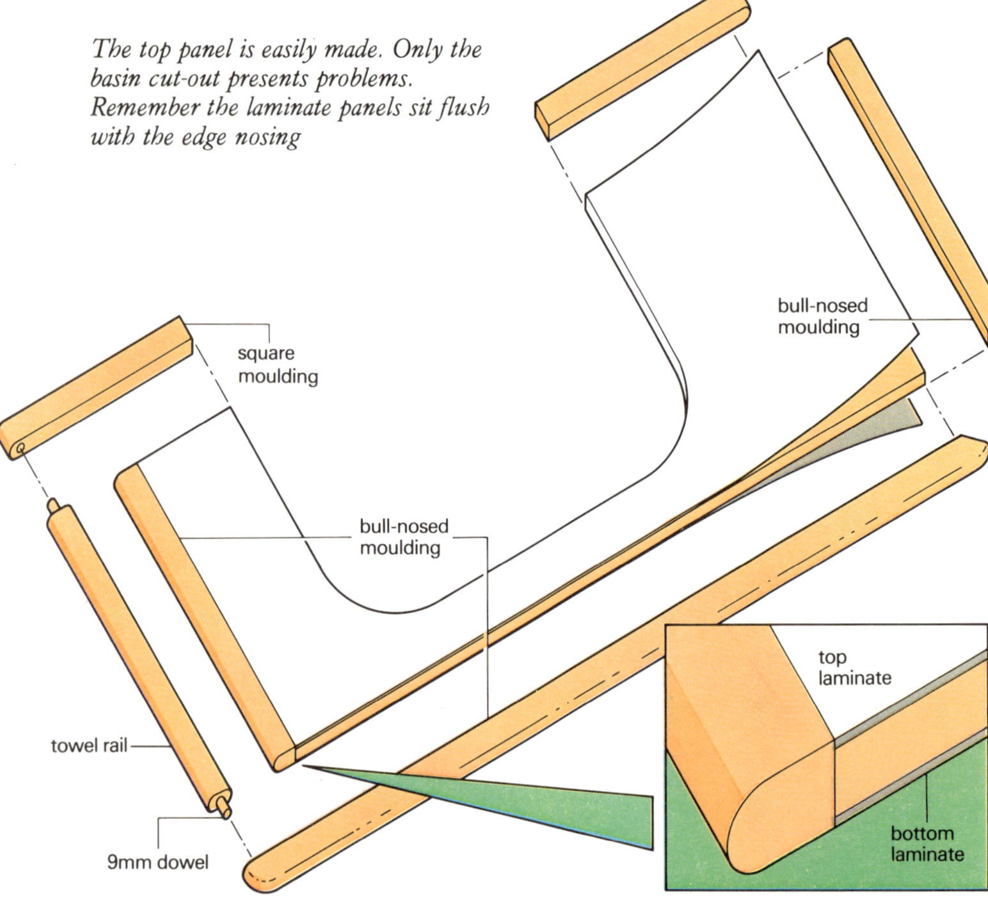

mately 25mm longer than the width of the top and mitre the front end.

• Try the two pieces for fit where they meet, then pin and glue them to the top leaving enough of a lip to take in the thickness of the facing (ie the nosing should sit flush against the facing when the latter is finally glued in position).

• Cut the front nosing to the correct length and use the top assembly to mark off and cut the remaining edging—the rear pieces and the towel rail side nosing.

• Cut two wall fixing battens to extend from the back of the bowl to the side panel battens. Pin and glue these flush with the backs of the rear edging pieces and drill two clearance holes in each of the battens to take No. 8 screws.

• Pin and glue the rear edging piece on the non-towel rail side and the remaining piece of nosing to the top, leaving a lip for the facing as before. Saw off the long side nosing flush with the rear edging.

• Clamp the other rear edging piece to the top then cut the towel rail dowel to fit between this and the front nosing.

Drill the dowel ends and the edgings to a depth of 10mm and slip glued dowels into the towel rail. Cut a groove along the length of each dowel first to allow excess glue to escape. Apply glue to the rail ends and to the rear edging, then bring all the parts

together and clamp them. Strengthen the rear edging by pinning through into the top in the usual way. When all the parts are completely dry, round off the front corners of the edging and the insides of the towel rail as shown, using a rasp or planer file to leave a perfectly smooth surface that won't catch on delicate fabrics, and is ready for finishing.

Making the template

The most critical part of the entire job is transferring the shape of the basin to the top board. To do it simply requires a sheet of stiff card which you can cut out to the correct shape, and the exact centre line of the front of the basin.

To find the centre line of the basin lay a timber batten across the basin and clamp it in place. Measure the exact width of the

unit, mark the centre of the batten and, using a carpenter's square, align another batten with this mark so that it overhangs the front of the basin. Mark the centre of the basin front with a chinagraph pencil or felt-tip pen.

Now take a sheet of card, lay it on top of one half of the basin and mark out the rough shape of the cutout from underneath with a pencil. Cut out the shape (try to cut it too small at first), then offer it up to the basin to check the fit. Keep on trimming the card until the shape is exactly right then mark on it the position of the basin's centre line. Check its fit with the other side of the basin.

Now lay the template on a larger sheet, aligning the rear edge of the template with one side of the sheet below. Draw out the basin's half-shape, mark the centre line, then flip the template over, match up the centre line again and draw the other half of the outline.

Cut out the shape of the basin from the larger sheet of card, and offer it up to the basin to check the fit once and for all.

Final assembly

It's best to delay fitting the top for as long as you can so that you have more room in which to mark up the doors and shelves.

Cut the door panels to size by direct measurement from the unit. Allow 1mm clearance for each edging strip (1.5mm if they're laminate) and a further 2mm closing clearance. Try the panels for fit in the unit before using them as templates to cut your chosen facing material.

With the doors faced and edged as required, place them in the unit once more and mark off the hinge positions against the nosing and the door edges.

Screw the hinges to the doors first, then hang the doors against the side panels. When both doors close perfectly—you may have to modify the depths of some of the rebates first—fit the magnetic catches so they close flush with the kickboard edge.

Cut the adjustable shelves to size, notching the rear corners to clear the fixing battens as before.

Having checked that the shelves fit properly, screw in the shelf supports where indicated in the diagram on page 32 and lay them in position.

Now position the top and mark through the fixing battens into the wall. Drill and plug the wall to take the appropriate fixings.

Screw the battens firmly to the wall and pin through the top into the side panels. Finally, glue the top facing in place.

BATH PANEL AND STORAGE

One place that is almost always short on storage is the bathroom—and yet the annoying thing is that usable space is often wasted. A common example is a gap between the end of the bath and the wall. This project shows you how to get the most out of it by installing a removable drawer. It also shows you how to panel in your bath so that you give your bathroom a new, streamlined look together with valuable extra storage space.

The drawer runs on wheels—like a trolley—and is made from melamine, so it's easy to clean and there is no complicated carpentry involved in making it. It is housed in a frame which is fixed to the walls and topped with a melamine board to add a handy shelf to the end of the bath.

The bath panel is made from decorative wall board braced with battens and held in place with magnetic catches—this makes the whole panel easy to remove to gain access to the plumbing.

The project can be adapted to suit many different bathroom layouts. And all is not lost if you don't have enough room to accommodate the storage drawer as well as the panelling—it's easy to adapt the design so you can just box the bath in neatly. But you must think ahead before you start.

Planning considerations

No two bathrooms are alike, so although the idea behind the design will remain constant, its dimensions will vary according to the size of your bathroom. The first thing to do is to take accurate measurements and from these make up your own working drawings—see diagram above. What you will need is a sketch similar to this but showing how the same features will fit into your space. It doesn't need to be very detailed, but it must show the dimensions.

Materials you need

You should be able to get all the materials from any large do-it-yourself store without any trouble.

•The bath panel and facing for the drawer are made from decorative wallboard—Laconite is a popular example. Wallboard is light and has a waterproof surface. It comes in a large range of textures and designs so you should be able to find a pattern you really like. The standard sheet size is 2240mm × 1120mm, which will be ample for the job.

•The drawer and top are made from 16mm white melamine made in different widths from 152mm to 914mm, usually in 2438mm and 1829mm lengths—calculate how much you need from your drawings.

•The edging strip for finishing off the drawer is 19mm wide and is bought by the roll—1800mm should be enough.

•The battening for making the panels and drawer frame is all 50mm × 25mm. Make sure that all the lengths are straight or you will end up with bent panels.

•The runner guides are made from 25mm × 25mm softwood.

•Plastic fixing blocks hold the whole drawer construction together—you will need at least 14. Screws are usually supplied with the fixing blocks when you buy them.

•The drawer wheels should not be more than 40mm in diameter. Fixed wheels are better than revolving castors. These should also be supplied with their own screws; but you may have to buy new ones since the design requires 16mm chipboard screws.

•Magnetic catches hold the side panel in place. There are several types—get surface mounted ones, preferably with slotted screw holes which will make positioning them that much easier, so count up how many you need from your drawing.

•Corrugated fasteners hold the battens together to make up the panels—buy them in the 30mm size.

•Drawer handles come in lots of different shapes and sizes—the choice is yours. Make sure that your handle or knob can be fixed to melamine—some are attached with a long screw which may come through on the other side and snag your laundry.

•Contact adhesive is used to glue the wallboard to the side panel and front of the drawer. Either buy a large tube or a small tin to make sure you have enough. Spreaders are normally sold with the adhesive but if not, you can make your own by cutting notches in an off-cut of the wallboard.

•Additional materials you need are: 38mm No. 6 chipboard screws for the drawer base

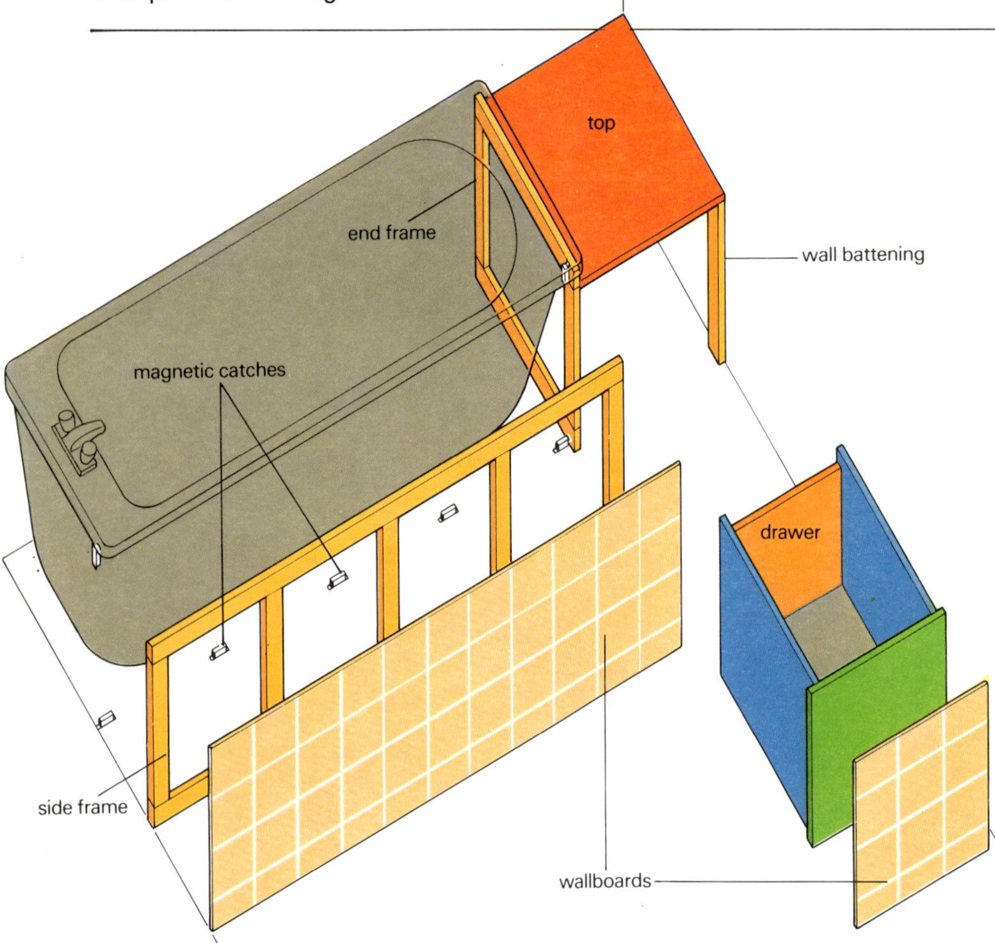

A batten framework fits round the bath. The side frame is held by magnetic catches so it can be removed, and is panelled with wallboard. The end frame supports a top shelf over the drawer

and 50mm No. 8 screws and plugs to fix the battening to the walls (your choice of plug will depend on what type of wall you are screwing into—masonry plugs for a brick wall, cavity plugs for a timber framed wall), 38mm panel pins for attaching the runner guides and PVA wood glue for all the joints.

Tools you need

Most of the job can be carried out with standard carpentry equipment: panel saw, tapemeasure, screwdriver, drill and bits, counter-sink, spirit level, trimming knife, hammer, straightedge and bradawl. The only special tool you need is an ordinary household iron to fix the melamine strip.

Panelling the bath

Start by making a frame from 50mm × 25mm softwood, ensuring that it fits accurately around the side and end. This can then be panelled in with wallboard.

Hold the lengths of your frame timber up to the side and end of your bath in turn so that they fit under the rim as shown in the diagram on page 37. Mark the wood off and use a panel saw to cut it to length. Use the two battens you have cut as patterns to make two more similar lengths in order to make the bottom of the frame.

To complete the frames you need a number of vertical struts—all the same length. To find out how long to make them, lay two of your frame lengths one on top of the other and cut a further piece to span the gap between them and the rim of the bath. You need to cut two strips of this length for the end plus a number for the side panel. Here, the vertical struts should be equally spaced not more than 40mm apart—but remember that it is better to insert an extra strut than to leave one out. If you intend to have a join between two panels of wallboard, make sure that you fit an extra strut where the extra join occurs.

To assemble the frames, lay all the pieces flat on the floor and make sure that all the corners are square. Hammer home the corrugated fasteners—two to each joint.

Hold the two completed frames up to the bath to make sure that they fit under it and against each other properly. Use a spirit level to check that they are vertical. Mark the position of the end frame on

1 *Measure the frame templates directly from the bath, fitting them underneath the rim of the bath*

2 *Assemble the frames with corrugated fasteners, and then check that the frames are square*

the wall and on the floor, then remove both of the completed frames.

Screw two plastic fixing blocks to the back edge of the end frame and two to the bottom edge—all the blocks should be on the side towards the bath. Reposition the frame and mark through the holes in the blocks onto the wall. Drill the wall and insert wallplugs or cavity fixings as appropriate, then screw the frame in place.

The side frame is held up against the bath with magnets placed at each corner behind each strut. To find the positions of the magnets on the floor, wall and end frame, hold the panels up against the bath using a spirit level to check the vertical. Mark off the positions of the magnets, and their corresponding plates, then screw them in place on the frame.

Try the completed frame up against the

bath to check that it fits. Then lay it down on the wallboard to mark the panel for cutting. Lay it on the face of the board—this allows you to align the pattern. Mark up carefully, about 2mm oversize all round, and score the lines with a trimming knife and straightedge. Cut the board with a panel saw, supporting it firmly on both sides of the cut. Smooth the rough edges with glass-paper and a sanding block, then with a plane or planer file after fixing. This allows you to finish the edges to match the frame exactly by using the frame itself as your guide. It's the best way to get a really good fit.

To stick the wallboard to the brace, spread contact adhesive evenly on the bracing battens and onto the rough side of the wallboard. Leave both wallboard and battens until the adhesive is touch dry.

With the end frame in place, carry the

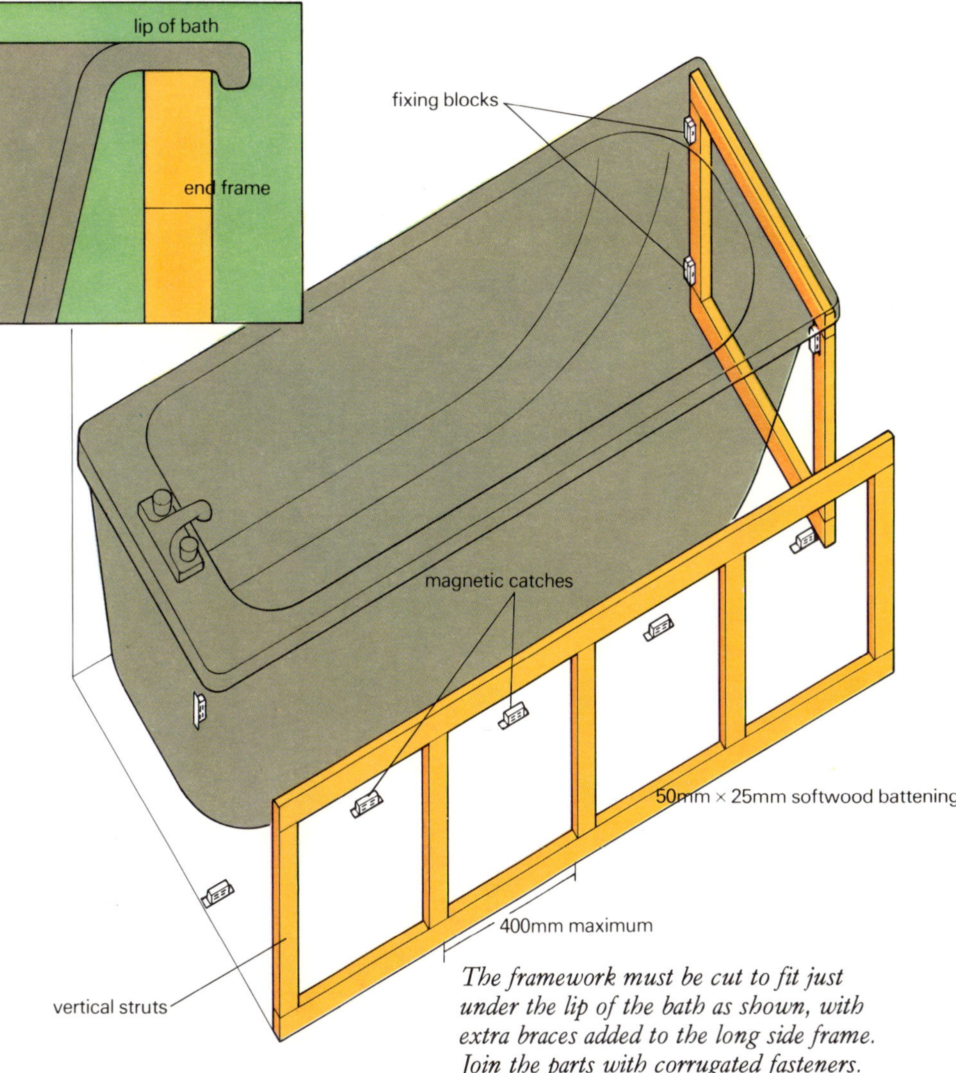

> ## ★ WATCH POINT ★
>
> If you have a strong pattern on your wallboard—imitation tiles for example—cut it so that the pattern is complete along the top; it is best to keep cut patterns low down near the floor. Mark the board for 'top' and 'bottom'.

framing round onto the wall to support the top panel. Before fitting the top, you must position the runner guides for the drawer.

The drawing (overleaf) shows the general layout, but you will have to cut everything to fit your space accurately.

Start with the wall battens which support the top panel. Cut these from 50mm × 25mm softwood—the one on the end wall is the same length as the end frame; the upright and the one against the back wall should be cut to span the gaps remaining.

Position the battens on the wall using a spirit level to ensure that they are horizontal. When you do this, allow for the thickness of the melamine top above them—it must sit on the battens so that its top edge is just below the lip of the bath.

Mark the line of each batten on the wall, when the first batten is in place, then take

The framework must be cut to fit just under the lip of the bath as shown, with extra braces added to the long side frame. Join the parts with corrugated fasteners. Screw the end frame in place and fit the side on magnetic catches

it away for drilling. You need 4.5mm countersunk holes every 300mm or so. Drill and plug corresponding holes in the wall, then screw the battens into place with 50mm No. 8 screws.

3 *Fit the end frame under the bath and screw it to the wall with plastic fixing blocks*

4 *Hold the side frame in place, check it is vertical and mark positions for the magnetic catches*

5 *Remove the frame, mark the dimensions on the wallboard panel and saw it to fit*

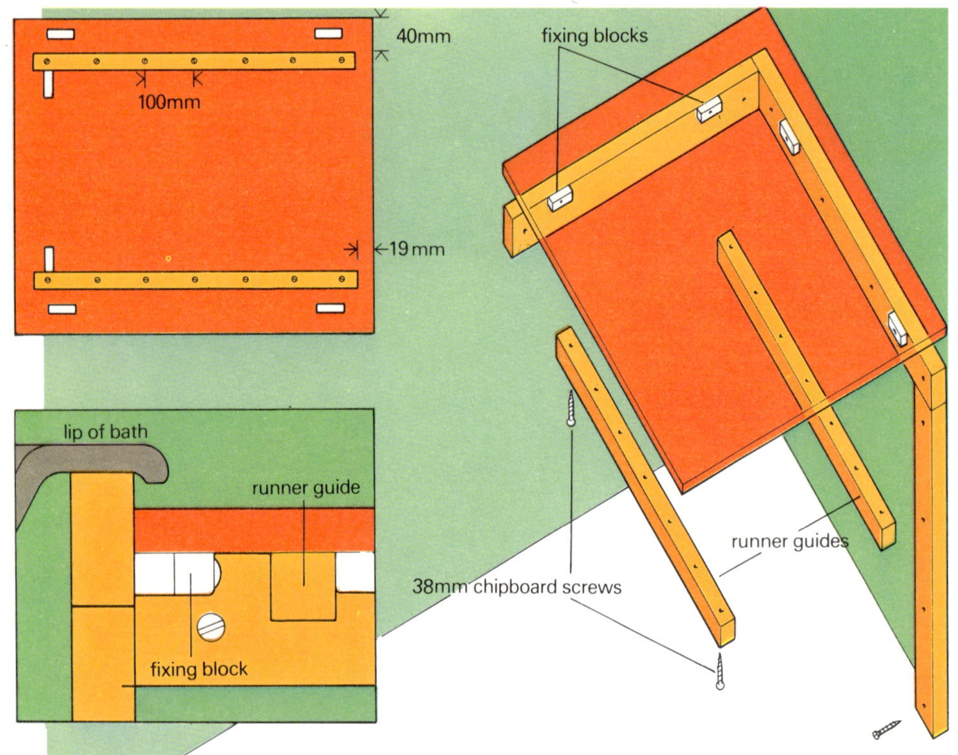

Fit the top onto the battens and mark their positions all round. Then remove the top and screw on plastic blocks—two on each side and two at the back to align with the battens. Replace the top and screw it firmly in position. Then screw the runners to it from underneath.

Making the drawer

The drawer is a simple box made from melamine and fitted with wheels. It's easy to make, but measure it accurately for a good fit in the space under the top.

Start with the front panel, which should be cut to fit the opening between the frame and wall batten at each side and between the top and floor—less about 3mm clearance all round. Once again, it's worth making a template to ensure that you get it right.

With this as a guide, you can make the other parts. Cut two sides, the same height as the front and the depth of the top less 50mm. Cut a back, 80mm narrower than the front and 30mm lower. Finally, cut a

The melamine top fits under the lip of the bath, fixed to wall battens with blocks. The drawer runners are screwed to the underside

To make the top, you need a piece of melamine which fits exactly on top of the battens and against the end frame. You can measure this up, but to ensure you get a good fit, it's worth making a template from hardboard or stiff card first. Cut the melamine out with a panel saw. Tape the cutting line to minimize the unsightly splintering of the surface that can happen when cutting laminates.

Before you fix the top in place, add the runners to its underside. They are made from 25mm × 25mm softwood, cut 50mm shorter than the depth of the top. Position them 21mm from the front edge of the panel and 45mm in from the edges. Make sure that they are parallel, then mark along them. Drill every 100mm or so and screw in 38mm No. 6 chipboard screws. Then remove the runners while you fix the top to the battens.

6 *Cut the wall battens to length, level them and screw to the wall at the right height*

7 *A card template cut to fit on the battens will help you to mark the melamine panel*

8 *Position the drawer runners under the top and screw them in place temporarily*

9 *Remove the runners and fix the top with blocks. Finally, refit the runners to the drawer*

The drawer consists of five pieces of melamine board and a batten framework. All the parts are cut to fit the space available, leaving the relevant clearances where necessary. The sides are joined to the front with block fixings, leaving a clearance at each side so they align with the runners. The back is fixed between them with a clearance above it for the runners. The batten subframe is screwed inside the main box; the triangles at the corners which support the castors are fixed to give 10mm clearance for the wheels. The base is simply dropped into place on the subframe. To trim the front, it is panelled with wallboard and edged all round with melamine strip

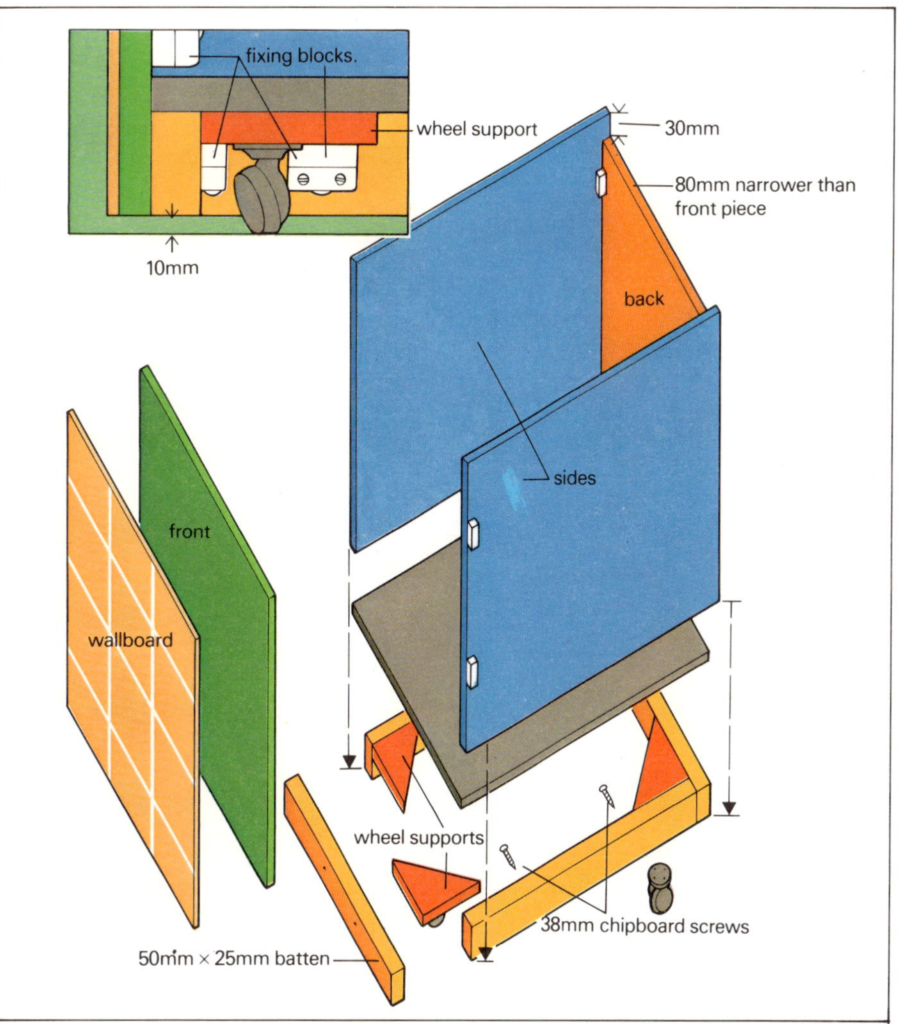

base, the same width as the back and the same length as the sides less 15mm.

To assemble it all, use plastic fixing blocks and battens. The drawing (right) shows how the parts fit together. Screw plastic fixing blocks to the outside of each side, one near the top, one near the bottom, then screw the sides to the front. To make sure they are the right distance apart, lay the back between them and centre it so that both sides are the same distance from the edge of the front panel.

Fit the back in place and secure it with two plastic blocks on each side, one near the top and one at least 75mm up from the bottom. Note that while the bottom edge of the back should be flush with the sides, the top edge is 30mm lower. This allows clearance for the runners above it.

Now cut four lengths of 50mm × 25mm batten to fit inside the drawer assembly as shown in the drawing. They don't need to be a perfect fit as they will be concealed from view. Drill and screw them to the melamine using 38mm No. 6 chipboard screws.

The four wheels on which the drawer runs are mounted on triangular plates which fit inside the corners of the frame. Make the triangular plates from some spare melamine; cut two 100mm squares, then saw them diagonally. Screw the fixing plates of the wheels onto each triangle, making sure that the wheels will have enough room to revolve freely inside the frame.

Line up each triangle inside a corner of the frame so that its wheel projects 10mm below the bottom of the frame. Screw the triangles into position with fixing blocks.

Drop the base inside so that it rests on the battens and fix with plastic blocks.

Finally, face the front of the drawer with wallboard so that it matches the bath panel. To do this, cut out a piece of wallboard that slightly overlaps by about 2mm all round.

10 *Assemble the main frame with blocks then screw in the subframe*

Make sure that its pattern will match up with the one on the bath. Score the surface of the melamine with coarse sandpaper to help the glue to bond and then glue the wallboard to the melamine as when making the panel. When it is finally stuck, smooth down the edges of the wallboard with glasspaper or a planer file.

11 *Position the corner supports carefully so the castors project 10mm*

Finish off the edges of the drawer front with iron on edging strips. Lay the strip along the edges of the melamine and wallboard keeping it flush with the front. Protect the surface with brown paper and iron it on. Finish off all exposed edges in the same way. The last part of the project consists of fitting a handle to the drawer.

MAKE A BATH BAR

This bath bar will keep all your bathing paraphernalia just where it's needed and give order to the clutter that's probably already there. The bar is simply fixed to the wall alongside the bath.

Its design incorporates a clever wall fixing method which gives the unit the impression of having no means of support.

The shelves are actually fixed to battens screwed to the wall, but they're located within the thickness of the shelves for neatness. A normal, flat shelf would sag with the arrangement, but the vertical sections act as braces to stiffen the unit.

The bath bar is straightforward to make from plywood (for the shelves and uprights), ramin (for the wall battens) and stout dowelling (for the front trim). Two thicknesses of ply are stuck together to form the lightweight shelves—plus the hidden fixing method—and the surfaces are clad with plastic laminate in your choice of colour. This gives a smooth, waterproof, easy-clean surface—important in the steamy atmosphere of the bathroom. (If you want to use the unit in another room you may prefer to stain, varnish or paint the shelves instead of laminating them).

Materials and tools

Study the cutting diagram on page 41 to see just how the bar fits together. You can cut out all the plywood pieces you need from two 1220mm × 610mm sheets—one 12.5mm thick; the other 9mm thick.

In addition to the plywood you'll need the following:
- Enough sheets of 1.5mm thick laminate to face the top and underside of the shelves and also both sides of the uprights. Two 1220 × 610mm sheets should be sufficient, but if the colour choice isn't good in this size, you may have to buy a larger 2440mm × 1220mm sheet.
- 1 litre of contact adhesive (ideally the emulsion type) to stick down the laminate.
- A 3m length of 12.5mm square ramin (hardwood) for the shelf batten.
- A 3m length of 44mm diameter softwood dowelling for the front edge trim.
- Sufficient 19mm No. 8 countersunk wood-screws to fix the shelves to the battens.
- Sufficient 600 No. 8 countersunk wood-screws to attach the battens to the wall.
- Enough 19mm panel pins to fix the two halves of the shelves together.
- Enough 65mm panel pins to fix the dowel edging trim in place on the shelves.
- PVA adhesive to stick the plywood halves of the shelves together. To mark out, cut and assemble the bar, equip yourself with a try square, tape measure, long straightedge, jigsaw with adjustable sole plate, hammer, screwdriver and tenon saw. You'll also need an electric drill with 4.5mm and 2mm bits, a laminate cutter, trimming knife and fine file, plus a sliding bevel, smoothing plane or coping saw.

How the bar fits together

Each shelf of the bath bar is made from a strip of 12.5mm plywood bonded to a strip of 9mm plywood.

The thinner ply strip overlaps the thicker one at the back by 12.5mm; the ramin wall battens fit in the recess for a flush fitting. The vertical shelf components are made in the same way and the main battens are positioned on the 'shadow' or underside.

The shelves are fixed to the vertical

sections with mitre joints, reinforced with glue and screws.

The unit is intended to be fixed into a return wall at one end, although a mid-wall version can easily be made: it should simply be shorter in length to prevent sagging.

The entire shelf unit is faced with a plastic laminate of your choice, which is applied with contact adhesive.

The front edge of the bar is trimmed with stout 44mm diameter softwood dowelling, which is stained or varnished. The mitred corner joints are rounded off for neatness once the trim has been fixed in place.

Making the shelves

Each shelf is made up from two strips of plywood bonded together. The 12.5mm thick lower half is topped with a thinner 9mm strip, which overlaps at the back to take the wall fixing batten. It's best to cut the ply into strips and stick the two halves together before you cut each piece to the length of the shelf.

Mark out the 12.5mm thick plywood sheet in 137.5mm wide strips, using a tape measure and a long straightedge. Make sure the edges of the ply are sound and straight—any unevenness will make laminating awkward.

Place the sheet on a firm, flat surface—ideally a workbench—and cut out each strip, using a power jigsaw.

Mark out the 9mm thick sheet of plywood for the other shelf components. These strips should be 150mm wide to give the front-to-back dimension of the shelves (including an allowance for the overlap).

You can now stick the two halves of the shelves together, using PVA adhesive.

Lay the 137.5mm wide strips face down on a flat surface and apply a generous amount of PVA adhesive to their backs. Spread it out thinly with an offcut of card, making sure the edges are well-covered.

Position the 150mm wide strips on top and align the edges. Push the panels into a right-angled corner to make sure the edges align: you can make a simple frame from slim battens nailed together in a right-angle, or just use the corner of a room at the level of the skirting board.

Drive in 19mm panel pins to secure the strips together, working from the thin panel side. Space the pins at 50mm intervals, 10mm from each edge. Insert a row of pins down the centre of the strips.

Clamp all bonded strips together with

1 *Measure the ply into strips 137.5mm and 150mm wide and cut them out. Use a batten clamped to the workpiece*

2 *Temporarily pin a length of ramin to each 137.5mm strip. Glue the 150mm strip on top and cramp the two together*

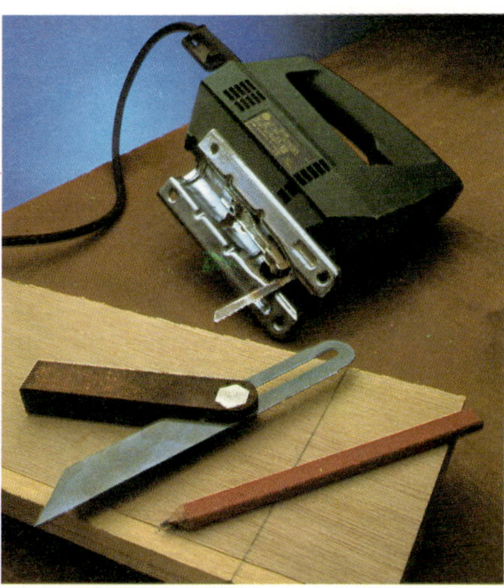
3 *Use a sliding bevel to mark 45° angles on the edges to be mitre-jointed. They can then be cut with a jigsaw*

If your jigsaw hasn't got a fence, make your own. Measure the distance from the saw blade to the side of the sole plate then transfer this dimension to the wood, measured from your cutting line. Clamp a long straight-edged batten to the work-piece so that the edge is on the line. To ensure a true cut, keep the jig-saw's sole plate against the batten.

G-cramps—using battens to protect the ply from damage by the cramp jaws, and to distribute pressure. Set the strips aside for the glue to dry.

When the glue has dried, remove the cramps and mark off the bonded strips in shelf sections. Start at the ramin-edged end, labelling this for later identification.

Measure off the lengths of the shelves—two at 550mm, one at 525mm and one at 400mm—and draw lines across the ply against a try square.

The shelves are mitre-jointed to the uprights, so mark 45° angles on the edges of the strips, using a sliding bevel to set the angle. Continue the lines across the other face of the strips. Notice that the two end shelves are square-ended and the lowest 525mm long shelf is mitred inwards at each of its ends.

Cut out each shelf and label it, then mark out and cut the two short (125mm) and one long (250mm) uprights. Make sure you cut the mitres the correct way round, so that the fixing batten will be on the 'shadow' or underside of the shelf unit.

Sand smooth the cut edges of the shelves and uprights, but don't round them off or you'll find it difficult to fit the laminate accurately in position.

The 400mm long shelf has a cut-out to incorporate a towel rail, and you should cut this now. Measure 75mm in from the front

It's important that the two halves of the shelves are fixed together squarely, so cut and temporarily pin lengths of 12.5mm square ramin to one long edge of each 137.5mm wide strip—they'll then match the 150mm strips. The end shelf abuts a return wall, so pin a ramin strip to the relevant end of the narrower ply.

4 *Fix each horizontal and vertical batten to the wall, carefully aligning each mitre with your try square*

6 *Use your home-made jig to hold the dowel firmly in place while you mark the lines necessary to chamfer the flat*

edge and draw a line across against a straight edge. Measure 50mm in from each end and draw lines from front to back.

Cut out the recess using the jigsaw freehand—this tool is excellent for cutting around curves. But don't force the blade.

Fixing the shelves

The next part of the job is to assemble the shelves on the wall: all of the finishing—laminating and edging—can be carried out with the unit fixed in position. First you have to attach the wall battens.

To mark the positions of the horizontal shelves, first decide at what level you want the lowest, 525mm long shelf: for con-

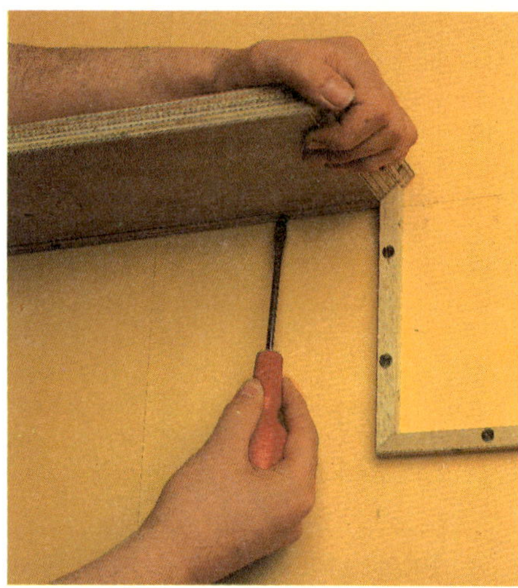

5 *After gluing the overlap and the adjacent edge of the shelf, hold it on its batten and secure the shelf with screws*

7 *By fitting an end stop to your home-made jig you can also use it to plane off the chamfer on the dowelling*

venience this should be about 350mm above the rim of the bath.

Mark the wall at this point in pencil and continue the line at this height for the length of the bath, using a straightedge.

The overall depth of the unit is 300mm—the height of the deepest vertical. Measure up this distance from your first guideline, subtract 21.5mm to give the baseline of the shelves, then make a second line. Continue the line onto the return wall to indicate the end shelf batten position.

Now measure from the end wall in increments of 525mm, 400mm and two at 550mm—the length of the shelves. Measure 21.5mm back from the lines marking the shorter uprights and 21.5mm in the opposite direction from the long up-

8 *When using your mitre box to cut mitres on the dowelling, use the saw carefully to avoid damaging the slots*

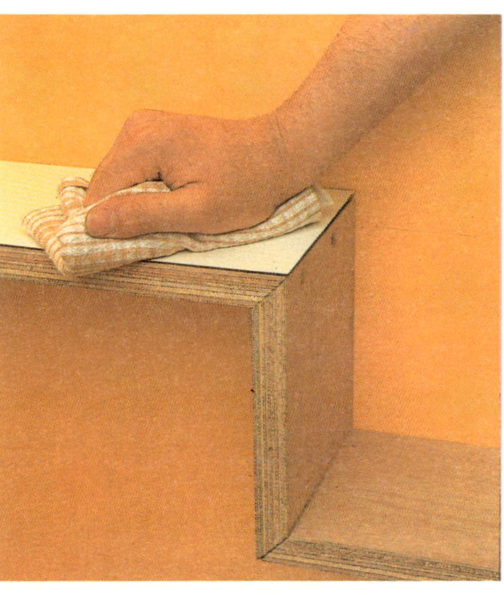

9 *As you position the laminate face panels, press down firmly with a cloth to bond them and eliminate air*

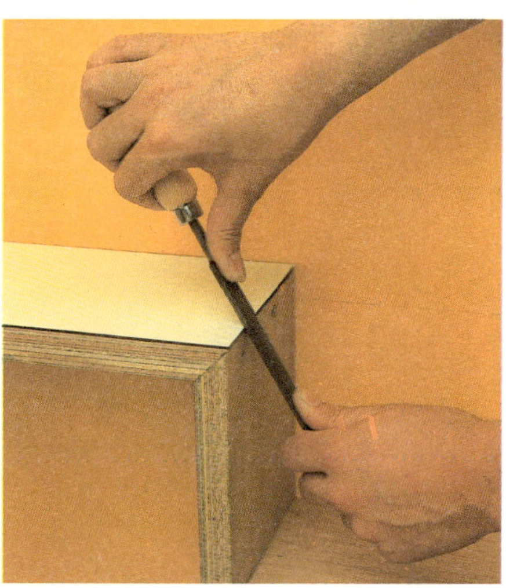

10 *Smooth the trimmed edges of the laminate face panels by quick strokes with a file or laminate trimmer*

right: this gives you the batten positions.

Prise off the ramin battens from the shelves—remember to label them first—and mark and drill 4.5mm clearance holes through their sides to take 35mm No. 8 screws. You'll need four holes per shelf, two per short upright and three per long upright. Space the holes about 70mm apart.

Mark and drill 4.5mm clearance holes to take 19mm No. 8 screws through the overlaps on the shelves—make sure they don't coincide with the holes drilled in the battens—then replace the battens temporarily. Drill 2mm pilot holes into the battens through the holes in the shelves. Countersink all holes by means of a hand countersinking bit.

Offer up the end wall batten to your pencil guidelines and check it for level by placing a spirit level on top. Mark the fixing positions on the wall through the screw holes, then drill the wall and insert wallplugs. Return the batten to the wall and attach with screws.

If your wall is a hollow partition, you'll have to align the vertical battens with a stud: simply screw them to the timber. Attach the shelf battens using screws and special hollow wall fixings.

Fix the other battens along on the long wall in the same way, making sure the mitres are aligned. Check the level of each batten with your spirit level.

As soon as you've fixed the battens to the wall you can attach the shelves, using PVA glue and screws for a firm fitting.

Take each shelf in turn and apply adhesive to the overlap and its adjacent ply edge. Position the shelf on its batten and secure by driving 19mm screws through

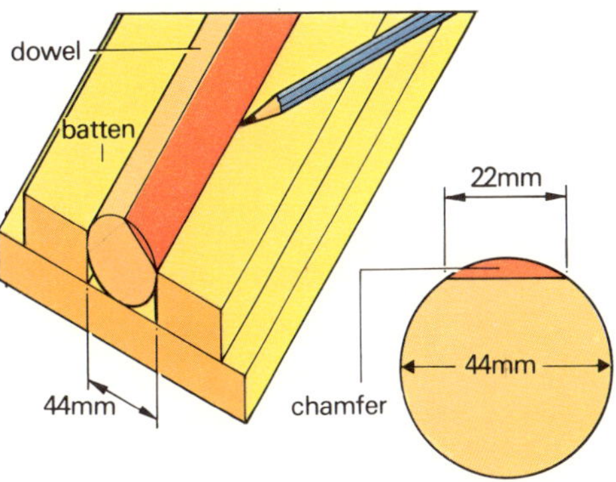

A home-made jig with battens nailed to a softwood base is a useful way of holding the dowel to mark the chamfer

the top into the battens (locating in your pre-drilled pilot holes). Screw the verticals in place in the same way, and check that all mitre joints are fitting accurately.

When all the shelves are fixed, drill pilot holes through the mitres and add screws for extra strength. Check that all screw heads are recessed below the plywood components before fitting the laminate.

Fitting the dowel trim

44mm diameter softwood dowelling is fixed to the front edge of the bath bar with glue and pins. The corners are mitred for neatness and the back edge planed flat to fit against the shelves.

Dowelling isn't easy to mark out and cut unless you have a holder to grip it firmly. You can make a jig from a 600mm long piece of 150mm × 25mm softwood with two 38mm × 25mm battens screwed along

its length, spaced 44mm apart.

Slip the dowel into the channel—it should be a snug push-fit—and use a pencil to mark the chamfer. Draw a line down one side of the dowel against the batten. Continue this line across the end of the dowel, 22mm from the top, and where this line meets the opposite side of the dowel mark a second line down its length against the second batten.

You can either remove the chamfer with a coping saw (holding the dowel carefully in a vice) or with a smoothing plane. If you use a plane to chamfer the dowel, fit your jig with an end stop, clamp the device in a vice and use it as a holder while you plane.

Mark out the length of the trims from the shelf lengths. Aim to cut as many lengths as you can from a single length of dowelling, and remember to label each piece so you know where it fits on the bar.

Use a mitre box or a vice to cut the dowel to length, but be sure to wedge the trim in place while you saw. Make the cuts with a fine-toothed tenon saw.

To make the mitres, simply place the chamfered edge of the dowel against the front edge of the appropriate shelf and mark off the angle on the dowel to correspond with that on the shelf. Then cut the mitres in a mitre box using a tenon saw. Take care to make the cuts at precisely 45°.

Fit each length of dowel trim to the edge of the shelves using PVA adhesive and 65mm pins. Allow the glue to dry, then fractionally round off the corners with medium- followed by fine-grade glasspaper to give a smooth finish. Finally seal the bare wood with stain and polyurethane varnish, or just varnish in gloss or matt finish.

SHELVES AND STORAGE

Make use of every available space in your home for storage and shelving. Turn wasted space above doorways into attractive storage cupboards. Build an adaptable cube storage system, ideal for a living room or bedroom, or a bedhead unit which combines comfort with extra shelving. Even a complete built-in wardrobe system should not be beyond your grasp—it can be constructed quickly and simply using ready-made components.

SPACE SAVING STORAGE

Here's an innovative and exciting way to add an otherwise boring practicality to your home—storage space that doesn't waste space. Planned and co-ordinated, it's both functional and highly decorative. And with just a few basic building considerations—always useful things to know—you could get down to this job before, during or after you've done your other decorating.

At first sight, the project is simply a rather sturdy false ceiling above the smallest room you can find, generally the lavatory. But made with strong, flooring grade tongue-and-groove boards, the ceiling doubles-up as the floor for an overhead cupboard. Cupboard doors provide access from outside the room through one of the walls, and double as features in their own right.

Planning considerations

First of all check that you've got enough height. In the UK, the Building Regulations require that rooms have a minimum headroom of 2.3m—about 300mm above most common door frames. This means that to provide a useable space, your ceilings must be about 3m high. Any windows in the room also affect your choice—make sure that the tops will be lower than the new ceiling level (that is, less than 2.3m high).

The next check is on the floor area. This must be small enough to give a side-to-side span of just 1200mm—floorboards alone will be strong enough to span this width.

There should be few other problems. Pipes and cisterns may get in the way, but with a little adjustment the ceiling would conceal them too. You must of course check that the hole in the wall is in a place which is easy to reach—preferably immediately above the existing door to the room. But don't worry about what the wall is made of—the project can be adapted to fit solid or frame types.

What to buy

The amount of building materials you need will vary with the size of the room, so measure it carefully and make a buying list. All the wood is available in standard sizes from any timber yard or DIY shop, while accessories can be bought from DIY shops or hardware stores.

You need enough 150mm×25mm

tongue-and-groove floorboards to cover the floor area—bear in mind you'll be cutting them across the short width of the room.

Use 50mm×25mm battens for the ceiling supports—buy enough to run round all four walls—and buy similar lengths of decorative moulding to trim the joints.

For the door frame, buy a 1m length of

75mm×50mm timber to make the lintels and some 150mm×25mm softwood for the frame itself. To trim the frame, you need architrave moulding to match the existing doors and some 25mm×12mm beading for a door stop. Use a 19mm blockboard for the doors—you can probably find a suitably large offcut. To hang them, you

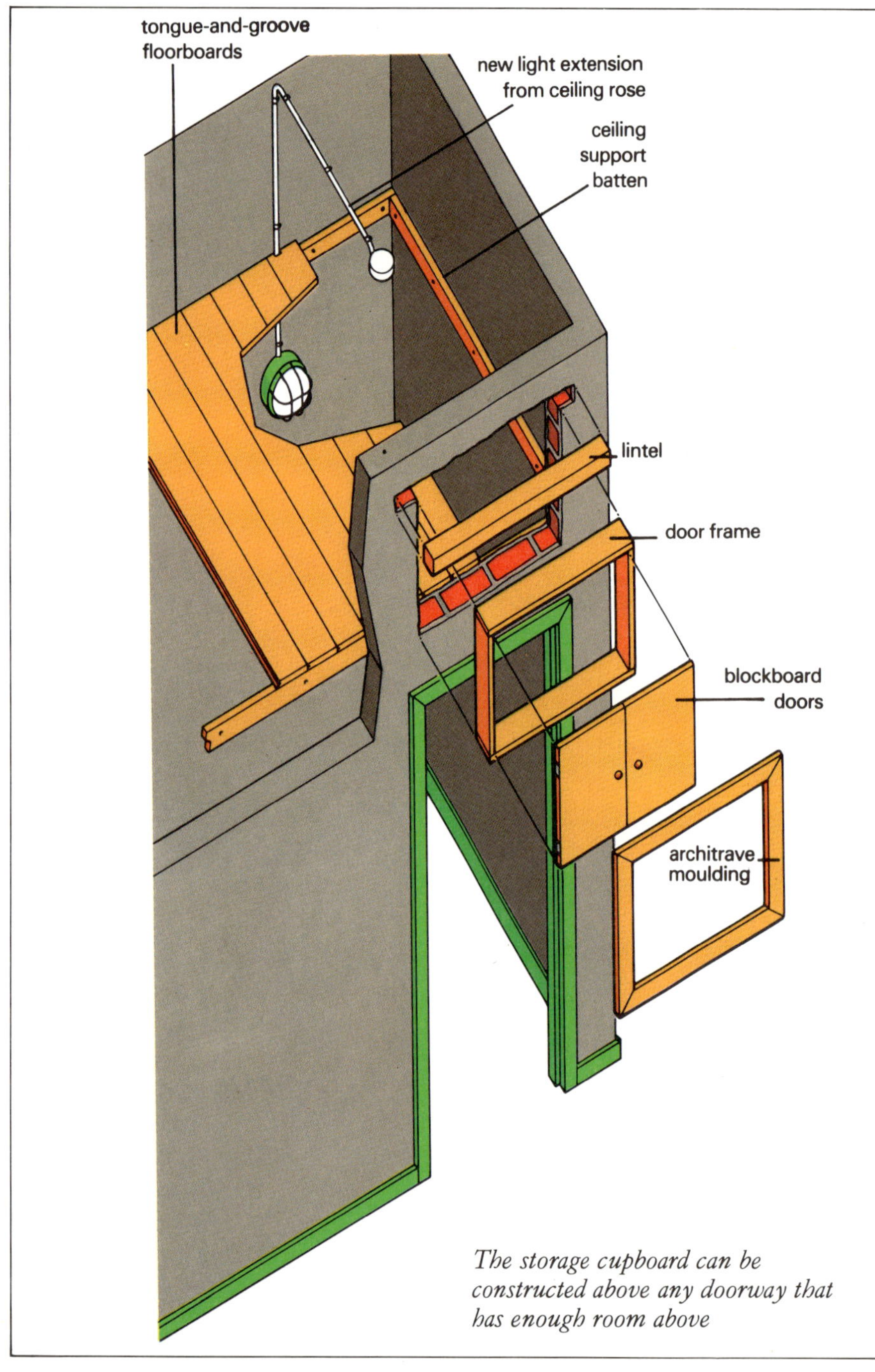

*The storage cupboard can be
constructed above any doorway that
has enough room above*

it, above the door frame. It is mainly concealed by the architrave, and the area around the hole is finished with interior filler or plaster, then painted or papered.

The doors are made from 19mm blockboard fitted with 50mm hinges and magnetic catches. They can be painted, varnished, or even papered to match the decor of the walls.

The ceiling is supported by a 50mm × 25mm batten, screwed to the wall 2.3m above the floor. The panelling is 150mm × 25mm tongue-and-groove floorboards simply nailed in place across the width of the room. The room must not be wider than 1200mm, or the boards will need to have additional support.

To light the room, an extension is taken from the existing ceiling rose with new 0.5mm² lighting flex to a wall mounted light below the new ceiling.

Making the holes

This section covers the hard option—masonry walls. Refer to the diagram on page 48 if you are dealing with a frame wall.

Tap the wall above the door with your fist—if it sounds dull and solid, it is probably a masonry wall. To check, drill an exploratory hole about 350mm above the door frame with a masonry bit—watch for red brick dust, or grey dust which will indicate concrete blocks.

With a spirit level, extend the width of the lavatory door frame upwards over the hole position. Allow for the thickness of the new door frame, then mark the width of the hole you need to cut. Don't mark the upper or lower lines until you have removed some plaster to reveal one whole brick.

Take up or cover all your carpets and accessories—the job is likely to be messy. Take extra care to cover the fittings.

Working from a step ladder or high table, remove a small area of plaster from the wall

need two pairs of 50mm flush hinges and two magnetic catches, plus the cupboard door knobs of your choice.

You also need a wall mounted light and some 0.5mm² lighting flex—enough to run from the ceiling rose, down the wall to the new wall light.

To put it all together you need a quantity of 50mm oval nails, 63mm No. 8 screws and wallplugs and an assortment of panel pins, as well as a 2kg bag of ready-mixed mortar. The finishing material—whether gloss paint or varnish—depends on your taste and decorations.

How the cupboard fits

A hole, cut through the wall and fitted with two small doors, gives access to the redundant overhead space. The hole is trimmed with a 150mm × 25mm wooden lining that also acts as a door frame; 25mm × 12mm beading is pinned to the frame as a door stop. Decorative architrave—chosen to match the other doors—gives the cupboard an integrated look.

To support the wall above the hole a 75mm × 50mm wooden lintel is built into

about 400mm above the door with a bolster and hammer. When one whole brick (or block) and mortar course has been exposed,

1 *Remove some plaster to reveal a brick and mortar course: their location determines the upper and lower boundaries of the hole*

2 *Chop the plaster back to the edges of the hole*

3 *Drill the mortar around the first brick. Drive in the bolster to loosen it*

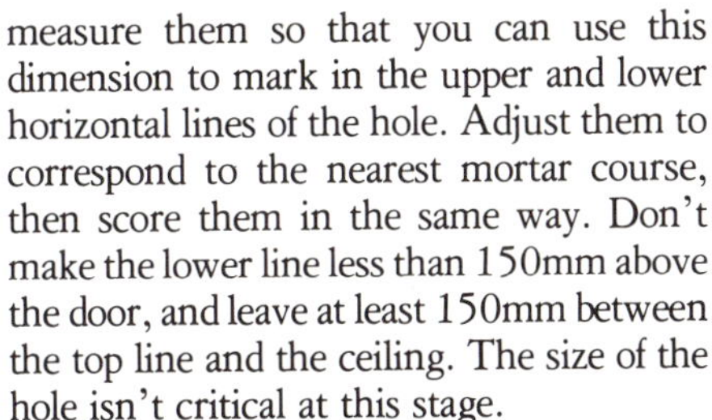

4 *Insert the lintel next placing it on the bricks on either side. Make sure that it is straight, and level it with mortar*

5 *Allow the bedding mortar to cure, then ease out the bricks beneath the lintel, carefully chopping downwards*

6 *Use ready-mixed mortar to pack gaps at the edges. Most will be concealed by the architrave*

measure them so that you can use this dimension to mark in the upper and lower horizontal lines of the hole. Adjust them to correspond to the nearest mortar course, then score them in the same way. Don't make the lower line less than 150mm above the door, and leave at least 150mm between the top line and the ceiling. The size of the hole isn't critical at this stage.

With a bolster and hammer, remove the plaster from both sides of the wall. Drive the bolster at an angle in towards the brickwork in regular, neat chops. At the edges, drive the bolster at a steep angle towards the hole to make a clean line.

Above the topmost line, mark in the position of a 75mm × 50mm wooden lintel set flat to take the weight of the remaining bricks. Make this approximately 75mm longer on either side than the width of the hole. Score the lines and remove the plaster.

When you have removed all the plaster, begin on the brickwork, starting near the top of the proposed hole. Remove only enough bricks to fit the lintel: leave the rest of the opening until later.

Start with a drill and large masonry bit. Repeatedly drill into the mortar all around one of the bricks near the top of the hole. Remove as much mortar as you can by this method then drive your bolster into the joints to loosen more.

Ease out the loose brick. If it refuses to budge, break it up with the bolster but try to keep the surrounding brickwork intact.

Once two or three bricks are out, others should follow with ease. Prise them gently from the mortar, working along the line of the lintel. If you need to cut a brick, chop downwards to splinter it bit by bit.

Now slip the lintel into the gap and level it up with a spirit level. Wedge it in place temporarily with slivers of wood. Mix up some ready-mix mortar with just enough water to make it workable.

Remove the lintel, then trowel a bed of mortar into either end of the hole. Slide the lintel back into place. Use the spirit level to check and adjust its position, packing mortar underneath or on top. Finally, pack all the gaps with mortar and leave to cure.

When you return to the job, continue removing the bricks from the opening. Leave the sides until last—you will have to trim alternate bricks flush, using the bolster and hammer. After this has been done, pack fresh mortar into any gaps left in the sides with the edge of your trowel. Knock off projecting pieces when the mortar is dry.

Opening up a frame wall

A timber framed wall sounds loud and hollow when you tap it with your fist. At doorways, there is a frame member on each side of the opening, running from floor to ceiling. A shorter one commonly runs from the top of the door frame to the ceiling.

Start your hole by cutting back the panelling to the frame timber on either side. First mark the plasterboard or other wall panel-

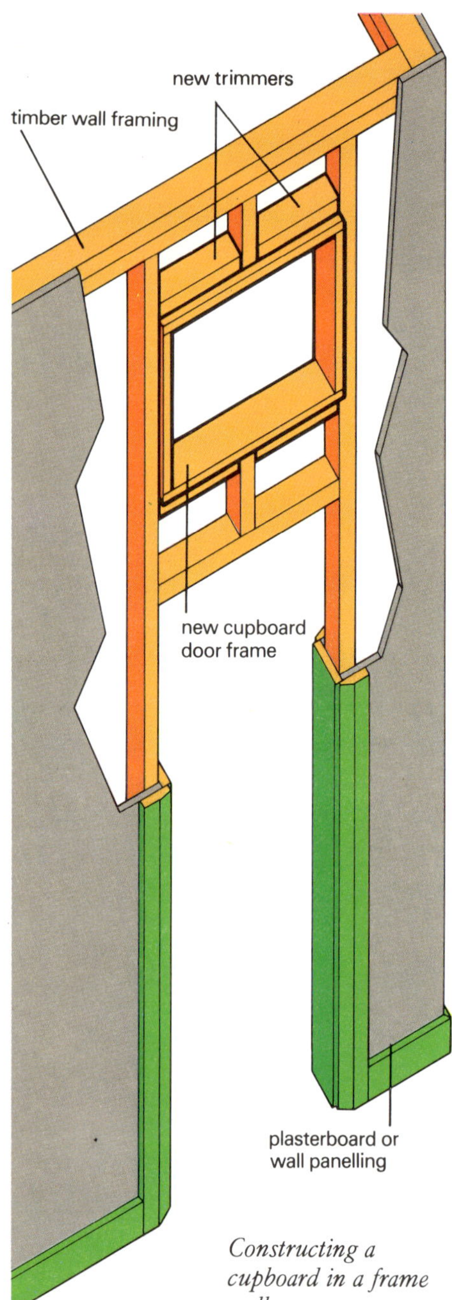

Constructing a cupboard in a frame wall

ling, then drill small holes to insert a padsaw—or a thin blade fitted to a trimming knife—and cut along the marked lines. Cut the sides of the hole back to the timber frame. If there is a central one, cut this off level with the horizontal edges of the hole.

To support the top and bottom of the opening, insert 'trimmers' made of wood the same size as the rest of the frame (usually 100mm×50mm). Cut them to span between the sides of the hole and slip them under the wall panelling. They are best held in place with L-brackets screwed to the corners. The cupboard door lining and the doors then fit in the same way as on a masonry wall.

Fitting the door frame

The new door frame also serves to line the hole. Use standard 150mm×25mm planed-all-round (PAR) timber (or a width to fit the thickness of your walls).

Start by holding a board across the bottom of the hole and marking off a length to fit it. Use a try square to level the ends,

7 *Nail and glue the frame together and brace it across the diagonal*

8 *Mark and drill fixing positions, then screw into wallplugs. Plug gaps*

9 *Pin architrave to the frame's edges to conceal the gaps*

then cut two pieces to exactly this length.

Place both pieces together across the bottom of the hole. Hold a further length of the wood up to them and mark the point at which it meets the bottom of the lintel. Cut two pieces.

Join all four pieces with woodworking adhesive and 50mm oval nails. Drive the nails through the ends of the long pieces into the tops of the shorter vertical pieces. Check

that the frame is square by measuring the two diagonals—they should be the same.

Drill two 4.0mm countersunk holes near the top of each of the uprights and two at the bottom. Drill two holes in each horizontal.

Place the frame in the hole in the wall and adjust it until it is flush with the wall and level. Wedge it in place with scraps of wood.

Mark through the holes onto the wall by poking a nail through the holes you have made. Remove the frame and drill holes at these points with a No. 8 masonry drill (use a 2.0mm twist bit to drill pilot holes in the wooden lintel). Plug holes with wallplugs.

Screw the new frame into place with 63mm No. 8 screws. Tighten gradually, checking that the frame continues to remain square and upright.

Any roughness on the wall behind the frame does not matter—it will be concealed later on in the construction.

Cut four lengths of architrave moulding all about 100mm longer than the frame they fit over. Cut mitres at the four corners with the aid of a mitre box so that the architrave fits just short of the inner edge of the frame. Nail the architrave to the frame with 50mm oval nails.

Adding the doors

Make the doors from an offcut of 19mm blockboard sheet. Use a tape measure or piece of batten to mark the width and height of the hole and transfer them to the sheet.

Extend the lines with a try square and ruler, then saw it to size. Score the cutting lines with a knife to avoid splintering the surface. Cut the panel down the middle to make two doors, then sand the edges.

Add two 50mm flush hinges to the edges of both doors about 50mm from each

10 *Measure and mark the blockboard. Score lines*

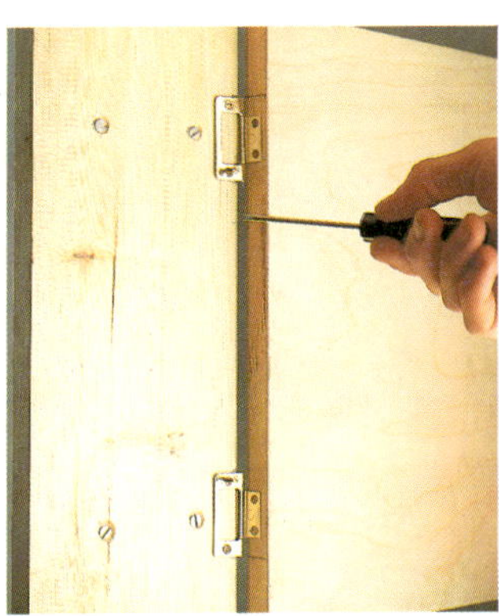

11 *Hinge and fit the doors to the cupboard*

12 *Pin 25mm × 12mm beading to the frame*

13 *Attach catches to doors and frames*

end—see Fitting the hinges (above). Screw the hinges to the frames and test-close the doors. If they have been properly marked and fitted, it's unlikely that the doors will stick. If they do, mark the areas that are sticking and sand until they close smoothly.

Cut a length of 25mm × 12mm beading to fit the width of the door frame. Shut both doors so that they are flush with the front of the frame. Lay the beading flat on the top part of the frame so that it butts up snugly against them. Nail it in place with 25mm panel pins.

Fit the knobs of your choice to each of the doors, then add the magnetic catches. Screw the striking plate to each door, then—one at a time—close the door and align the catch body with the striking plate. Mark through the fixing holes onto the frame and screw the catch body in place.

Fitting the hinges

50mm flush hinges are perfectly adequate for this job. Their main advantage is that you don't need to cut recesses in either the door or the frame—all you need to do is align them properly and securely on the edge of the door, then on the frame.

With a try square, mark points on the hinge edge of each door, 50mm from each end. Place a closed hinge against one mark. Adjust its position until the shoulder sits against the edge of the door, then mark through the screw holes of the inside leaf.

Use a bradawl or 2.0mm drill bit to make pilot holes at these points, then screw the inside leaf home with the screws provided. Do the same for the other hinges.

Place a door in the frame with the hinges closed. Adjust its position to give an equal gap at top and bottom. Then lightly mark the frame to indicate the top and bottom of the hinges themselves.

Open the door, align the hinges with your marks on the edge of the frame, then screw into place. Test-close the door. If it sticks at any point, smooth the area with a sanding block.

Wiring the light

You will need to fit a new light below the position of the lowered ceiling. With most light fittings, all you need to do is replace the existing flex from the ceiling rose with a longer one and connect the other end to a wall light before you install the ceiling.

The boards of the ceiling must be level with the bottom of the door frame, so allow for the thickness of the boards and the support batten below them. Mark this point, then use a spirit level to extend a line round the walls. Mark the position of the light below this.

Before you start any work on the light itself, switch off the fuse board main switch so that there is no chance of getting a shock.

Unscrew the rose cover to reveal the wiring beneath. Whatever the wiring system in use, note the connections of the existing flex to the light, remove the old one and replace it with the new flex in exactly the same position.

Take a length of 0.5mm² (3 amp) lighting flex sufficient to reach from the rose to the light position. Remove about 50mm of the outer sheathing then strip 10mm of the coloured insulation from each wire, and twist the individual strands together. Loosen the terminal screws holding the old flex, then slip the flex from the rose cap. Reverse the process to wire the new flex. Remember: the blue wire goes to Neutral (the old wire may have been black), the brown goes to Live (the old wire may have been red). If cord grips are provided, clamp the wires in them.

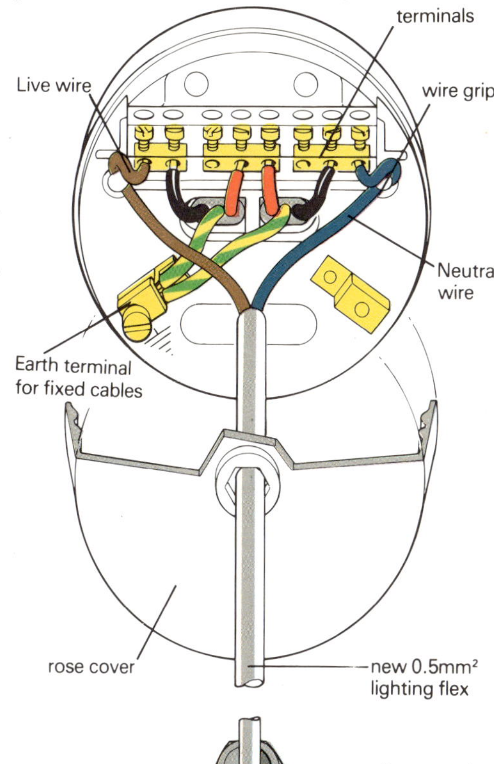

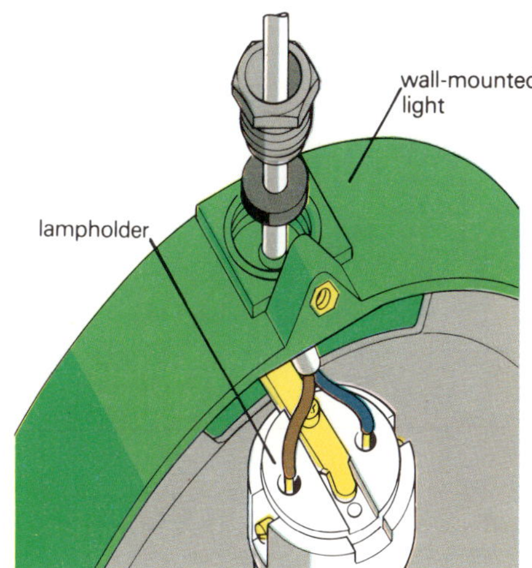

14 *Switch off at the mains. Remove the rose cover and note connections. Remove the old lighting flex and replace it with new flex. Connect to the terminals*

Run the flex across the ceiling and down the wall to the new light position. Cut it to the length required, then bare the wire ends to make the connections to the light itself.

Remove the base from the light, thread the flex through the flex entrance hole and connect the wires to their appropriate terminals.

Mark the light fixing holes and screw the base to the wall, then attach the body.

Switch on the mains supply, then try the light. If it works secure the flex to the ceiling and wall with cable clips.

Installing the ceiling

Start the installation by sawing up 50mm × 25mm battens to fit along the walls, just above the lines you marked, before repositioning the light. Two lengths of wood will be slightly shorter than the wall to allow for an overlap at the corners.

When the batten crosses the flex to the light, cut a notch in the back. Saw part-way through the wood, then cut out the waste with a narrow chisel so that the batten rests against the wall without squeezing the flex.

For masonry walls, drill 4.0mm countersunk clearance holes at 500mm intervals. Hold the battens in place then mark the fixing positions on the walls. Using a No. 8 masonry drill, drill holes at the points you have marked. Insert wallplugs, then screw the battens to the wall.

For frame walls, tap the walls to find the frame members. If necessary, drill an exploratory hole to find one—the rest should be at 400mm or 450mm intervals, which makes them easy to locate. Mark the walls with their positions, hold the battens in place and transfer the marks to the battens. Drill 4.0mm countersunk holes at these points on the battens. Hold them in place and mark the wall in the same way, but drill 2.0mm pilot holes onto the wall. Screw in place as above.

Cover the screw heads with fine surface filler. When dry, sand the filler flat.

Cut the tongue-and-groove boards to fit the width—not the length—of the room.

Measure them as for the support battens. A slightly rough cut at the end will not matter as it will be hidden from view by the battens. Starting at the end away from the door and working from below, drop the boards on to the support battens and nail in place with 38mm oval nails. Slot the tongue of each board into the groove of the next.

As you approach the new opening, it will be easier to work through it. You will probably need to cut the final board along its

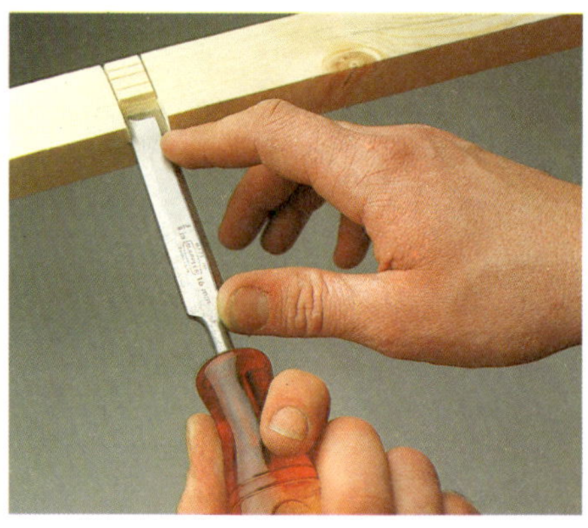

15 *Mark where the batten crosses the flex. Saw two lines partway through, then cut out the waste*

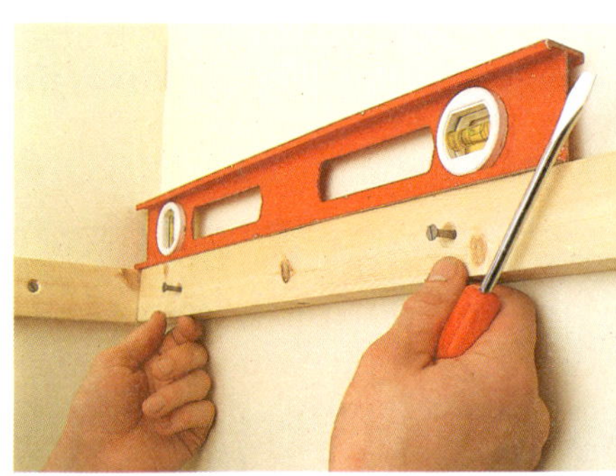

16 *Drill countersunk clearance holes in the batten. Level it, then mark fixing positions. Screw the batten on*

17 *Cut the floorboards. Nail each board to the batten. Slot the tongue of one board into the groove of the next*

★ WATCH POINT ★

To measure the length of a wall without a tape measure, hold two shorter pieces of wood against each other. Slide them apart until the ends touch either side wall, then use both pieces together to mark the wood you want to cut.

length to make a neat fit, so lay the last few boards loosely to check. Measure the gap, or mark it off on a piece of scrap batten, and use this to make the last board. Saw it down its full length.

Lift the remaining unfastened boards slightly so you can fit the tongue of the last board into the groove. Push the boards into place together, then nail them down.

Finishing off

A nice finishing touch is to nail thin decorative moulding to the support batten so that it looks like a cornice. Add it to the corner between the boards and batten, to the

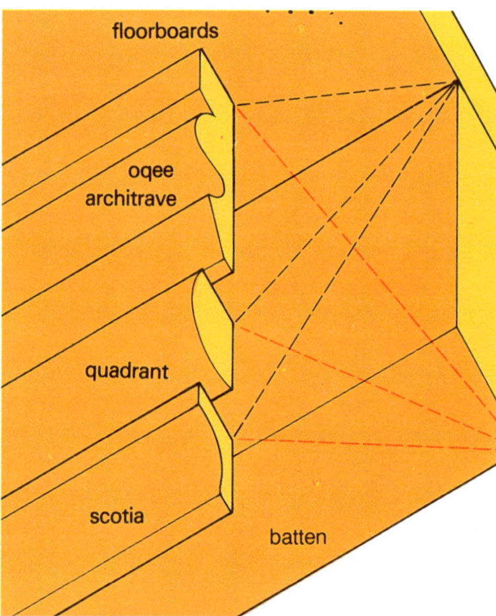

18 *Nail a moulding to the batten. Punch nail heads below the surface with a nail punch and insert filler*

★ WATCH POINT ★

Apply the primer, then rub down with fine glasspaper a second time. The painted surface reveals blemishes far more obviously than an untreated surface does.

bottom of the batten, or to both.

When you have chosen your pattern, nail the mouldings on then punch the heads below the surface. Fill all holes and gaps with interior filler, then rub down with fine glasspaper. Prime all the wooden surfaces.

Alternatively, fill the holes with plastic wood filler then varnish all the surfaces for a natural wood finish.

CUBE STORAGE UNITS

Most cube storage systems look easy to build but aren't, because it's hard to get the panels to fit together squarely. Finishing the edges of the panels can be a problem too; you will normally be restricted to using melamine-faced chipboard with a matching iron-on edging strip.

The cube system (right) solves the fitting problem in an ingenious way: all the panels are cut to the same size and are then butt jointed to edging pieces made from square section hardwood. This also gets round the edging problem—because none of the panel edges are exposed, you can use plywood or blockboard as your main material and then stain, varnish or paint it to match your other furniture.

Another interesting feature of these cubes is that they can be joined to each other to form rigid larger units, which you tailor to fit the available space. This is achieved quite simply by using proprietary plastic male/female connector screws to link the different units together.

A choice of versions

The basic cube is easily modified to make better use of the space inside. Horizontal shelves can be fitted on shelf support studs; or vertical slide-in dividers on sections of hard-wood channel moulding. Taking the work a stage further you can fit a door made to match the other panels and hang it on standard flush hinges. And if you feel really ambitious, add one or more drawers—use proprietary plastic drawer kits faced with the panel material.

If you consult the diagram which shows how the various versions of the cube are put together, you'll see that the parts have been kept to standard sizes as far as possible. This makes it well worth your while setting up a 'production line' rather than trying to build each cube individually. Make full use of the instructions given on templates for cutting and marking out, and this part of the job will automatically become easier. It will also lessen the chances of introducing minor discrepancies between cubes, which could spoil the finished result.

Tools and materials

The basic panel material for the cubes is 12.5mm plywood or blockboard. Both are

about the same price, but plywood is slightly stronger and may well have a superior surface finish. If you plan to paint the cubes, make a point of inspecting the surface of every sheet you buy for large knots, dents or chips.

Standard sheet sizes are 2440mm × 1220mm (enough for up to twelve standard panels, plus a door, shelf or divider) and 1220mm × 600mm (enough for up to three panels plus offcuts for drawer fronts). Obviously it makes sense to buy the largest sheet size, but you should also be able to get offcuts that fit the panel dimensions with less waste—ask your timber merchant.

Consult the diagram opposite before making up your cutting list. For each basic cube you will need:
- 5 panels of 12.5mm board (ply or blockboard) measuring 350mm × 350mm;
- about 4.5m of 12.5mm square ramin (hardwood edging);
- a generous supply of 12mm veneer or moulding pins and PVA woodworking adhesive;
- stain and/or polyurethane varnish or primer, undercoat and gloss paint to finish.

For a shelf cube add (per shelf):
- one panel of 12.5mm ply or blockboard measuring 350mm × 219mm;
- four screw-in plastic shelf supports;
- 350mm of 12.5mm × 6mm ramin edging.

For a divider cube add (per divider):
- one panel of 12.5mm board measuring 338mm × 264mm plus 540mm of 12.5mm square ramin channel of 6mm square ramin.

Note: for thinner dividers use 4mm or 5mm ply and narrower section channel moulding.

For a door cube add:
- one panel of 12.5mm board measuring 334mm × 328mm (or 334mm × 334mm if your opt for a handle other than the one shown);
- about 1040mm of 25mm × 12.5mm ramin edging (for the door handle);
- two 25mm flush hinges and a magnetic door catch, plus fixing screws.

For a drawer cube add (per drawer):
- one plastic drawer kit;
- 700mm of plastic drawer runner;
- 3mm white-faced hardboard (drawer base);
- 6mm square ramin to hold drawer base;

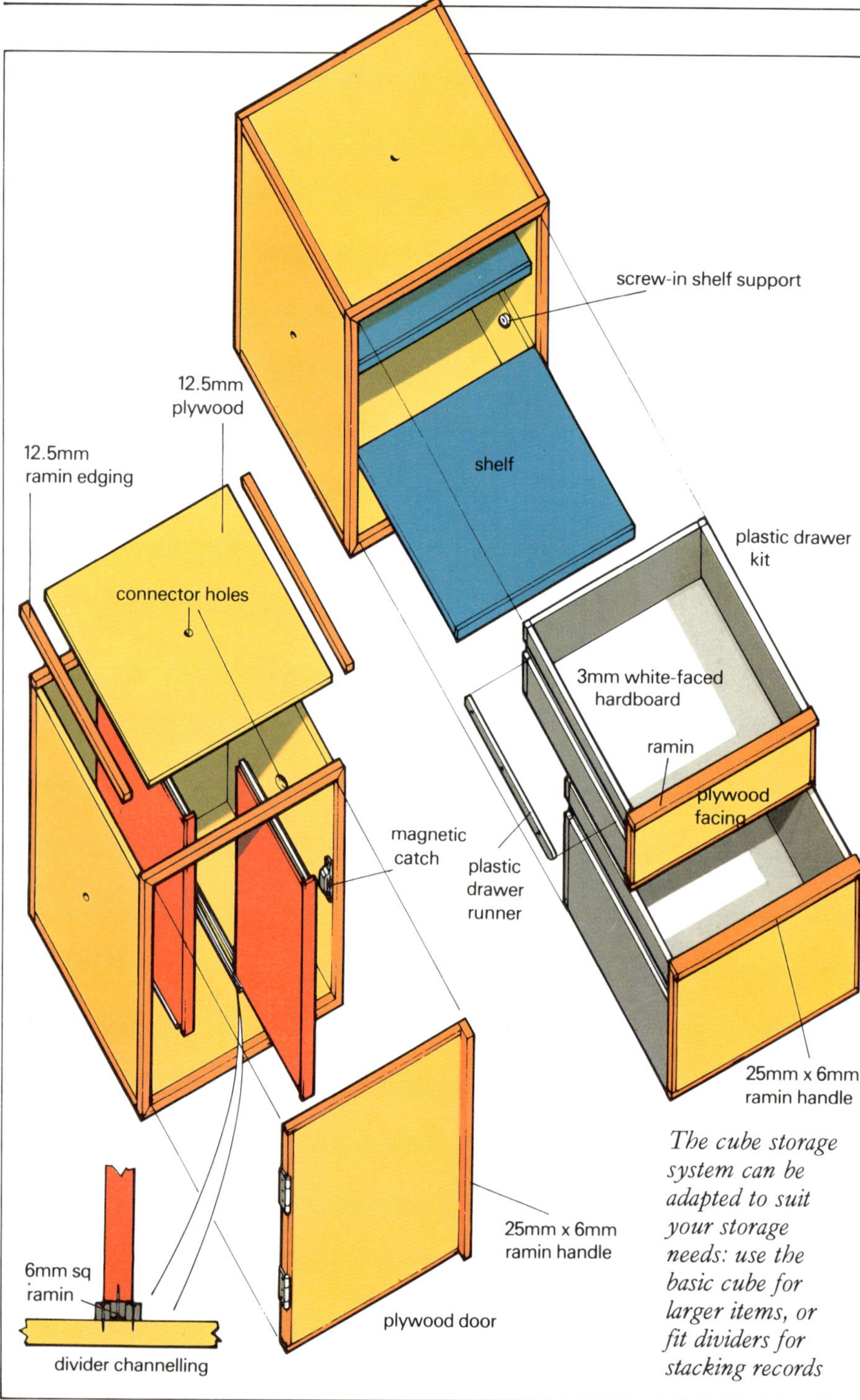

The cube storage system can be adapted to suit your storage needs: use the basic cube for larger items, or fit dividers for stacking records

and try square to 350mm square, then rule diagonals across it and check that they are exactly the same length.

Cut the template out very carefully and align the edges with the plywood sheet on a flat, firm surface.

Align the edge of the rule with the template and the ply before marking each line. Draw around the template with a pencil to mark the panels and check that they're accurate before scribing over the top with a marking knife. Press down firmly as you run the marking knife along and be sure to keep your fingers behind the blade. Repeat for each panel.

Marking along the template with a marking knife held against a steel rule is not only more accurate than using just a pencil, but also scores the surface of the ply and prevents it chipping when you cut it.

When you come to do the cutting, make sure that the sheet is well supported on each side of the cutting line.

If you're using a jig saw, align the blade with the cut and then clamp a straight-edged piece of wood against the sole plate, parallel with the cut, to act as a guide. Don't try to force the saw through—concentrate on keeping the blade on the line. Be sure to support the sheet with your free hand as you near the end of the cut.

If you are sawing by hand, make sure that the saw is sharp and use long but gentle strokes—too much force will certainly cause the surface to split.

Cut the ramin edging next. On each cube there are four pieces 350mm long with square cut ends and eight pieces 375mm

• 12.5mm board for drawer front;
• 346mm of 25mm × 12.5mm ramin edging (for drawer handle).

Construction calls for mainly standard woodworking tools. To mark out the panels accurately you'll need a steel rule, marking knife and try square. You'll find a portable workbench useful for supporting and cutting the panels and you must have a good saw for the cutting work itself—either a sharp panel saw or a power jig saw.

You'll also need an electric drill and 6mm twist bit for making pilot holes for the

cube connectors, and a mitre box for cutting the ramin edging accurately.

Making a basic cube

The hardest part of this job is cutting five panels of plywood to the same size. Take care to get it right and the cube will go together with the minimum of fuss.

The safest way to mark out the plywood for cutting is to make up a template from thin cardboard. Mark this out with a rule

long with the ends mitred. Measure, mark and cut one of each size using a rule, try square, marking knife and tenon saw. Then take the longer of the two and cut the mitres at the ends using a mitre box—be sure to get them the right way round on each strip.

For maximum accuracy, you should now use the two lengths as templates to cut the remaining sections of edging individually. Check the fit of the mitres as you go and sand the cut ends very lightly—just enough to remove any roughness—but beware of rounding off the edges.

1 *Mark out the sheet in 350mm squares then cut out using a panel or jig saw*

2 *Cut the ramin edging to length: you'll need four square ends, four mitred*

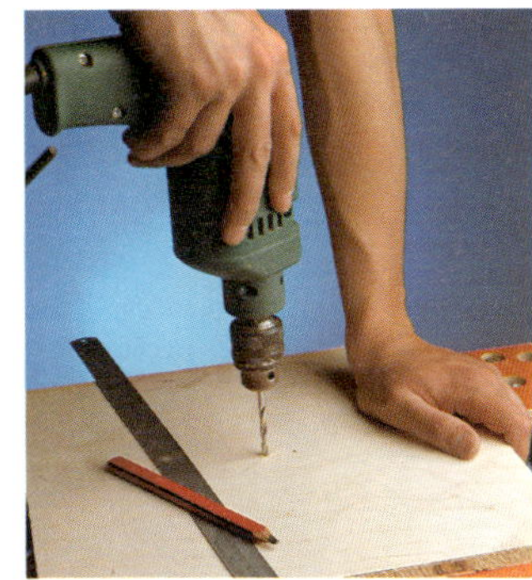

3 *Drill a hole for a connector and a countersink in the opposite face*

4 *Glue and pin two square-ended ramin strips to opposite edges of panels*

5 *Glue and pin four mitred ramin edging strips around one of the ply panels*

6 *Take the two edged panels and assemble with the remaining unedged panels*

7 *Glue and pin the framed panel to one end of the shell to form a 'box'*

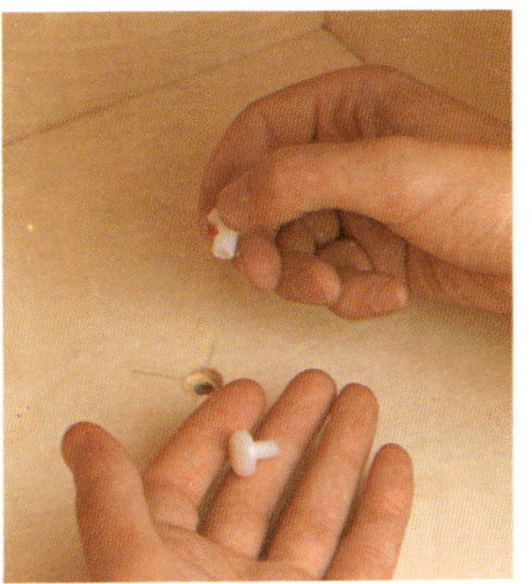

8 *You can test the joining method using plastic screw-threaded cabinet connectors*

Now, using a 6mm twist bit, drill pilot holes for the connectors at the marks you have made in the centre of each panel. Follow by recessing the holes on one side with a suitable countersink to accommodate the connector heads. With the connectors shown, the recess is 16mm in diameter and 3mm deep; with other brands you may have to vary the sizes slightly for a neat finish.

If you want to stain the cubes, do so at this stage, bearing in mind that the edging should be a contrasting colour for best effect. The components will then be ready for assembly, which runs as follows.

Take two of the panels and pin and glue 350mm lengths of ramin exactly flush along two opposing edges on each one. Punch the pin heads below the surface using a centre punch or a nail.

Take another panel and glue and pin four 375mm mitred lengths exactly flush around the edges. Fill any gaps in the mitring (and the pin head recesses) with a mixture of ramin, sawdust and glue.

Take the first two assemblies and the remaining panels. Glue and pin together.

When the shell is dry, take the edged panel and glue and pin it to one open side.

Take the remaining mitred lengths of edging and glue and pin them to the exposed edges.

When everything has been allowed to dry thoroughly, sand down the square edges of the ramin until they are fractionally rounded (1mm radius) and sand the surface of the panels with fine abrasive paper mounted on a wood block. Varnish or paint the cube as you require.

When you've completed a second cube, try out the cabinet connectors. Test-fit a male and female half in adjacent holes in the cubes and screw them together. You may find that they need shortening, in which case note by how much, remove them, and trim with a fine toothed hacksaw. If this damages the thread on the end, restore it by filing off the burrs.

Dividers, doors and drawers

Because the cubes are all a standard size, fitting dividers, shelves, doors and drawers is simply a matter of adding extra parts before and during assembly.

On all the options listed below, start by cutting and edging five panels as for the basic cube. Keep your cutting template handy—it'll help when you come to mark the positions of the fittings. Measure and mark it out with the lines shown in the diagram opposite so that you can use it whatever the version you're building. You can, of course, vary the spacings between the shelves and dividers to suit the shape of the items you're displaying.

Shelf cube: Take one side panel, lay the template exactly over the top and refer to the diagram (left). Measure out and mark the required shelf support positions on the template, then make pilot holes through it into the panel using a bradawl. Press (stud type) or screw (screw type) the shelf supports to the panel, having removed the template, then repeat the entire operation on the other side panel.

Cut each shelf panel to 350mm × 319mm and sand the edges thoroughly. When the basic cube has been assembled, try the shelf for fit and sand or plane as necessary. Then use the width of the shelf as a template to cut a length of 12.5mm × 6mm ramin edging. Glue and pin this to the

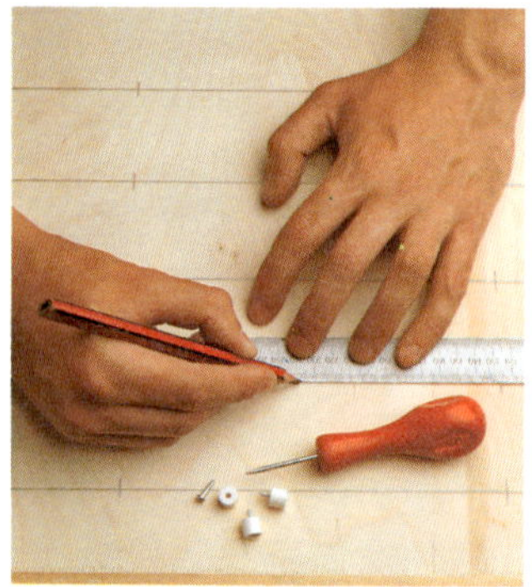

9 *Mark the shelf support positions on one side; make pilot holes*

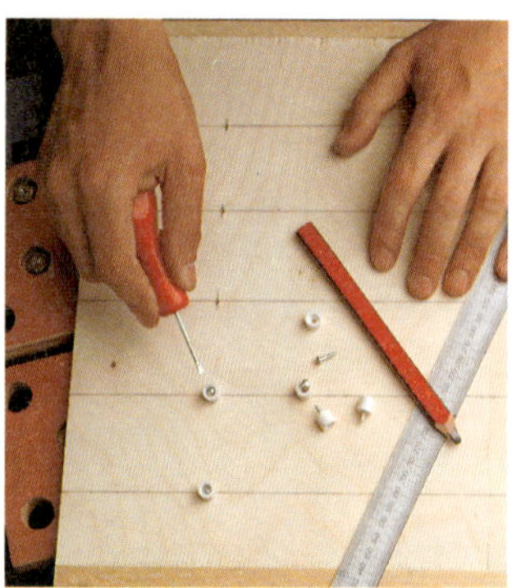

10 *Fix the stud shelf supports into the face of the side panels*

11 *Glue and pin a ramin strip to the leading edge of each shelf panel*

12 *Slide the shelves into the cube so they rest on the shelf studs, edge out*

13 *Mark the positions of the divider channels then nail in place 6mm apart*

14 *Edge the dividers and fix runners. Slide in between channels*

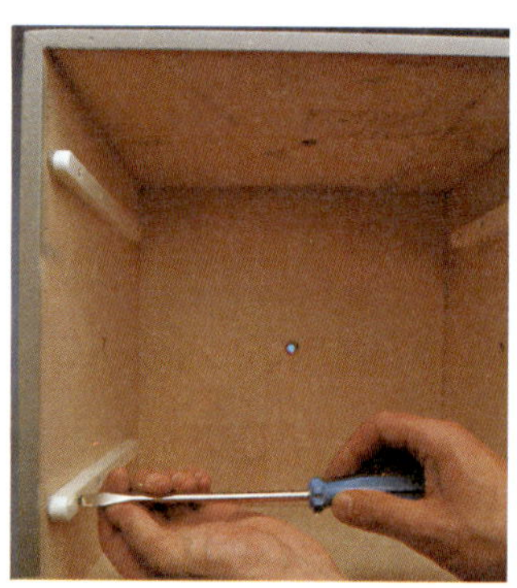

15 *Mark out the positions for the drawer runners and screw them to the sides*

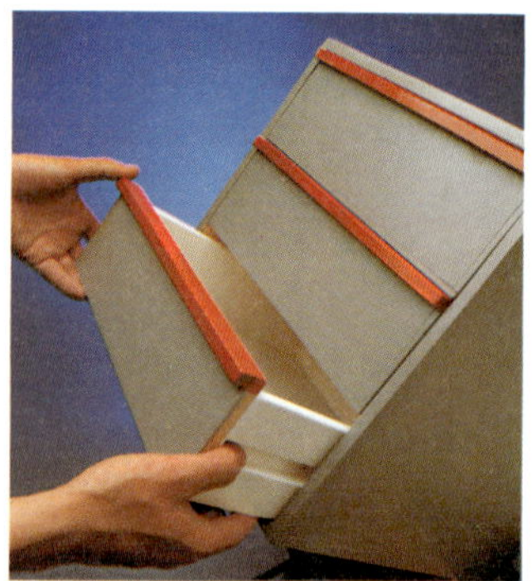

16 *Make up the plastic drawer kits. Slide onto runners*

shelf's front edge then slot the shelf into the cube to rest on its stud supports.

If you should want to alter the shelf positions later to accomodate larger or smaller items, remove the studs where necessary.

Divider cube: Prepare edged panels as for the basic cube. Then cut two lengths of ramin channel to 270mm for each divider, plus 338mm×264mm panels of the materials for the dividers themselves.

Take the cube base panel and lay the template over it. Refer to the diagram on page 52 and align a length of channel exactly with the appropriate line on the template (the shelf positions can be used as divider positions, too). Pin the channel into the base and top panels at 75mm centres, making sure the channel itself stays flush with the back edge of the base panel (not the edging). If you're using 12.5mm dividers it's easiest to make channels from 6mm square ramin strips pinned 6mm apart at each side of the dividers. Fix all the channels in position before assembling the cube.

Try each divider for fit in the cube and sand or plane the edges as necessary. Then cut a length of 12.5mm×6mm ramin edging to trim the front edge. Glue and pin

it in position, and then you can simply slot the divider in place.

Door cube: Make up the basic cube panels and cut the door to size (334mm×328mm with edge handle or 334mm square if you opt for a conventional door). Cut three pieces of 12.5mm×6mm ramin edging to 346mm: mitre both ends of one piece and one end of the other two. Cut the 25mm ×12.5mm ramin handle to 346mm.

Pin and glue the edging around the door so that the handle stands proud (note: if you're fitting a conventional handle simply mitre together four pieces of 6mm ramin). For simplicity you could butt the door edging together instead of cutting mitres.

When the basic cube has been assembled, mark the positions on the centre line of the opposite side. Convert the marks to pilot holes with a bradawl and then screw the hardware in position on the cube.

Try the door for fit and adjust by planing down the hinge edge as necessary. Then mark through the hinge leaves onto the door, convert to pilot holes and screw the door in place. Add the magnetic catch, centred on the centre line of the door. Most have slots so you can adjust the position.

Drawer cube: With this design, you can have three single drawers or a double and a single. Cut the drawer fronts to size (350mm×115mm for a single; 350mm×230mm for a double) plus the ramin edging and handles.

Mitre the side edging strips at one end and the base edging at both, then glue and pin the edging to the fronts. Alternatively, butt join the edging strips.

Cut the plastic drawer sides and back panels to length—this may vary according to the jointing method used—using a hacksaw. Smooth off burrs with glasspaper.

Cut the plastic drawer slides to length (350mm) with a tenon saw and sand the cut edges. Lay your template over a prepared side panel and align the slides with the appropriate lines, keeping them butted against the back edge of the panel (not the edging). Drill pilot holes through the slides and into the panel to take No. 6 roundhead screws, then remove both them and the template. Screw the slides in place. Repeat the procedure for the other side panel. Having assembled the cube in the usual way, make up the drawers and drawer fronts. Then slide the drawers onto their runners.

MAKE A BEDHEAD UNIT

This design has been created with flexibility in mind. The bedhead itself can be as long as or as short as you want it, and adds only 50mm to the overall length of the bed. It features removable upholstered panels which you pad with foam and cover with the material of your choice. And there's plenty of room inside to run the wiring for reading lights, switches and so on.

At 300mm deep, the side units can easily accommodate hi-fi units, speakers, a radio and the like. Leave them with open shelving or fit half doors, and adjust the positions of the shelves to suit what's going inside.

The main construction material is sturdy 19mm plywood, which can be painted, stained or varnished as you wish. The exposed edges are covered with hardwood lipping, and adjacent panels are ingeniously butt-jointed against quadrant moulding to give a truly high quality finish.

Equally ingenious is the way you prepare the panels: simply mark out your sheets of plywood exactly as shown in the diagram on page 57 and then run down the cutting lines with a power saw. This leaves you with a 'kit' of parts that have only to be pinned and glued together.

Planning the construction

The dimensions given here are for a standard size double bed measuring 1600mm wide by 495mm high. Obviously, there's some room for manoeuvre, but if your bed size is significantly different, you need to adjust the lengths of the horizontal bedhead members or the vertical side unit panels accordingly. This in turn will affect the cutting plan given on page 57 and you may therefore need to rearrange the panels so that you're not left with too much waste.

Buying the materials

Start with the plywood. To build the bedhead shown here you'll need one full sheet measuring 2240mm × 1220mm, plus another measuring at least 800mm × 650mm—you may have to buy a half sheet and keep some spare for another project. Because you'll be cutting the sheets with minimal waste allowance it's vital that the plywood you buy has sound edges, free of chips and marks. You need:

• 2.3m of 19mm ramin (hardwood) quadrant moulding, from which you cut four side unit top edges to 306mm, four bedhead edges to 50mm and four corner reinforcers to 200mm.

• 6.2m of 25mm × 25mm PAR softwood from which you cut eight headboard battens to 768mm.

• 12m (15.6m if you have doors) of 19mm × 6mm ramin lipping to edge the plywood.

• Four pieces of 50mm high density foam measuring 768mm × 156mm plus a latex or contact adhesive to fix it. Buy all this at an upholsterers or specialist foam supplier.

• The fabric of your choice—cut four pieces to 1030mm × 420mm.

• 16 pairs of small magnetic catches.

• A supply of 19mm and 32mm panel pins.

• A good supply of PVA woodworking adhesive.

• Finishing materials—wood stopper or

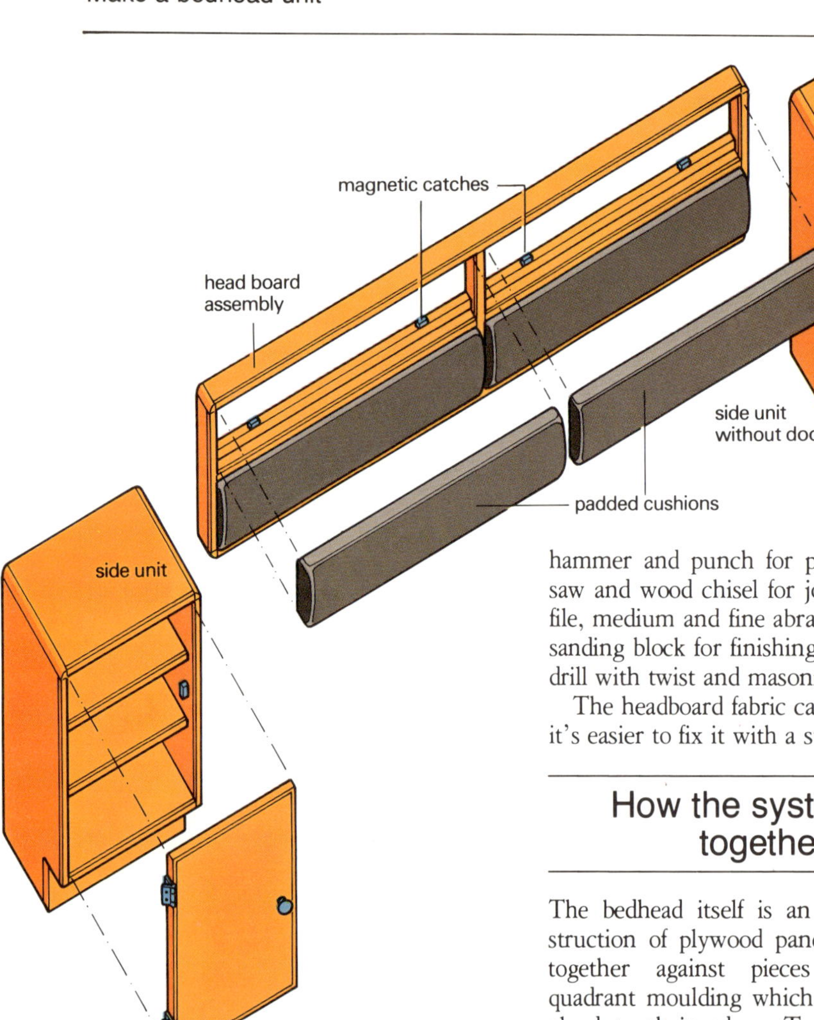

interior filler to cover the pin heads, plus paint, stain or varnish as required.

If you decide to fit doors, don't forget the hardware: buy two pairs of 38mm flush hinges, two round wooden doorknobs and two further pairs of magnetic catches.

Wall fixings can be made with 32mm No. 8 steel woodscrews. If you have a stud wall, aim to screw directly to the studs; otherwise buy standard plastic wallplugs.

Tools for the job

Although the construction of this project is quite straightforward, cutting 19mm plywood by hand is a laborious process and difficult to do with any sort of accuracy. Consequently, it really will pay you to make sure you have a power jigsaw or circular saw equipped with a fence, plus a decent saw table or adjustable workbench so that you can support the sheets on both sides of the cutting line.

Among the other tools you'll need are a tape measure, try square and steel rule or straight edge for marking out; a pin hammer and punch for pinning; a tenon saw and wood chisel for jointing; a planer file, medium and fine abrasive paper and a sanding block for finishing; and an electric drill with twist and masonry bits.

The headboard fabric can be tacked, but it's easier to fix it with a staple gun.

How the system fits together

The bedhead itself is an open box construction of plywood panels, butt jointed together against pieces of hardwood quadrant moulding which are pinned and glued to their edges. Two more panels, halving jointed where they cross, divide the box into four 'compartments'. Square section softwood battens are pinned and glued inside each one, flush with the back, leaving recesses into which you fit the padded headboard panels. The panels are held by magnetic catches; the unit is secured to the wall by screwing through the appropriate battens.

The side units employ the same butt joint/quadrant moulding construction, and feature false plinths cut out of the sides. The tops, lowest shelves and kickboards are all pinned and glued for structural strength, but the centre shelves rest loose on shelf supports.

Cutting the plywood

With a power saw and a proper bench, this job is much easier than you might think. But take extra care with your marking up—mistakes at this stage could prove costly later when the panel edges don't match up.

Refer to the diagram on page 57 showing how the panels can be cut out of standard sized sheets with a minimum of waste.

You'll notice in the pictures that the cutting lines are in fact double, with 2mm between each one. Although this takes longer to measure and mark out, it does enable you to take the kerf—the width of the saw blade—into account while still having clear lines which you can saw by.

If you are building the unit to dimensions other than those given, the usefulness of the marking diagram may be limited and you may have to draw up your own.

Measure out your sheets, section by section, making V-shaped marks in sharp pencil. After each section is completed, measure back against the one before to check for cumulative error.

Do the actual marking out with a trimming knife held against a steel rule. As well as being more accurate, the blade scores through the surface layer of the plywood and cuts down the risk of it chipping when you saw it.

When cutting, simply make sure the saw blade doesn't stray from between the two guidelines. If you haven't got a fence, it may be worth clamping a straightedged batten along the line of the cut; align it by starting the cut then holding the batten hard against your saw's sole plate.

After cutting, smooth—but don't round—the cut edges with medium abrasive paper mounted on a block. Then sort out the four headboard panels and round the edges of these to a radius of about 2mm. Mark all the panels with the appropriate key letter to identify them.

You may find, if you have cut the plywood with a jigsaw, that the cut edges

1 *Mark cutting lines on the plywood for adjacent parts about 2mm apart using a craft knife to break the surface ply*

2 *The gap between cutting lines allows you to use a power jigsaw without worrying unduly about slightly wavering saw cuts*

3 *Trim the cut edges down to the marked lines using gentle strokes with a planer file, then sand—but do not radius —the edges*

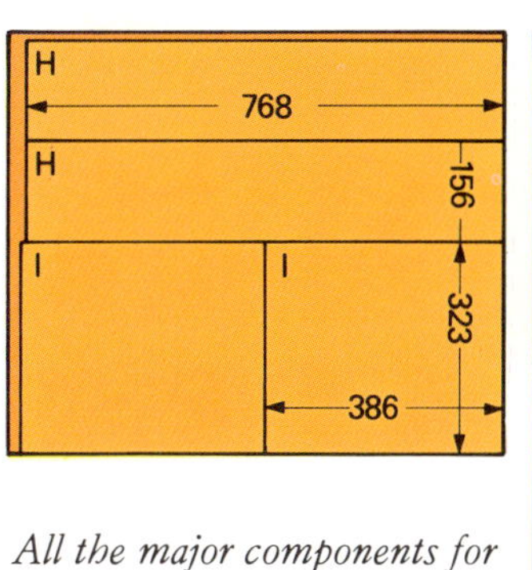

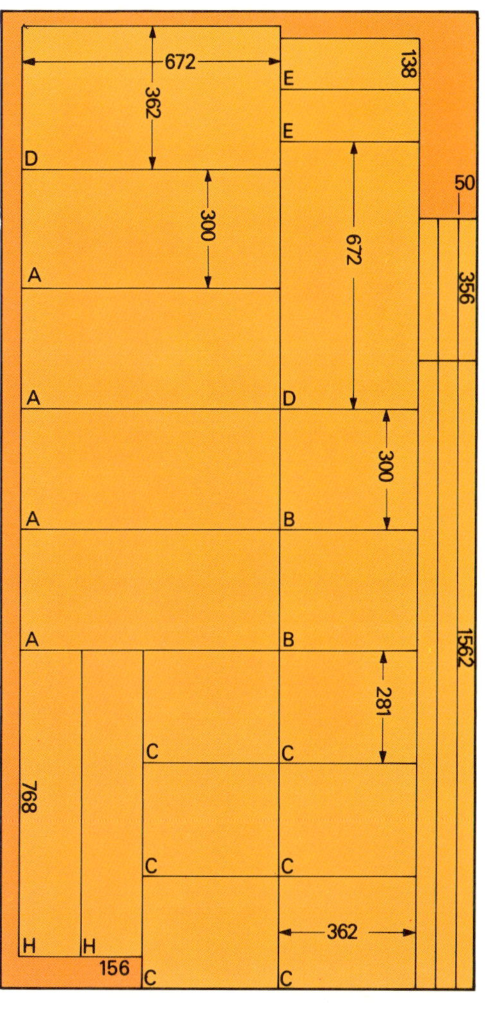

All the major components for the bedhead unit can be cut out of one and a third sheets of 19mm plywood. The square section battens to which the four cushions are fitted are made from 25mm × 25mm PAR softwood

are slightly too wavy to be sanded down easily. Simply smooth them off with a planer file, but don't remove too much material—the edges are apt to splinter so leave a small amount above the cut line for sanding perfectly smooth.

Assembling the side units

Start with the top panels by cutting the hardwood quadrant for the top edges and corner reinforcers to size. Clamp one top panel in a vice with the back edge to your left, using offcuts of ply to protect the workpiece. Glue the side edge and the corresponding edge of a piece of quadrant then lay the quadrant in place, flush with the back edge. Strengthen by pinning in four places, taking care that the moulding doesn't slip out of alignment as you do so. Repeat for all four side edges.

Now cut two pieces of ramin lipping to fit the front edges. It's best to cut them slightly oversized, then try them in place and sand the ends as necessary. Secure the lipping with glue and three equally spaced pins. Afterwards, set the top panels aside to dry.

Tackle the sides next. First mark out and saw the cut-outs for the false plinths, using the same techniques as before. Sand the cut edges smooth, but not rounded. Then pin and glue lengths of ramin lipping to the front edges, flush with the tops.

Mark out the shelf bracket positions on the inside faces of the panels, working from the top edges at all times. Depending on the type of bracket you're using, pin them in place or drill 10mm recesses and glue them.

If you want doors, mark and drill the hinge and catch positions at this stage (see Adding side door units).

Now pin and glue ramin lipping to the front edges of the lowest shelves. If the units are being left open, lip the centre shelves too. Finally, mark and drill the wall fixing holes in the back panels where shown in the assembly diagram.

4 *Clamp the shelf side panels together and mark the 'plinth' cutouts simultaneously*

5 *Pin and glue the quadrant moulding to the shelf side panels and punch the heads down*

6 *Use a webbing strap and offcuts to hold the top and side panels while you pin them*

To assemble each unit, start by laying the side panels on edge on the floor with their feet against the wall. Insert the centre shelves between them to give the correct spacing, then tie them in this position—or,

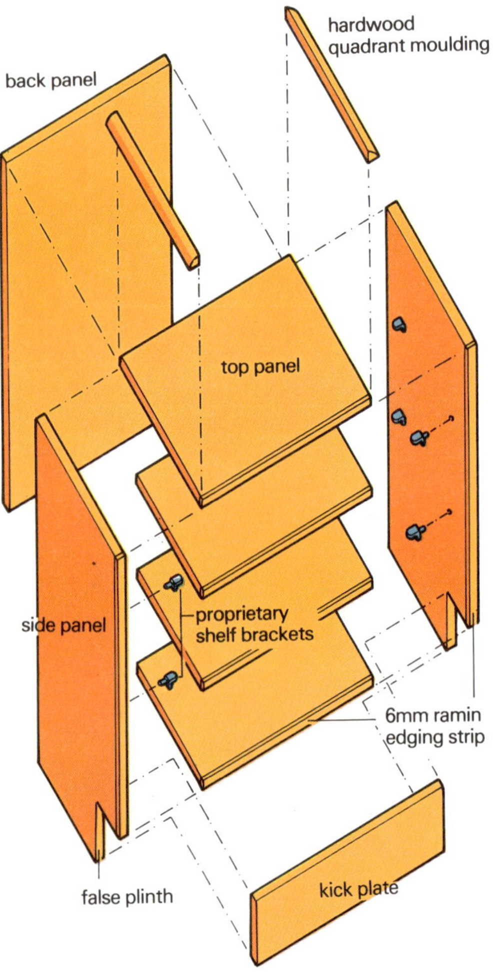

The shelf units are simple in construction. The quadrant moulding overlaps the top and sides to neatly match the lipping along their edges

if you have them, use sash clamps.

Pin and glue the top panel first, using four pins per edge and punching the heads just below the surface of the quadrant. Make sure that the top remains flush with the sides at all times.

Now untie the assembly or remove the clamps and flip it round so that the top is against the wall. Glue the sides of the lowest shelf and ease the side panels apart just enough to slip the shelf into position. Holding it there, turn the unit onto its side and pin through the side panel into the shelf edge at four places.

Complete the side unit by turning it on its front and gluing on the back panel. Use a centre shelf (or if you're fitting doors, an off-cut) to support the top of the back while you pin it to the lowest shelf. Then stand the unit upright and pin through the top. Finish by pinning through either side at 100mm centres. Glue the corner reinforcers into the corners between the top and the sides, flush with the back panel.

Adding side door units

Fitting a door to one of the side units is simplicity itself if you use flush hinges—with these, one leaf folds over the other so there's no need to cut recesses.

You can have either full doors, in which case both centre shelves are cut back by 19mm, or fit half doors and leave one of the centre shelves full size.

Mark the hinge positions on the insides of the side panels before you assemble the unit. The leaves should be exactly flush with the edges of the panels, leaving the barrel protruding.

Cut the door to the required size and pin and glue ramin lipping to all four edges.

When this is dry, mark the hinge positions along one edge as you did on the side panels.

If the cut edges are very clean, of course, you could dispense altogether with lipping: simply use iron-on edging strip.

Screw the hinges to the door, then fit the door in place in the unit. Sand the lipping as

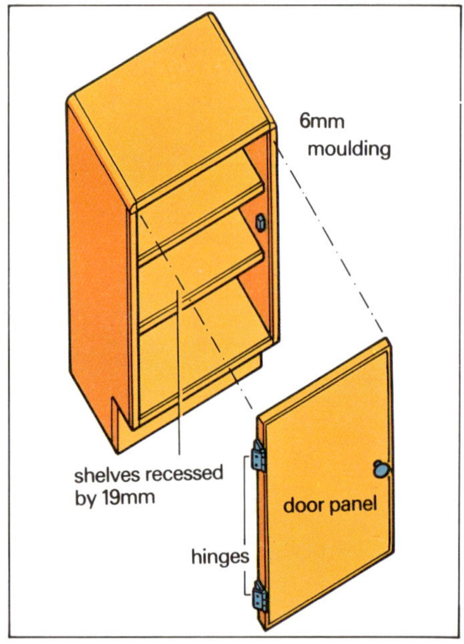

necessary so that the door swings free, then fit a magnetic catch and catch plate. Finish the door by screwing on a wooden knob.

Building the bedhead

As with the side units, assembling the bedhead is perfectly straightforward providing you take care to keep the panels aligned as you pin them.

Start by cutting the edging quadrant to size. Pin and glue it to the side panels as you did on the side units. Make sure the mouldings are flush with the back edges so that you can follow by pinning and gluing ramin lipping to the front edges all the way around the unit.

Make the centre halving joint next. Find the middle of the centre upright and mark a 25mm × 19mm slot across it on what will be the back edge using a pencil and try square. Do the same on the front edge of the centre horizontal member.

Cut the vertical slot lines in the usual way with a tenon saw.

Saw the headboard battens to length by marking and cutting one, then using this as a template to mark and cut the others. Locate two of the battens flush with the back edge of the centre horizontal, separated by the halving slot. Glue them in this position, then pin in four places to strengthen the joints. Fix two more battens to the underside of the horizontal in the same way.

Pin and glue the remaining battens flush with the back edges of the top and bottom panels, using the centre upright as a spacer.

The depth lines are normally cut with a chisel, but in the case of plywood, this is hard to do cleanly. A better method is to drill holes at either end of the line, well inside the waste, and then join them with a padsaw. Afterwards, sand or rasp the corners of the slot to a sharp edge.

Screw the magnetic catches to all the battens, 150mm from each end, as shown in the diagram. Finish by drilling 4.5mm clearance holes for the wall fixing screws through the battens on the top and bottom panels, level with the catches.

The bedhead is now ready to be assembled. Lay the top, centre and bottom panels front edge uppermost on the floor. Take the centre upright, coat all the mating surfaces with glue, and slot it in position over the centre horizontal panel. At the same time as you are doing this, locate the

ends in the top and bottom panels.

Now try the end panels for fit. If this is poor, leave the assembly to dry then sand down any protruding edges with a planer file to get a good finish.

When all is well, glue and pin the end panels in place with the bedhead supported against the wall. Follow by pinning through the top and bottom panels into the centre upright. Make sure all the pin heads are punched below the surface. Then complete the bedhead box by pinning and gluing ramin lipping to the exposed front edges of all the panels—which also gives you the chance to disguise any imperfect joints.

Making the headboards

First measure and mark out the catch plate positions on the backs of the headboard panels and screw the plates in place. Then turn the boards over and glue on the foam padding, following the adhesive manufacturer's instructions. If necessary, trim the foam flush with the edges of the boards using a handyman's knife. If you have access to a staple gun use this to secure the fabric, rather than tacks and a hammer.

Lay each board foam downwards over its fabric covering and adjust until it is roughly central. Fold the first long edge of the fabric over, without pulling it, and take or staple it to the back of the board. Then fold over the other long edge, this time stretching it taut before you fix it. Repeat this procedure with the side edges, pocketing the corners as you fold them.

Finishing off

Thanks to the attractive colour contrast between the ply and its hardwood edging, just about any combination of stain and varnish is possible—as well as an all-over painted finish.

Begin the finishing process by double checking that there are no sharp edges or ill-fitting joints. If you need to sand the plywood, feather the edge evenly or bumps will show up when you apply the surface finish of paint or varnish.

The pin holes must be filled next. If you're painting the bedhead, use fine surface interior filler; otherwise use a wood stopper matched to the colour of the wood (you'll need two—one for the ply, one for the ramin). Press the stopper in with a knife and scrape flush with the surface—it's difficult to sand when dry.

Filler and woodstopper often changes

7 *Pin and glue the quadrant moulding and edge lipping to the longitudinal members*

8 *Clamp the three vertical members together and mark and cut them simultaneously*

9 *Cut halving joints in plywood using a tenon saw, a drill with wood bit and a keyhole saw*

10 *Wait until the frame is assembled before you cut and fix the softwood battens*

colour once it is stained or varnished, so it is a good idea to experiment with your chosen finish on a piece of scrap board. Leave the filler to dry hard (this will usually take three to four hours) before applying the finish. You may be able to darken the filler or stopper slightly by adding a stain or using some household cocoa. When you apply the filler, sand it down as carefully as possible, so that only a small amount shows. Once it dries, sand thoroughly, working in the direction of the grain to avoid damage.

Before you apply the finish, give all the surfaces a quick sanding with fine abrasive paper mounted on a block. Be sure to clean off all the dust before proceeding. If you're varnishing, remember to do it in a dust-free environment; sand and clean down throughly between coats—three applications should be sufficient. For a fine finish, dilute the first and last coasts with a little white spirit. The first coat will largely sink into the porous wood; the last coat will give a fine, almost dust-free, finish.

The bedhead frame is very simple. The ramin lipping merely hides the plywood's grain—you could replace it with iron-on veneer edging strip, or a carefully applied paint finish

Fitting the unit

Fit the bedhead first. Although there's plenty of room for manoeuvre when it comes to the height you fix it at, it looks best if the centre horizontal aligns with the tops of the side units—giving a height of 394mm if you go by the dimensions in the construction diagram.

Rather than use a spirit level to level the bedhead, it's best to get an asistant to hold it against the wall at the right height, then slide the side units against it and align them before marking the eight screw positions with a bradawl. Having drilled and plugged the wall and screwed the bedhead firmly in place, do likewise for the side units and your installation is complete.

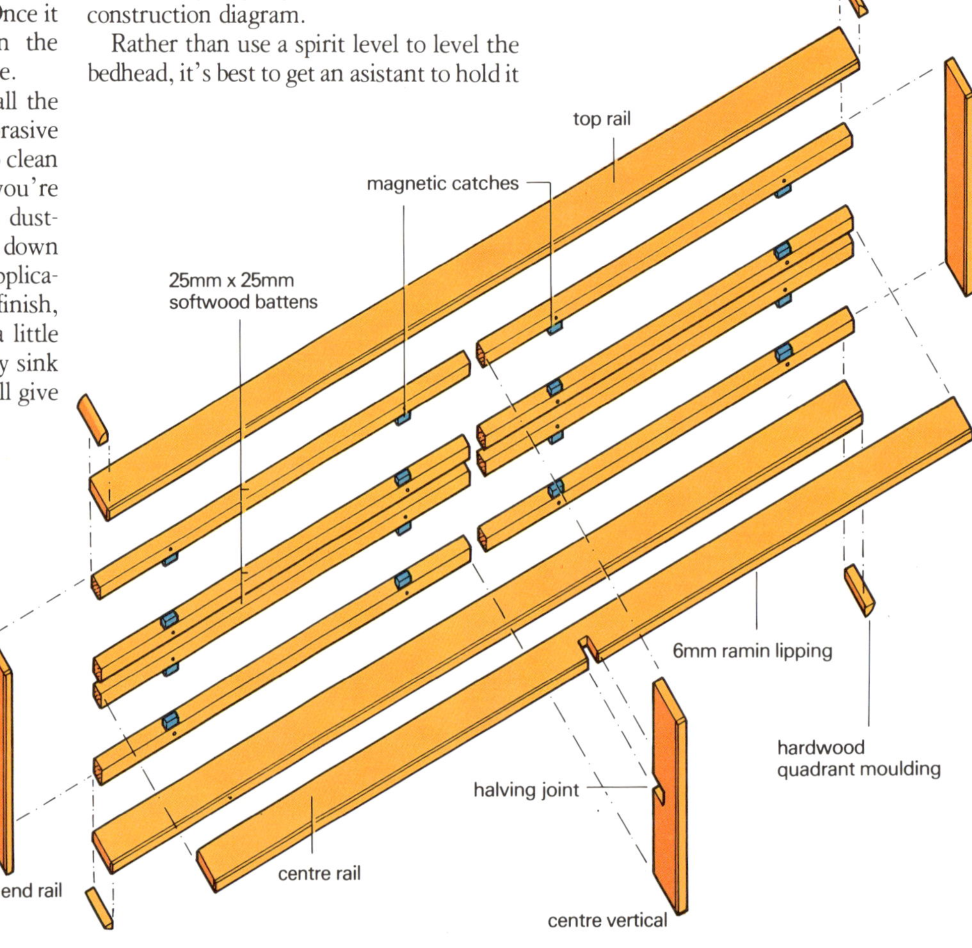

11 *Use a thixotropic glue to fix the foam. This will not react chemically with the plastic. Press the foam into position as you roll it out*

12 *Fold the material into a neat 'hospital' corner—by tucking the spare material underneath the fold—and staple it down securely*

13 *Fit the steel plates for the magnetic catches over the material to ensure a proper match. Try the padded cushions in position and alter as necessary*

FITTED WARDROBE SYSTEM

Built-in furniture is an ideal way to make the best use of space—and a well planned, well made unit can add to the value of your home. But shop-bought systems can work out to be a very expensive buy—and do-it-yourself wardrobes often need a lot of planning, construction and juggling to fit the space that is available.

As far as possible, this wardrobe system combines the best of both worlds. It's based on a simple—but sturdy—framework of melamine boards and softwood battens and—to cut planning down to a minimum—it's mainly built out of modular parts with only one section used to match it to the width of the room. To keep construction as simple as possible it's largely made from standard size materials—so not much cutting. And to keep costs low the number of components for the framework, the doors and fittings is kept to a minimum.

There shouldn't be any problems fitting it to your bedroom. It's width can be whatever you want—and at 2.3m its height is low enough to suit almost any ceiling. All you need is a wall free of major obstructions.

Any wardrobe's appearance depends mainly on its doors, and with this system you have a choice—fit standard sized ready-made cupboard doors or build your own.

Planning considerations

Although planning is kept to a minimum, check the options before you start, and get to know how the system fits together. Then you can tailor a unit to fit your room—and your needs—perfectly. The diagram on page 62 gives details of the wardrobe's main construction.

The system has three basic components which you can mix and match to suit yourself—the unit shown in the photograph uses four of them:
•**The hanging wardrobe** is fitted with a rail and has plenty of space for a variety of clothes plus extra storage below.
•**The two-door storage wardrobe** uses the same basic shell fitted out with shelves for folded clothes and linen.
•**The matching dressing table** has a drawer for storing make up, jewellery and other small items.

Above each unit is a roomy storage cupboard for bed linen, blankets or items you don't use very often, such as suitcases.

And it needn't stop there. There are also

designs for an easy-to-make set of shelves to make more use of the hanging wardrobe—plus ideas for fitting out the interior of the storage wardrobe.

You can put all these units together however you want, but it depends on your space. So start by measuring the width of the wall. It will help to draw a simple sketch plan. Each of the wardrobe units is 630mm wide, so you can easily work out how many will fit your wall space.

It's virtually certain that a whole number of units won't span the wall exactly, so to adjust the width you have two options. The first is that the dressing table is of variable width—anything from 500 to 1500mm. This should cover the majority of situations. But if you are left with an awkward small gap to span—usually running along the top of the wardrobe, or at the sides—you can fill this as described on page 65.

The height of the system should be suitable for most ceilings. But in a room with a higher ceiling you can span a small gap with a filling panel or alternatively cover in the top (see page 65).

Based on this information you should be able to refine your sketch to show where each unit fits and the width of the dressing table plus any infill panels. From the sketch you can then work out what materials—and their precise quantities—you need.

Materials you need

What to buy depends on the size of your room and choice of units. But as most of the components are standardized it shouldn't be difficult to work out what you need by looking at your sketch plan and checking off the parts against the list below. Note that this covers the main structure of the wardrobe's framework only—interior fittings are detailed on page 66.

Check which of these parts you need:
•**Plinth frame:** This is all made from 50mm × 25mm softwood. Buy enough to span your room twice plus 475mm for every 600mm width of the unit.
•**Plinth base:** This is made from 600mm wide 15mm melamine faced chipboard. You need a total length to span the whole room.
•**Wall battens:** You need two 2235mm lengths of 50mm × 50mm softwood plus 2235mm of 25mm × 25mm softwood per upright panel.
•**Upright panels:** Each of these is 2235mm long and can be cut from a 2440mm × 525mm panel of 15mm melamine faced chipboard.
•**Shelves:** These are cut from 525mm wide 15mm melamine. Against a wall they are 620mm long; between two uprights they are 600mm long. The shelf above the

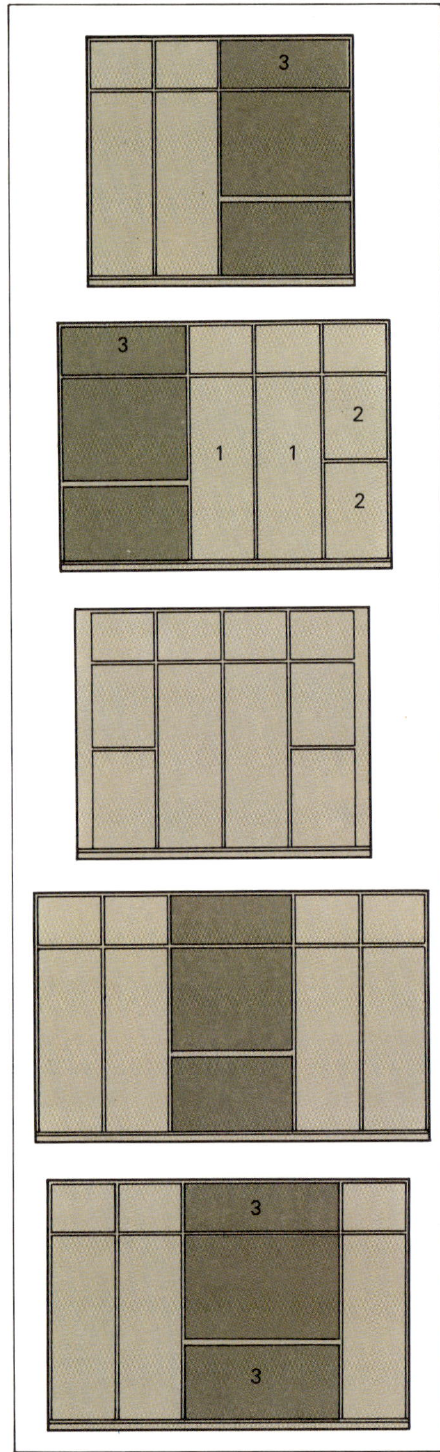

Careful choice of hanging wardrobes (1), storage wardrobes (2), and variable sections (3) will fit the system into almost any room

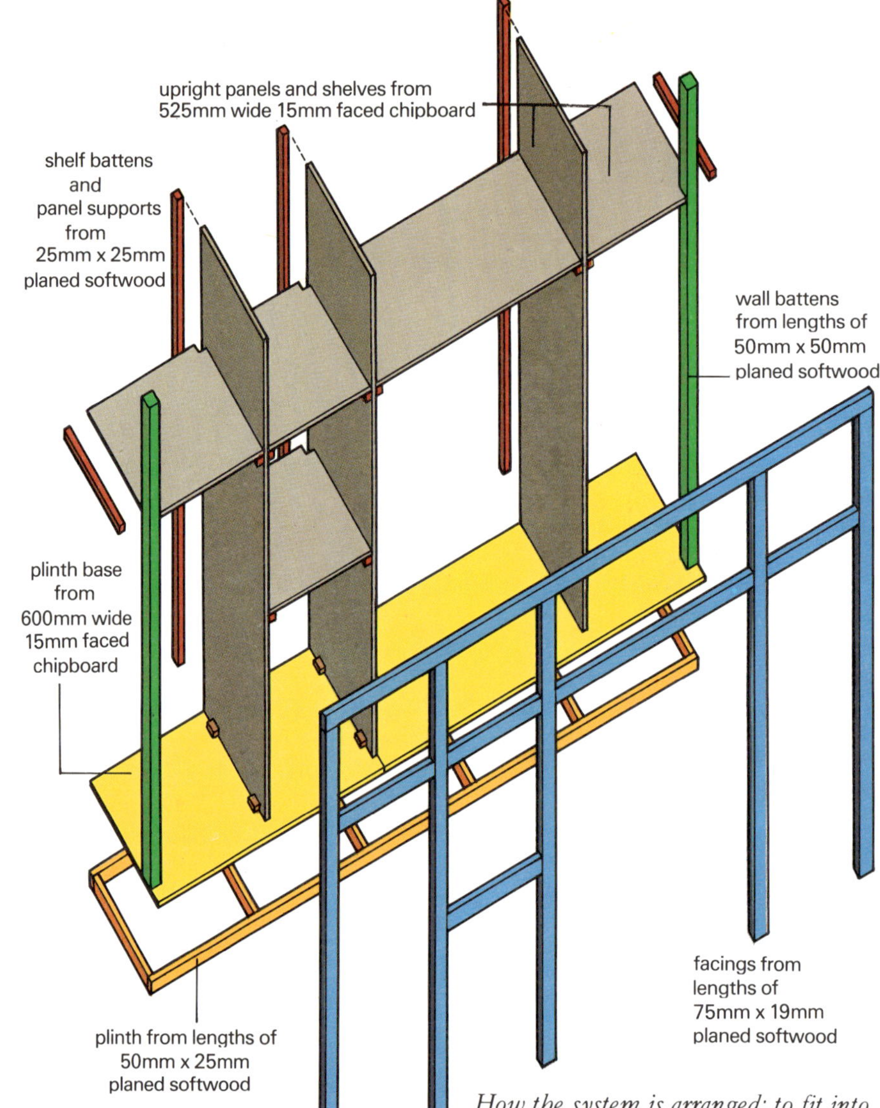

dressing table depends on your room.

•**Shelf battens:** These are 25mm × 25mm softwood. You need a total length of about 1100mm per shelf.

•**Dressing table:** Cut two lengths of 525 mm melamine depending on your room.

•**Top board:** Cut to span your room from 75mm × 19mm softwood.

•**Shelf-facing:** Cut from 75mm × 19mm softwood, 150mm less than the room width.

•**Wall batten facings:** These are 2160mm long from 75mm × 19mm softwood.

•**Upright facings:** These are in two lengths—485mm and 1675mm, both from 75mm × 19mm softwood.

To hold everything together you need glue, nails, screws and plastic block joints. Once again the quantities are variable, but it's worth buying by the box. Get 75mm and 50mm No. 8 screws and 38mm and 25mm No. 6 chipboard screws. Buy ½kg of 50mm oval nails and ½kg of 38mm panel pins. A small bottle of PVA woodworking adhesive is more than sufficient for this job. For wall fixings buy either plastic

How the system is arranged: to fit into irregularly shaped rooms, the wardrobe system isn't fixed directly to the walls. Instead it stands on a plinth on the floor and between battens fitted to the walls. By fitting these carefully to the irregularities of the room and ensuring that their outer faces are perfectly square, you can standardize the wardrobes.

The wardrobe construction could hardly be simpler. The sides are panels of melamine-faced chipboard screwed to the plinths and fixed back to the wall with 25mm battens. Shelves in the same material are added on battens fixed to the sides.

All the front edges are trimmed with pine boards. These serve two functions—they stiffen the structure and make it easier to fit doors.

The dressing table is essentially a sturdier version of the shelves in the units. The cupboard above is of similar construction to the top of the wardrobes—only the door fitting differs

wallplugs or cavity fixings, depending on your walls. Block joints are quite cheap so buy a few extra.

Building the plinth

The first step in construction is to build and level the plinth on which the wardrobe units are going to stand. Before you start, roll the carpet back well out of the way. If it is held by carpet grippers, prise these away along the wall and out for a distance of 600mm on the side walls. When you have finished, the carpet can be rolled back again and cut to fit along the plinth.

The plinth consists of a framework of 50mm × 25mm softwood, glued and nailed together, with a sheet of 675mm wide melamine faced chipboard on top and slightly overlapping the frame at the front.

The sheet of melamine and the front and back battens must span the whole room between the skirting boards at either side. Although this should not be a problem with the softwood, in a large room you will not be able to do this with one piece of melamine—there must be a joint somewhere. If you can, arrange this where it will be least noticeable. If you haven't ordered your wood cut to length, do so at this particular stage.

Construct the frame first. Lay the front and back battens out on the floor. To separate them you need a number of cross bars 475mm long—one for each end, plus one every 600mm. Cut all of these from one pattern, so you know that each batten is identical.

Assemble the ends first. Apply woodworking glue to the ends of the framework's cross bars and nail them with two 50mm nails at each corner.

Check that the frame is reasonably square. If it isn't, it should be simple to push it back into shape at this stage. Now glue and nail it to the cross bars.

When the frame is ready, lay it in position about 50mm from the back wall. Lay the melamine board on top. It helps if you cut it fractionally short. Don't worry at this stage how well the back fits.

The plinth provides the whole basis for the construction, so it's essential that it is flat and level. Hold a spirit level on top of the melamine—on both directions. Adjust with packing pieces slipped beneath or by shaving the bottom of the plinth frame to fit the floor (see Scribing to fit). When you are satisfied that the plinth is flat, screw the frame down using plastic block joints.

Now replace the melamine board. If it

1 *Cut the pieces to length, then nail and glue the corners of the plinth frame together*

2 *Check everything is square and add further braces at intervals of about 600mm, nailing and gluing in place*

3 *Lay the melamine plinth top and check level. Adjust by packing or shaving the base*

doesn't fit snugly, scribe it to the irregularities of the wall. When the boards fit properly, drill 4mm holes through them

<table>
<tr><td style="background:#f5d76e">★ WATCH POINT ★</td></tr>
</table>

To prevent the wood splitting, stagger the nails so that they aren't both going into the same grain line. It also helps to blunt the points by tapping each a couple of times with a hammer.

and into the frame below at roughly 250mm intervals. Countersink all the holes, then screw the boards down with 25mm No. 6 chipboard screws.

Putting up the wall battens

With the plinths providing a level platform for the structure, it's time to fit the side battens. These must establish true verticals for the wardrobe units to fit against.

Both of these battens are 2235mm long made from 50mm × 50mm softwood. They fit onto the side walls of the structure, so that their front edges are 525mm out from the corners of the room.

Stand each one in turn against the wall with its base on the plinth. The skirting will probably prevent the bottom of the batten from fitting back against the wall—so you will have to notch it out. Mark the width and height of the notch on the wood, then saw it out with two cuts of a tenon saw.

Use a spirit level to check that the batten is vertical, both sideways and front to back.

4 *Make sure the battens are vertical, checking both front to back and side to side*

Look for gaps behind the batten too. If the wall is at all uneven or out of square, the batten has to be scribed to fit against it properly before fixing (see Scribing to fit). Then, line the batten up again and double-check that it is truly vertical.

Drill fixing holes at intervals of about 300mm, starting near the bottom and using a 4.5mm drill bit. Countersink each hole in turn. Hold the batten up and mark through each hole.

In a masonry wall drill 6mm holes at each point and insert plastic wallplugs. In a cavity wall drill 6mm holes and insert cavity fixings—unless you are lucky enough to coincide with a stud position, in which case you can screw directly to it. Screw the battens firmly in place using a quantity of 75mm No. 8 screws.

Putting up the wardrobe sides

Each of these is 2235mm length cut from a 2440mm × 525mm sheet of 15mm melamine faced chipboard. They are fixed to the plinth with simple plastic block joints and to the wall with battens.

Mark the position of each one on the plinth. Those adjacent to the side walls are set with their closest face 620mm away from it. Those in the centre of the unit are set with their faces 600mm apart.

Stand each panel in turn in position. Use a spirit level to check that it is upright and try it back against the wall for fit. If, as is probable, the wall is uneven, you will have to scribe the back edge to match it (see Scribing to fit). Use a plane or planer file to trim the melamine, then double-check that it fits. Mark each one with a letter so that you can fit it back in the correct position. Draw a line on the wall to show where each panel fits.

Next, screw support battens to the back wall along the lines you have marked. Cut them 2235mm long from 25mm × 25mm softwood, and fix them with 50mm No. 8 screws and wallplugs.

Drill fixing holes along the back edges of the panels to attach them to the battens. Use a 4mm drill bit and set them 15mm from the edge. Countersink all the holes for neatness.

It's easiest if you attach shelf support battens before you screw the sides in place. Refer to the construction plan on page 433 and to your own sketch plan to see where these are required. The main ones are for the division of the top cupboard; these are set 590mm down from the top of the

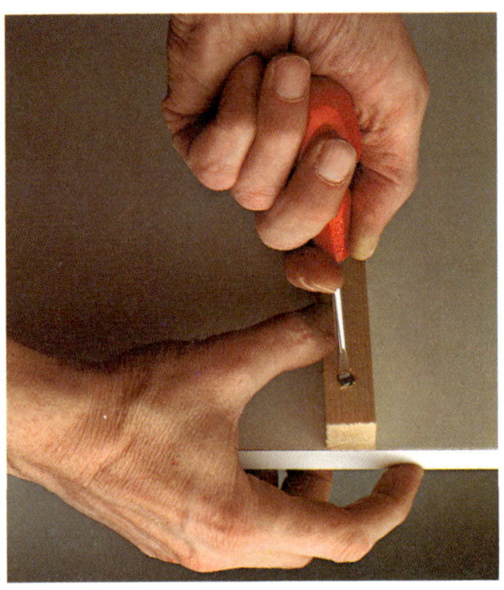

5 *Fix the shelf support battens in place, taking care to get them square*

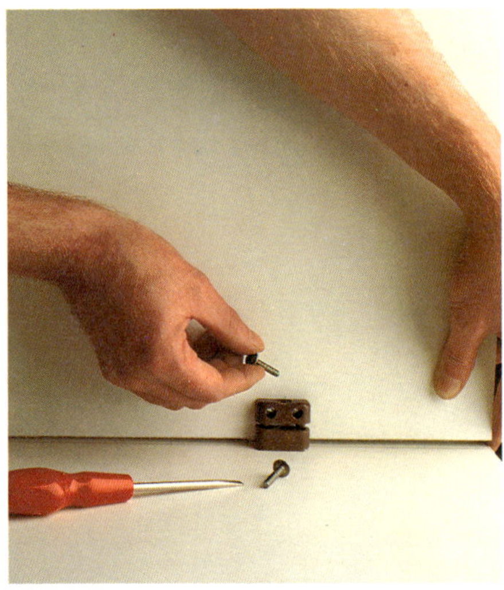

6 *Drill screw holes along the back edge, ready for fixing it to the wall batten*

7 *When fixing panels direct, use chipboard screws; countersink the heads*

panels. The divider for the storage wardrobe is set 900mm up from the plinth. Other shelf positions are optional.

All the battens are made from 25mm × 25mm softwood in 500mm lengths. Mark their positions carefully using a try square to make sure they are set squarely across the boards—and mark the boards at each side of a shelf together so that you are absolutely sure both supports are at the same height. The battens must be aligned with the front edge of the panels, not the back.

Screw the battens to the boards with 38mm No. 6 chipboard screws every 150mm or so. Spread a little PVA adhesive on the back of each of the battens for an even firmer fixing.

Now screw the block joints along the base of each of the side panels, flush with the edge. Set two block joints on each, 150mm from the corners.

Stand the panels back up in place—ideally get a helper to hold them upright for you—and mark the positions of the holes in the block joints and along the back edge. If you use a bradawl it should save drilling a pilot hole. Screw the boards firmly in place with 25mm No. 6 screws.

The panels should now stand up by themselves but to steady them further you can temporarily tack battens across the tops of them.

Scribing to fit

Use scribing whenever you have to fit a component snugly against an uneven surface such as an irregular wall or floor.

The first step is to fit the part as closely back to the surface as it will go. It's usually important to keep it in a particular alignment—such as with another component or against a spirit level—so check this point carefully, too.

It's essential that the part does not move while you are scribing, so fix it temporarily or get someone to help you by holding it firmly in place. Mark its position so you can refit it exactly.

To scribe it you need a pencil or marker, plus a block of scrap wood slightly wider than the largest gap behind the part of the structure you are scribing.

Tape the pencil firmly to the block. Then run the block down the wall, keeping it firmly against the surface, so that the pencil marks a line down the edge of the part. This line will be an accurate mimic of the outline of the wall.

Once you have done this all along the

edge you can remove the part and trim it to the line. The best way to do this depends on how close the line is to the edge, and how thick the material is. To remove small amounts you can use glasspaper. For larger amounts use a plane or planer file—you could even use a saw if the material is thin enough to cut easily in this way.

Adding the shelves

The shelves stiffen up the whole structure and complete the main carcase ready for you to fit out the interior and add the doors.

Start by screwing shelf support battens to the walls in line with those on the upright panels. These too are made from lengths of 25mm × 25mm softwood. Cut them to fit the spaces and screw them in place with 50mm No. 8 screws every 150mm or so. In the outer units use a spirit level to make sure that they are positioned accurately along the back and side wall.

The shelves can now be dropped into place. All of them are lengths of 525mm wide 15mm melamine. Those adjacent to the walls are 620mm long. The others are 600mm wide. The shelf over the dressing table, and the dressing table top itself, must be cut to fit the space between the chipboard sides exactly. Cut three panels this size —the dressing table top is made out of a double thickness of melamine.

Try all the shelves in place to check that they fit properly. They may need to be scribed at the back so they slide back flush with the front edge of the uprights. They also need 25mm square notches at both back corners to clear the wall battens.

When you are satisfied with the fit remove each shelf, labelling where it goes so you can identify it later. Then drill a series of 4mm holes along the sides and back of each shelf, 15mm from the edge and at 200mm intervals. Apply woodworking glue to the tops of the battens, put each shelf back in place and spike through all the holes with a bradawl. Drive 25mm No. 6 screws through each hole to hold the shelf down to the batten. But note that while you can do this for the shelf above the dressing table, keep the dressing table boards to one side and don't drill them at this stage.

Once you have fitted all the shelves, apply the pine trims to the wardrobe fronts. These are simply glued and pinned to the edges of the melamine.

Start with the two outer trims on the face of the wall battens. These are 2160mm long and cut from 75mm × 19mm softwood. Use a spirit level to set them

8 *How the front frames and shelves are fitted in the completed frame*

9 *After cutting to fit, nail and glue the softwood trims to the melamine*

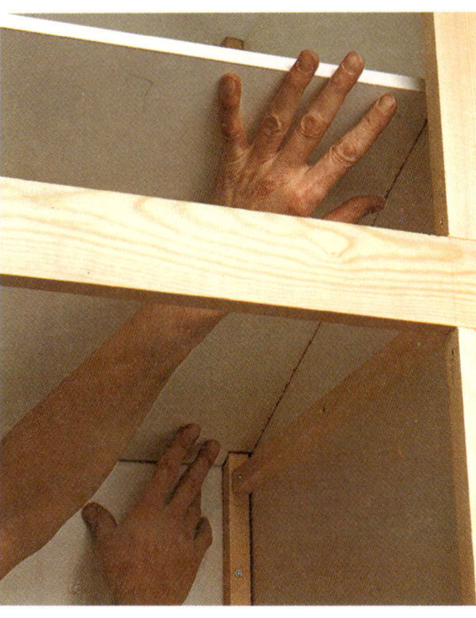

10 *Drop the notched shelves onto the support battens*

upright. To do this, you may need to move them out into the room by a fraction if you have scribed the wall batten to fit. Glue the wall batten and nail them in place with 38mm panel pins every 250mm or so. Use a nail punch to sink the heads below the surface of the wood.

To span the top of the unit you need a long board running wall to wall. In the basic design this is cut from 75mm × 19mm softwood, but if doing this would leave a slight gap you could use something wider. The alternative is to fit a coving over the gap afterwards (see below).

Cut the top board to span exactly. Try it in position to check its fit, then glue and pin it to the wall battens and the edges of the upright panels.

There is a similar board spanning the front of the top shelf—this is again cut from 75mm × 19mm softwood but runs between the side trims, rather than above them. Cut this to fit accurately, then glue and pin it to the front of the shelves. It must be positioned so that the shelves run down the centre of the board.

Finally cut short lengths of 75mm × 19mm softwood to trim the uprights between these two boards, and longer ones to run from the plinth up to the lower cross boards. It's more accurate to cut these to fit the space than to measure them. Once again these should be set centrally on the uprights. However, don't just glue and pin them: they have to carry the weight of the doors and need stronger fixings—use plastic block joints at 200mm intervals screwed firmly to both parts.

Concealing awkward gaps

There are two places where you may be faced with an awkward gap around the standard units—at the top or at the side. Fortunately these are usually easy to conceal neatly.

The only time you are likely to have a gap at the side is if you want to fit several wardrobe units and the remaining space is not large enough to construct a dressing table—that is, less than 500mm.

The answer here is not to leave this as a relatively large gap on one side but to set the other units centrally and leave a more manageable gap of 250mm on both sides. The interior of the units so created can then be fitted out with somewhat wider shelving. To get around the problem of needing a wider door, fit a front trim which is oversized by the amount of the gap.

Gaps at the top are even easier to deal

with. It's most likely that you will either have a very small gap—or a very large one in an old house with a high ceiling.

In the first case you can span it with an oversize top board. If this would create difficulties use an ordinary top board and cover the gap afterwards with a wooden or plastic coving moulding.

With a very wide gap, don't even attempt to cover it. Instead, construct the wardrobe completely and panel the top with a sheet of melamine faced hardboard pinned to the top of the uprights to keep the dust out.

Finishing the framework

Once the main framework has been erected you can add the finishing touches, making them as simple or as sophisticated as you like. For example, if you want a simple dressing table you can make a plain shelf using two lengths of faced chipboard placed on top of one another with a timber facing pinned along the front edge. But you can turn it into a proper dressing table with a make-up drawer underneath.

Similarly, you need only fit the inside of the hanging wardrobe with a clothes rail. But you can construct a small set of shelves to take up the wasted space in the bottom.

Inside the storage wardrobe you can fit plain shelves in the two halves or add adjustable baskets.

Decide which interior fittings you want and then incorporate these into your original sketch plan using the construction diagram on page 62 as a guide.

Above: A wide variety of fittings such as sliding baskets adds versatility to the basic framework

Fixtures and fittings

The materials you need fall into two sections—the doors and the interior fittings. **Doors:** All of the wardrobe and door fronts fitted to the system are standard size and can be bought ready-made—except for the flap-up cupboard door above the dressing table which is almost certain to be an odd size. You can trim the ends or sides of a standard door; but if the amount to be removed is more than say, 100mm, you will probably find this impossible.

The easy option in this case is to cut a plain panel to the required size from

Below: The main fittings detailed here— dressing table (yellow), shelves (orange), baskets (red), doors (blue)

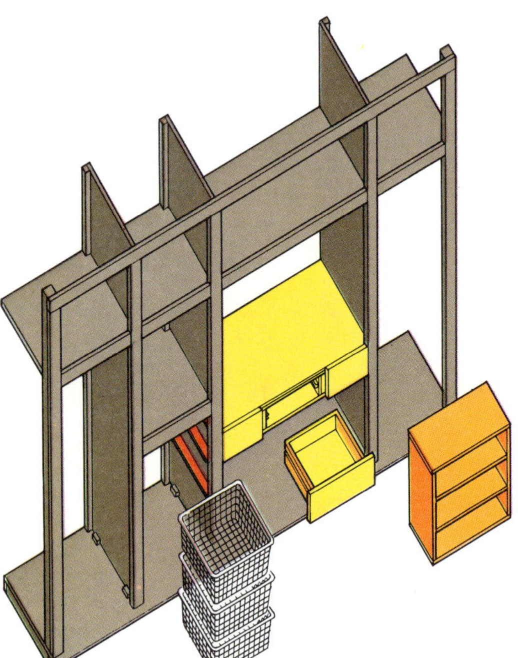

laminate or plywood and hang this in place of a door. But there's a good chance that you can trim this in style with the rest of the fronts, providing you can buy some smaller doors (see page 70).

Apart from this, for each hanging wardrobe buy a 1680mm × 610mm door, and for each top cupboard a 610mm × 460mm door. The storage wardrobe requires two doors, one 760mm × 610mm door for the top and one 900mm × 610mm door for the bottom.

- **Door fittings:** Buy three 50mm brass or chrome-plated hinges for the large doors and two hinges for each of the others. You also need a matching handle or knob for each door, plus a magnetic catch. For the door above the table buy a lift-up stay.
- **Interior fittings:** The materials you need here vary according to the exact design of your system. So look at your sketch plan and check off the parts against this list:
- **Hanging rails:** For each hanging wardrobe buy an 18mm diameter tube plus two ends and one centre support. If possible buy a little oversize and cut to length.
- **Dressing table:** For the basic dressing table without drawer all you need is a piece of 25mm × 19mm softwood, cut the same length as the front edge of the table.

For the dressing table drawer use a ready-made plastic kit. Buy components to make a drawer up to 525mm deep, 100mm high and roughly half the width of the table (see Self-assembly drawer kits). You also need plastic runners and a hardboard base.

To build a framework for the drawer assembly you need some pieces of 525mm wide melamine faced chipboard and softwood cut into the following lengths:
- For the sides two pieces 525mm long, the same depth as the drawer plus 25mm.
- For the base one piece 525mm wide and the same length as the dresssing table itself.
- Two 525mm lengths of 25mm × 25mm battening to support the base.
- You also need a piece of 150mm × 19mm softwood or melamine the same length as the front edge of the table to make a fascia.
- **Pull-out basket system:** Buy as many standard 545mm baskets as you need. For each basket you need two 525mm lengths of 50mm × 25mm softwood and 25mm × 25mm softwood to act as runners.
- **Freestanding shelves:** This unit is made entirely from lengths of 300mm wide 15mm melamine. If you haven't enough offcuts, all the pieces can be cut from 3.5m of 300mm wide melamine sheet. You need:
- For the sides, two 570mm lengths.
- For the top and bottom panels, two 560mm lengths.

• For the shelves, two 530mm lengths.
Miscellaneous: Buy primer, undercoat and gloss (½ litre of each) for the front facings and support battens, plus paint or varnish for the doors, and general purpose filler.

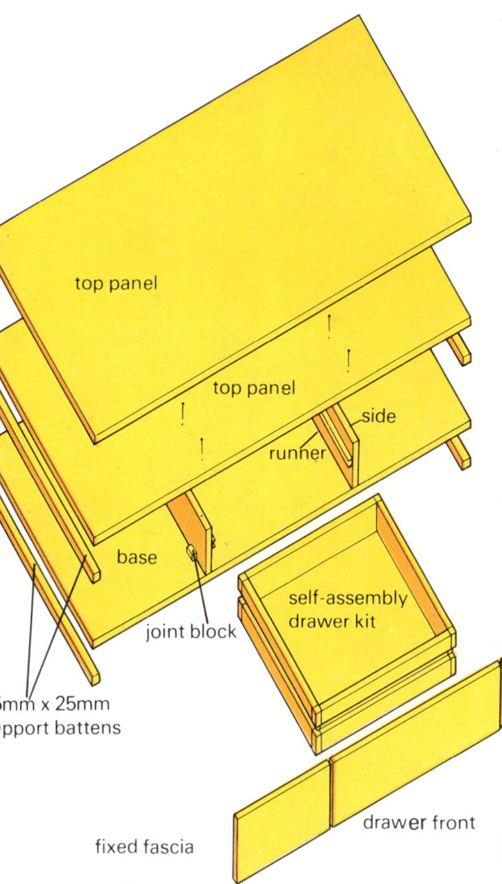

General assembly of the dressing table

Constructing the dressing table

The simple dressing table is built from two layers of faced chipboard lipped with softwood facing. For the dressing table with drawer you need a few additional parts.

To construct the simple dressing table without drawer simply lay the two prepared pieces of chipboard face down on a flat surface one on top of the other. Then drill and countersink screw holes at regular intervals around the outer edge and across the centre. Spread a little glue between the sheets and screw them together.

Turn the assembly over and slot it between the wardrobes so that it is resting firmly on the support battens at either side. Then pin the facing to the front edge of the dressing table.

If you want to fit a drawer to the dressing table, you must erect a solid framework for the drawer to sit in as shown below.

Take the base of the assembly and lay it down flat. Position the two side pieces on it with the gap between them measuring the width of the drawer plus 10mm, and an equal gap on either side. Make sure they are square to the base and level with the front edge. Attach them by fixing two block connectors down the outside edge of each.

Now fit the drawer runners. Position them 55mm up from the base, drill and screw in place.

On the main wardrobe sides, measure down 125mm from the tops of the dressing table support battens. You need two more battens with their top edges in line with these marks, to support the base of the dressing table. Cut these and screw in place.

Drop the base on these supports. Lay a top over it and check that it contacts its supports, plus both side pieces. Remove it, drill and screw the base to support battens.

11 *Joint the sides to the base, then screw on the plastic runners*

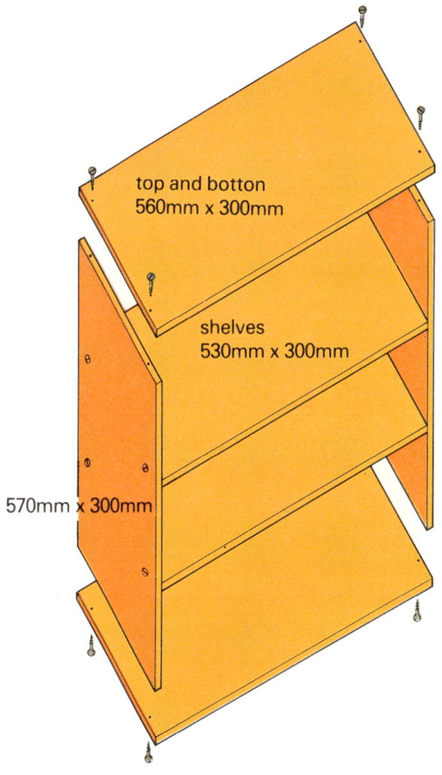

12 *Screw support battens to the wardrobes in line with the base and add the assembly. Fit the tops after the base is in place*

Now fit the top panel. Drill through and screw it to the supports at each end, and the side pieces where it contacts them—but check that these are upright.

Sand lightly over the upper surface of the top panel and the underside of the remaining top panel. Glue the two together with contact adhesive—the sanding provides a key. Nail on two fascia pieces.

Now fit the drawer together (see Self-assembly drawer kits) and try it for size. If it is satisfactory, remove the drawer and add the front. Drill and insert the screws from inside the drawer so you don't damage the front face. Position the front so that it fits level with the fascia either side. It will then project enough underneath the drawer to provide a hand grip.

Building the wardrobe shelving unit

This freestanding storage unit is designed to be placed in the bottom corner of the wardrobe so it can be used for storing shoes, socks and other items. It is made entirely from melamine faced chipboard, glued and screwed together.

Before you start, examine the construc-

The whole assembly consists of just six pieces of melamine. Measure and drill accurately, and use chipboard screws to put it together

13 *Cut all the pieces to length, joining the outer frame first*

14 *Add the shelves. The cut edges can be lipped with edging*

tion plan. Cut out the pieces and label each of them with a letter or number. Construct the main frame of the unit first by gluing and screwing the two uprights to the top and bottom panels. Mark off the shelf positions at 200mm intervals, then glue and insert the panels and fix them by screwing through from the sides. If you want to add a back panel, glue and pin it in place.

Hold the panels in position temporarily for drilling with a few strips of masking tape. You can then check they are square before finally screwing the pieces together.

Self-assembly drawer kits

Plastic DIY drawer kits—which come in different designs—enable you to construct different size drawers quickly and easily.

All you have to do is to decide the depth and size of drawer you require. The kit consists of profiled drawer sides with a groove moulded down the outside to accept runners and one on the inside to take the base, plus four snap-fastening corner pieces. There are also moulded plastic drawer runners, if required.

There are two ways to use the kit. The easiest is to make all four sides of the drawer in plastic and add a front trim afterwards. The alternative is to make three sides in plastic—the drawer front itself forms the fourth. This type of construction is more complicated and for this design a four sided construction is used. Apart from the kit itself, you need a piece of hardboard to make the base of the drawer.

The side profile can be cut to length with a fine toothed saw, such as a tenon saw. Use a try square to make the cutting line accurately. When you work out the lengths you need, remember to allow for the thickness of the corner block. The makers give a formula for working this out and it's most important to get it right. Similarly when you come to cut the base of the drawer to size you have to allow for the thickness of the sides—less the slots.

To assemble a four sided drawer first lay out all the component parts of the drawer onto a flat surface. Slot the corner connectors into the back profile. Lift the baseboard into position followed by the two sides. Make sure that the baseboard is located firmly in the slotted recess cut around the inside of the profiles. Finally add the front corner connectors and the front piece of edging profile.

Adding the hanging rails

The hanging wardrobes can be fitted out very quickly—it's just a matter of screwing the hanging rail under the top shelf.

There's a small amount of variation from make to make, but most fit in a similar way. There are two kinds of support brackets. The first is a socket which screws to the side of the wardrobe to take the end of the rail tube. The second is a drop bracket which screws under a shelf and has an arm with a ring on it to accept the tube.

Some rail systems only have one or other of these types of support. It's better to go for one which has both—since this will take the most weight. Fitting is simple, and in most cases the makers will provide full instructions. The important thing is to screw the brackets up firmly and in the correct alignment. If you are using a drop bracket in the centre, its length will determine how far down to fix the end brackets.

15 *Mark the rail tube to the required length. A piece of tape will allow you to use a marker pen and leave a clear line. Allow clearance for the ends*

16 *Align the tube carefully down the centre line and at the correct height. Screw on the support brackets at the ends and centre*

Start by finding the centre line across the wardrobe and marking it in pencil. Hold the rail to span the wardrobe and mark the position of the brackets. If you have to cut it to length, use a junior hacksaw. When you mark the cutting line, be sure to make allowances for the amount which is 'lost' in the two end brackets.

Check how the rails fit into the end brackets. Sometimes they drop into them from above after the brackets are screwed in place. Alternatively, some designs have to be slipped over the rail first and screwed in place all together.

17 *Three pull-out baskets make versatile use of space*

18 *Measure the heights of the baskets and add runners*

Above: Each runner is made from two pieces of softwood

Fitting pull-out baskets

These provide an alternative to the plain storage cupboard with shelves. They allow you easy access and help keep clothing tidy.

You need to fix packing pieces to either side of the wardrobe to act as runners. They can be made using a 25mm × 25mm batten to support a second piece as shown. The width they need to project depends on the baskets. You must screw them in place to leave a clear spacing of at least 50mm between baskets—so work this out and mark the position of each packing piece before you start. Measure the distance from the bottom of the cupboard every time so you can make certain that each runner is correctly aligned.

Drill and countersink screw holes through each runner at roughly 100mm intervals. Hold each runner in turn in position and spike through the holes with a bradawl to make pilot holes in the chipboard. Then screw the runner into place. When all the runners are positioned, try the baskets for size and check that they slide in and out freely.

If you find that any of the drawers are a little sticky, remove the drawer concerned and rub the top edge of each supporting packing piece with a candle.

Filling and finishing

Before you hang the doors, any gaps in the front facings and support battens must be filled, sanded down and painted. At the same time you can apply a suitable finish to the doors, if they haven't been treated.

Apply the filler with a filling knife, paying particular attention to the gaps between the facings and the walls. Here you may have to build up the filler layer by layer until it is just above surface level. Make sure you fill over the nail heads in the facings, too.

Leave the filler to set hard—this usually takes three to four hours—then smooth down with a piece of sandpaper on a block. Check the surface and refill if it is particularly bumpy. When you are satisfied, remove any excess dust before painting with a soft cloth dampened with white spirit.

<table>
<tr><td>

★ WATCH POINT ★

You will find it easier to work the filler into very tiny cracks and crevices and remove any excess if you wet the filling knife and run it gently over the surface.

</td></tr>
</table>

Paint in the order primer, undercoat and topcoat. Leave to dry thoroughly between coats and rub down each with a piece of glasspaper before applying the next.

If the wardrobe and cupboard doors have not been given a surface finish, now is a good time to do it so that all the paint can dry together. Prop the doors up against a nearby wall during painting, with a piece of rag or newspaper wrapped around the top to protect the wallcoverings.

It is worth taking the trouble to get a good finish on the doors. So before you apply the final coat rub the surface down thoroughly with a piece of fine glasspaper or steel wool. Clean off any dust completely with a soft cloth and white spirit and use a

19 *Fill blemishes in the doors and gaps in the frame. Paint mouldings carefully*

20 *When painting large areas of the doors take care to get a smooth finish, working in blocks from left to right*

good quality brush with soft and pliable bristles, to ensure a good result.

Apply the paint evenly and thinly, working in blocks running from the top left hand corner to the bottom right. Finish off by smooth upward movements of the brush to avoid streaking or paint runs.

Hanging wardrobe and cupboard doors

When all the paint is dry you can fit the hinges to the doors and hang them in place.

Sort out the doors so you know what fits where. Then check your construction plan to see which side of each of them is hinged. Mark this in pencil.

The doors are hung on single cranked hinges. These allow the doors to open in their own width without binding. They have the additional advantage of being easy to fit—the metal plates just screw to the back surface of the door and the face of the frame with no cutting in necessary.

Screw the hinges to the doors first. Space them evenly for appearance and to spread the load. Position one hinge 100mm from the top and one 100mm from the bottom of each door. On large, heavy doors it is advisable to fit a third hinge in the centre.

Take care to align the knuckle of each hinge with the edge of the door, and ensure that it is butted up hard against it. Mark the screw holes with a bradawl. With small fixing screws it shouldn't be necessary to drill holes for them.

With all the hinges in place, offer up each door in turn to check its position and mark the screw holes on the frame. With large, heavy doors or when working high up it helps if you have an assistant. Alternatively, prop the doors up for a short period with lengths of wood.

Check that there is a 25mm overlap of the door onto the frame all round, and that the door itself is square. Then mark through the holes in the hinges onto the face of the framework. If you use a bradawl to do this, you can insert the screws directly to hold the door in place.

When all the doors are in place, screw on the handles or knobs you have chosen. Mark them carefully to ensure that they all line up with each other. Don't try to fit them in thin panels; put them in the outer rails where the doors are strongest. Secure each door with a magnetic catch.

The only door which can't be added as simply as this is the flap above the dressing table, which you have to make up first. Cut a panel from plywood or hardboard to stiffen the flap. Depending upon how you fit the doors to it, this can be the same size as the opening—in which case the doors must overlap it by 25mm—or 25mm larger than the opening all round.

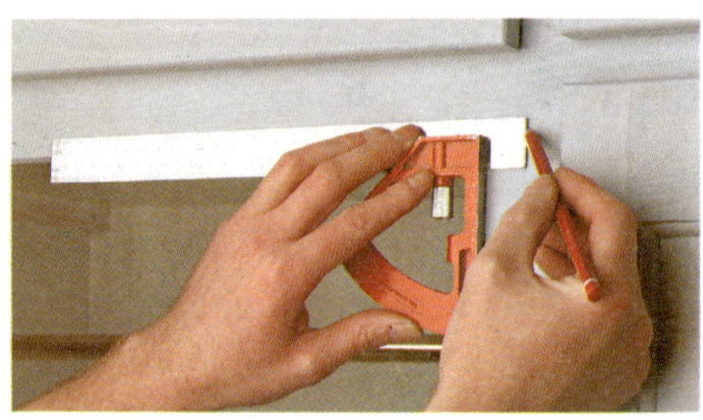

21 *Make sure that the doors overlap the front frames by 25mm*

22 *Fit the hinges to the doors then offer each one up in turn. Check that it is square and in correct alignment*

23 *Mark the positions of the hinge holes onto the frame*

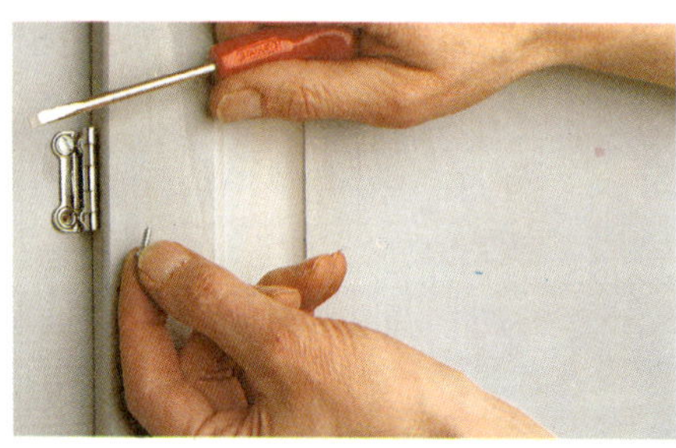

24 *Put in the fixing screws one at a time so that you can adjust the doors*

There are various ways to arrange one or more doors to fit onto the panel; some examples are shown on the right. It doesn't matter if you cut the doors drastically because the panel will support them.

Hang the flap from its top edge. To support it while opened, screw a fall flap stay to the inside of the cupboard.

Finishing off

Once you have cleared up all the dust and mess, roll the carpet into position and recut it to fit in front of the wardrobe units. Trim the carpet back with a sharp marking knife and butt it up against the plinth.

There are a number of additions you can make to the wardrobe system to improve its usefulness and appearance. For example, a mirror could be fixed to the wall behind the dressing table with a light above it.

There are also a number of proprietary wardrobe fittings—shoe racks, sliding rails and drawer systems—which you may want to add to your wardrobes or storage cupboards. These are available from most large DIY retailers and DIY supermarkets —so look around at what is on offer.

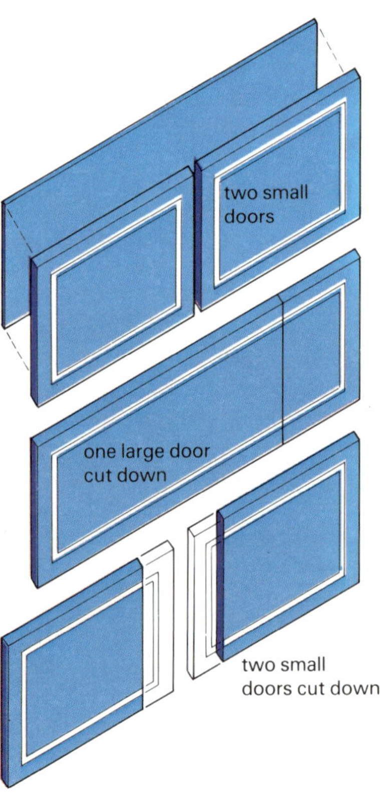

Above: Since you are unlikely to find a door of exactly the size you need for the flap, make a plain panel. To trim it to match the other doors, cover it with door panels cut down as necessary

CHAPTER 4

FLOORS AND WALLS

Putting up partitions, plastering made simple and a special project showing you how to floor your attic are all included in this chapter. These might seem to be daunting tasks, particularly for the beginner, but the correct approach, combined with careful planning, will yield professional results.

nailing rows of 100mm × 50mm blocking between two adjacent joists. It is easier, usually, to move the wall a few inches.

•**How will the top be fixed?** Along its top, the partition wall needs to be nailed or screwed to something rigid. Great strength is not needed, because a well built wall will 'want' to stand up, not fall over. But fixing to just lath and plaster or to ceiling tiles will not not be strong enough.

So you can fix to a single ceiling joist, or a row of joists or, at a pinch, to a securely nailed timber ceiling.

If both your floor joists and ceiling joists are parallel to the proposed wall, however, you may find that one set is not immediately above the other. In this case, you will have no option but to install some rows of blocking pieces in the floor or in the ceiling—whichever of the two is the easiest to get at.

So, before you decide on the exact position of the wall, some work with a steel tape and plumbline may be essential.

•**How will I deal with the skirting board?** Theoretically, the easiest way is to remove the skirting board (you drive wooden wedges down behind it) before you build the wall, and cut and replace it later.

But in some houses this is impracticable because the skirting board is 'trapped' behind a built-in cupboard. And in other, old houses it can be a messy job because some of the plaster comes away with the removal of skirting board.

If you decide that removing the skirting is not practicable, you do have an alternative—to build the base of the wall to fit around the skirting board. This does not affect the way you install the skirtings on the wall itself, because they are scribed (not mitred) to fit the existing ones. But it does affect the placing of the studs because, to maintain rigidity at the end of the partition, the end studs should be no more than about 300mm in. So you will need a detailed sketch plan.

•**How will I deal with the coving?** In timber framed houses, the moulding that covers the gap between the existing walls and ceiling is itself often made of hardwood. It can be prised off, trimmed and replaced in much the same way as the skirting board.

In masonry houses, however, the coving may be made of paper-covered plaster (like plasterboard). In this case, you can cut a notch to receive the top plate on one side of

A stud partition wall can split one large room into two, or create a small enclosed area in a corner or end of it. The main proviso is that there will be enough space in each part of the room after conversion—although there are more detailed planning considerations.

So before you start, it's important both to measure up the space you have available and to get a clear idea of how the new wall will alter it. If you have difficulty visualizing the effect, it may be worth putting up a temporary screen where you intend to build the wall. If the idea looks practicable, you can plan how to build the wall in detail.

Planning considerations

The instructions given here are for building a light partition wall only, such as might be used to divide a bedroom into two or provide walk-in wardrobes for adjoining rooms. A wall intended to carry heavy items—kitchen units, say, or heavy book-shelves—would need to be built of heavier timber and to be much more strongly supported underneath.

Even so, building a partition wall is one of those jobs where the planning takes longer than the doing. Before you start work, you must know the answers to these questions:

•**What will it stand on?** If you look at your existing floor and it is solid, the partition can stand anywhere on it; fixings can be made with screws and wallplugs. If you are dealing with a wooden floor, the situation is slightly more complicated.

The nail positions will tell you where the floor joists below it are situated. Ideally, a partition should straddle a whole row of joists. If this is not possible, because your partition will be parallel with the joists, it can stand on top of one joist or, at a pinch, *nearly* on top of one.

It is possible to provide extra support by

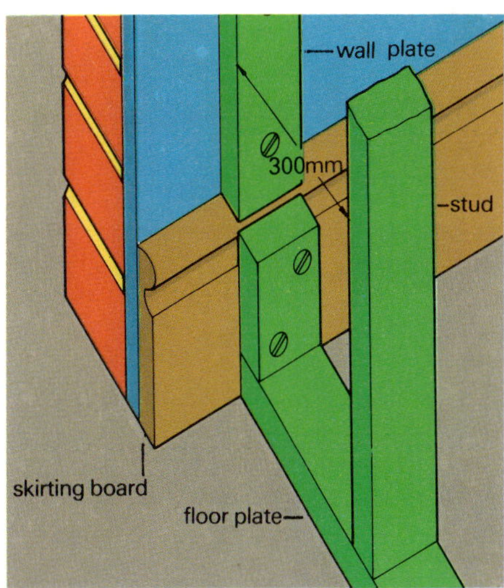

Skirting boards can be dealt with (above) by continuing the wall plate down the face of the board. Use timber of the same size, attached with 63mm No. 8 screws and fixed securely with wallplugs

the room, and remove a length of the coving on the other to fit in your new wall.

Alternatively, the coving may be of solid plaster. In this case it is risky to cut right through it—it tends to shatter. So it is easier to cut only about halfway through it, and shorten your new top plate accordingly. Or, if the plaster is not too thick, you can leave it intact and build round it in the same way you would build round a skirting board.

In Britain, you are not compelled by law to have a window in the room that your new partition creates. You can use 'borrowed light' (see Alternative Ideas) instead. But if you *do* decide to have a window, do not assume that you can knock through an outside wall to provide one; the building regulations on this point are particularly complicated.

In most other countries, you must have a window—often with a glazed area equal to one tenth of the floor area.

So, when you have designed your wall, your next step should be to submit your plans to the building control officer. Take a detailed floor plan, including the siting of the new window if any; a sketch of how the wall is to be supported; and a sketch of how it will be built (adapt the diagram of the frame on this page).

Tools and materials

As this wall is non-loadbearing—you are not removing any existing wall—it can be built from quite light materials.

For the top and bottom plates, use 75mm × 50mm sawn softwood in pieces long enough to span the room you are dividing—a wall with jointed plates is hard to handle. The studs and noggins are also 75mm × 50mm.

For the lintel, use the same 75mm × 50mm timber. You will also want some offcuts of 50mm × 25mm, plus a few scraps of plywood or hardboard, to use as packing pieces.

Most of the frame is fixed with 100mm roundhead nails, but buy 0.5kg (1lb) of 75mm oval nails—they are much easier to use for skew nailing awkward pieces.

Your plasterboard should be 9.5mm thick, in sheets either 915mm or 1220mm wide, depending on which will span the room with minimum waste. Try to buy the taper-edged variety, which produces neater joints than the square-edged type.

You will also need enough plasterboard jointing tape to cover the joints, and some jointing compound (the finer grade) to cover the tape and finish the joint.

Names for the nails used to fix plasterboard vary from one area to another, but if you ask for 'galvanized plasterboard clouts' you shouldn't go wrong.

Unless you want an open archway, you need a new door for the wall. Try to get one that matches the others in the house—size

Build the frame (yellow). Lift it into place and secure it with packing pieces. Level then add the wall plates. Add the noggins, then cut the wood from the threshold

doesn't matter as the wall is built round it. To frame it you need 100mm × 25mm planed softwood and 38mm × 12mm softwood. To hang it you need a pair of 100mm butt hinges and suitable screws—plus a catch and door handles and fittings.

To trim the wall, buy mouldings like those used elsewhere in the room—skirtings, door architraves and coving. Measure the quantities you require, plus a trimming allowance. Buy them from timber or builders' merchants.

Once built, you can finish the wall to match other decorations, so buy paint or paper as required. You also need some filler—although joint finish will do at a pinch—and knotting and primer for the woodwork.

Only 'everyday' tools are needed to build the frame and for finishing the plasterboard. Professionals use a taping knife, a plasterer's trowel, and a plasterer's jointing sponge—a circular plastic foam sponge mounted on a wooden handle which is used

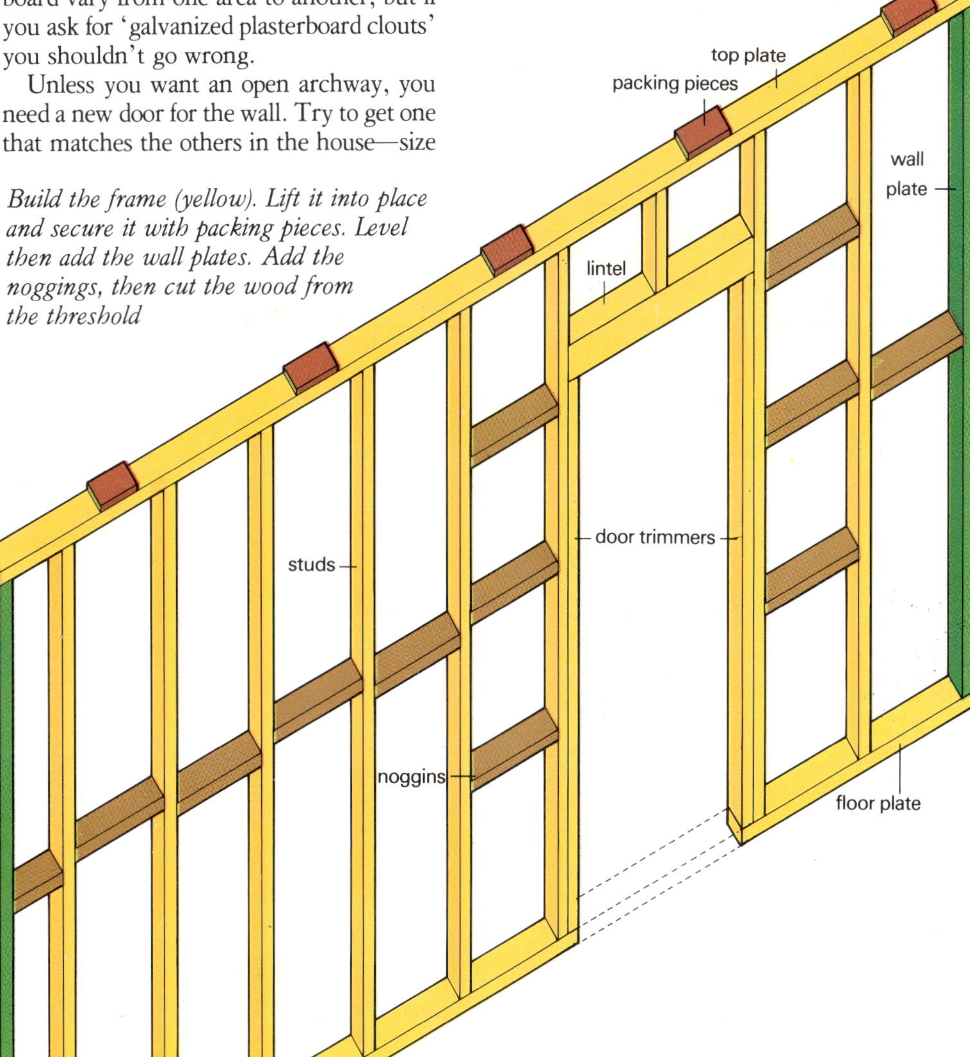

1 *Lay the top and bottom plates on edge. Mark in the position of the double studs for the door—allow a span for frame and door*

2 *Mark the positions of the other studs onto floor and ceiling plates. Use an offcut to keep them the correct distance apart*

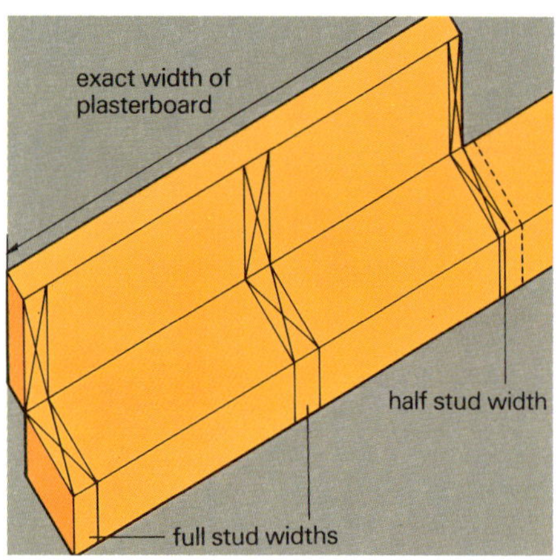

3 *Cut a batten of any size to use as a template. The half stud widths are important—you need to join sheets of plasterboard above a stud*

4 *Nail through the plates into the studs with 100mm round head nails*

5 *Nail on the lintel, then add the trimmers, allowing floor clearance*

6 *Lift the frame into position—you'll need the help of an assistant*

to feather off the edges of the joint filler. There's little need for such special tools as long as you're prepared to sand down thoroughly.

Building the frame

The easiest way of building a stud partition wall is to assemble it flat on the floor, then lift it into place. This avoids much awkward skew nailing, and also makes it easier to get the wall plumb.

However, you must take steps to see that the partition does not jam, either on the ceiling or on the walls on either side, as you lift it. To do this, you make the frame a loose fit and omit some components until it has been erected.

For your top and bottom plates, select your straightest lengths of timber. Cut them to length—either a fairly snug fit between the skirting boards (if you are leaving these on) or about 40mm less than the width

between the existing walls (if you are going to remove the skirting boards).

Lay the bottom plate in position on the floor. Using thick pencil marks, mark on the plate the positions of the double studs on either side of the door frame. Make the space between them about 60mm wider than the overall width of the door and frame so that the frame will be a loose fit. (When you install the door frame, you will use bits of hardboard to fill the small spaces on either side, and nail through frame and hardboard into the studs.)

Now mark the other stud positions, working outwards from the doorway. A 75mm × 25mm batten, cut to match the exact width of the plasterboard and with the correct stud spacings marked on it (see diagram) will help you to do this accurately.

Plasterboard must be supported by studs in the middle of the sheet as well as at the edges. For a sheet up to 915mm wide, use one intermediate stud. For wider sheets, use two intermediate studs.

7 *Plumb the frame level, then tap offcuts between the top plate and the ceiling*

With your bottom plate marked out, lay the top plate on the floor beside it and, using a try square, transfer the stud positions from one to the other—this helps keep the studs straight and plumb.

Next, cut to length all the full length studs. They should be the height from floor to ceiling, less the thickness of the two plates, less 19mm for lifting clearance.

The diagram on page 73 shows how much of the frame should be assembled before you lift it into place. To put this together, you will probably need to get an assistant to help.

Lay both plates on edge. Lay the full length studs (except the end ones) between them, bow sides upwards. Then, using two 100mm nails at each joint, nail each stud simultaneously at both ends, synchronizing your hammer blows so that the plates do not skid about. As you nail, watch that the top surfaces of the plate and studs are flush—to ensure this, you may have to kneel on one or the other.

The trimmers (short studs on either side of the door opening) are cut 5mm longer than your door frame will be deep—again, to help make the door frame a loose fit. The door frame will be the height of the door, plus about 30mm—more if you intend to fit a thick floorcovering. So cut the trimmers about 35mm longer than the door. Nail the trimmers both to the bottom plate and to the adjoining full length studs.

The lintel rests on top of the trimmers. It is nailed through the studs on either side, and also skew nailed to the trimmers (see Skew nailing). This uses more timber than one commonly used method—housing the ends of the lintel into single studs—but is easier and makes a stronger job.

The short length of stud between the lintel and top plate is easily nailed at the top. At the bottom, however, it too will have to be skew nailed into the floor plate.

Now lift the frame into position. Secure it temporarily with two 100mm nails part-driven into the floor, as near as possible to the middle of the bottom plate, and a wedge or two driven between the top plate and the ceiling—preferably under a joist.

Next, check that the bottom plate is straight. Do this by nailing a short piece of 50mm × 25mm wood to each end of the plate and stretching a line taut between them. Check that the distance between line and plate is consistent along the whole length of the plate. If it isn't, force the plate into line with your foot as you nail it, using two 100mm nails hammered into each floor joist (or at about 450mm centres if only one joist is below).

The final stage of erection is to fix the top plate to the ceiling joist(s), at the same time making sure that the wall is plumb. You will need some packing pieces of different thicknesses to wedge between the top plate and ceiling—trim them for a neat fit.

Start by using a plumbline on one of the door trimmer studs. Check that it is plumb in both directions and, when it is, nail through the top plate (and through a packer) into the ceiling above. Do the same on the other side of the door opening. Then work outwards in both directions, plumbing, packing and nailing as you go.

If you find that your nailing is beginning to crack the ceiling, use screws instead.

To finish the frame, first install the components coloured green in the diagram on page 73, then those coloured brown. Finally, cut away the length of bottom plate that is obstructing the door opening.

Skew nailing

Skew nailing is a simple method of joining two pieces of wood which you can use wherever it is not possible to drive a nail straight through two pieces.

Part-drive all nails before you place the workpiece (the component to be nailed) in position. The nails should be at about 50° to the face of the work piece.

As you drive the nails home grip the other side of the work-piece and wedge your foot against it, to stop it moving sideways. If it moves only a few millimetres, it will come back into line as you nail the other side.

Nail heads can be sunk with a nailpunch, particularly if you have a nail on the face, instead of the side, of the workpiece.

★ WATCH POINT ★

Don't nail where you intend to install architraves, coving and so on. The trim itself will pull the plasterboard back against the frame—this will prevent any gaps between plasterboard and trim.

Cutting plasterboard

For a straight cut, start by marking out the sheet with a pencil and straightedge—either a steel square or a straight length of batten.

Using the straightedge and a trimming knife, score through the paper and into the plaster on the face ('good') side.

Stand the plasterboard on end, supporting both sides as you do so, so that your cut is vertical. Then bend the sheet back on itself; this will sever the plaster core back to the backing. Finally, trim off the unwanted bit by running your knife down the back of the sheet.

Part nailing one end will help

Wedge a foot behind if you can

Clamp a block beneath noggins

For a two-way cut—for example, to remove a section that would otherwise cover a doorway—mark out on both sides of the sheet. (If you have trouble transferring the marks from one side to the other, push a

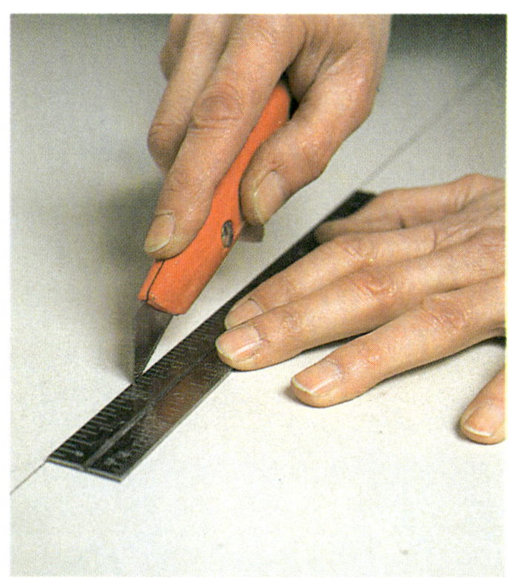

Score the cutting lines on the face side with a trimming knife held against a straightedge

Snap along the line by folding the sheet back on itself—if necessary, over a batten

Sever the offcut by cutting through the cardboard backing. Change blades if the cut tears

bradawl through the sheet to make a hole.)

To cut along the first line, use your knife. Score deeply on both sides until you cut right through the plaster.

To cut along the second line, use the 'cut and bend double' method described above.

Fixing the plasterboard

Now you can hang your plasterboard. Fix it with the ivory coloured side outwards, since it is not going to be skim-plastered.

The most important thing is that the sheets must lie flat against the frame, without any bulges. So start by lifting the sheet about 12mm from the floor, either by resting it on a piece of plywood or by using a foot lift to lever the sheet up.

Start nailing in the middle of the sheet and work radially outward, doing the edges last. Drive each nail so that its head is just below the surface—but not so far that it cuts through the paper.

For a secure fixing, space your nails about 100mm apart around the edges of the sheet, and about 150mm apart down the middle stud or studs.

After the plasterboard is nailed in place, there will be both cracks between the sheets and dents from the nails. All of these must be filled over to get a smooth finish.

On square edged plasterboard, the joints can be merely filled with a little joint finish, using a filling knife. This gives a reasonably level surface, but one which is likely to crack as the timber frame below dries out.

On taper edged plasterboard, however, you can get an almost invisible finish. Start by cutting a length of jointing tape long enough to cover one joint. Take about a cupful of the jointing compound, mix it according to the instructions on the packet or can, and trowel it down the tapered recess where the two sheets join. While it is still wet, use the knife to push the tape into the compound. Make sure there is enough compound behind the tape to ensure good adhesion, and try to avoid trapping air bubbles, which might cause cracking later.

Follow immediately with another coat of compound, this time bringing it level with the plasterboard on either side. Before it sets, moisten the sponge and wipe away any ridges that the knife has left at the sides of the joint. Then clean all your tools and utensils thoroughly.

If the compound subsides or cracks while setting, this indicates either that it is too wet or that you have applied too thick a coat.

Once the compound has set (about an hour), use the plastic trowel to apply a thin

8 *Make an improvised foot lift to lever the sheets into place and off the floor*

9 *Nail from the middle of the sheet, working outwards at 100mm or 150mm intervals*

layer of compound about 200mm wide, then immediately 'feather'—smooth off—the edges with a sponge, slightly moistened.

Let this coat too dry thoroughly. Then apply a second coat, about 250mm wide, and feather the edges with a sponge again.

When dry, sand the surface perfectly flat with medium grade glasspaper on a block.

To fill the nail holes, use either a filling knife or trowel. This can be done with small quantities left over from the joint filler or with filler paste.

Finishing touches

With the framework and panelling complete, the next thing to do is to fit all the trim. This includes skirtings and architraves—and most importantly the door.

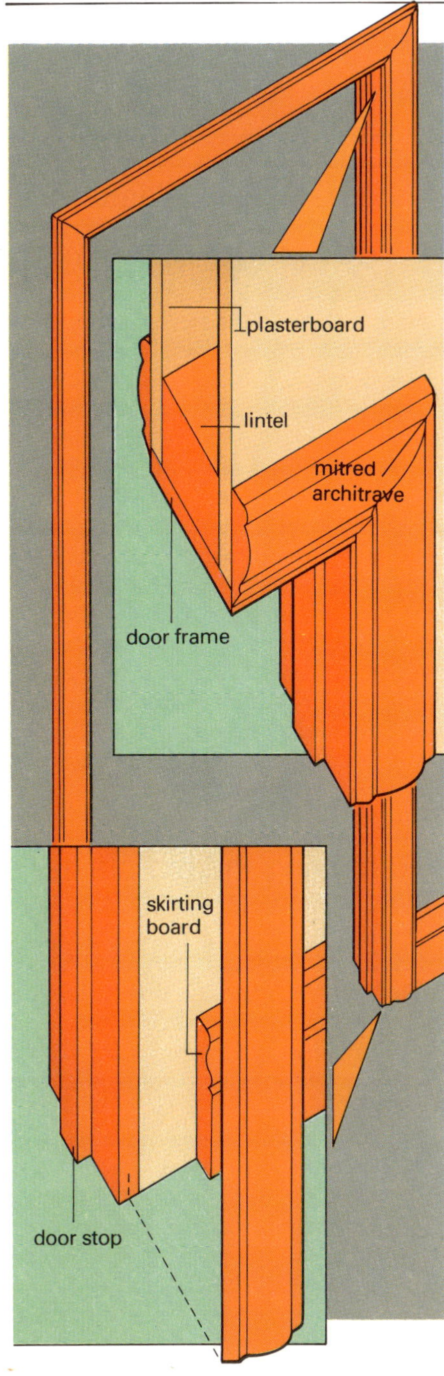

Finishing trim at the door opening (above). The door frame goes in first—it spans the studs and plasterboard. The architrave is mitred, then nailed to the edges of the frame. Fit the doorstop before or after adding the door—it's often easiest to fit the door, then butt the door stop up to it

Before hanging the door, you must make a frame to line the opening in the wall. This is made from 100mm×25mm planed softwood. Cut one length to span the opening under the lintel, and two lengths the same as the door plus about 5mm clearance—more if the floor is uneven or you plan to fit a thick floorcovering or deep pile carpet.

Nail the three pieces together and fit the door with a small clearance. Nail an offcut of batten across both sides temporarily to keep them in place, plus another diagonally across the whole frame to keep it square. Fit any frame into the opening and pack out any gaps with slips of hardboard or plywood. Make sure that it is flush with the face of the wall, then nail it firmly in place. Remove the bracing battens.

Decide which way round you want the door to hang. On the side where it opens outwards, measure the thickness of the door in from the edge of the frame. To make the door stop, cut lengths of 38mm×12mm batten and nail them to the frame, in line with this point.

Cut lengths of architrave to frame the doorway. The corners of these must be mitred. With a narrow moulding you can use a mitre box to guide the saw; alternatively, mark the architrave with a combination square or mitre square. Nail the architrave to the door frame.

It's easiest if you fit the skirting board at this stage. Cut lengths of the board to span the ends of the new wall to the architrave. They don't have to be accurately sawn, but don't make them any shorter.

Use a scribing technique to make the ends of the new skirting to fit over the existing skirting board—if you have removed it, saw it just short of the new wall and re-nail it first.

Hold the new skirting board in place and then use a small wooden block and a pencil to transfer the outline of the existing board onto it. Remove the board and saw along the marked line with a coping saw or similar to deal with the curved outline.

Now refit the board up against the existing skirting. Line up the skirting with the architrave you have fitted round the doorway and mark its width back from the door opening on to the skirting. Remove the skirting, square across from the mark and then saw to length. Finally, nail the skirting to the studs along the base of the new wall.

To complete the trim, cut lengths of coving and nail them to the top of the wall. Where they meet the existing coving, you can use a similar scribing technique to that used for the skirting, although it is difficult to do this accurately.

To complete the construction, hang the door in the frame on a pair of 100mm butt hinges. To do this you will have to cut hinge recesses in both door and frame. Add a catch and door handles at this stage.

Finally decorate the new wall to make it look like a part of its surroundings. Fill any small gaps carefully first. You can paint the plasterboard directly, or paper it as you wish. Before you paint the wood, seal any knots with knotting solution, then prime it thoroughly.

Alternative ideas

If one of the new rooms your partition creates has no window, you can use 'borrowed light'—light from the other room—by glazing the top of your wall.

Studs should be spaced evenly, at least across the glazed area, even if this wastes plasterboard.

To hold the glass in place, and cover the cut edges of the plasterboard, you can choose from several types of moulding—bullnose, bevel edges, architrave or door stop.

To calculate the width of the moulding, allow 4mm for the thickness of the glass and about 4mm for two thin beads of putty (to stop the glass rattling). Deduct the total from the actual, measured thickness of the wall and divide by two.

A small overhang of 1–2mm on either side will help conceal any irregularity in the thickness of the wall. The easiest way is to fix all the mouldings on one side of the wall; then apply putty; then insert the glass; and finally apply the second bead of putty and the 'other side' of the mouldings at the same time. In this way the mouldings can be kept flush with the plasterboard, while the putty helps to take up the irregularities of the fitting.

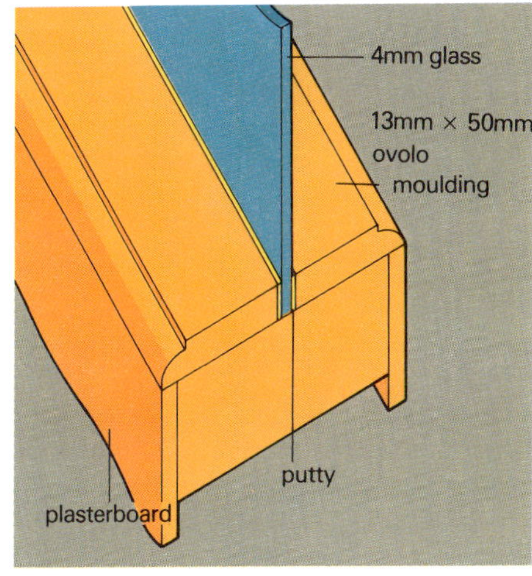

Borrowed light (above) may be necessary if there is no window. You could add a pane of glass between noggins, held and trimmed with a moulding

PLASTERING THE DIY WAY

Plastering or replastering an entire wall is not something to approach lightly. First you must be sure that it really is necessary. And then you should check that there isn't an easier alternative—drylining for instance.

Why replaster?

Patching a plastered wall is a great deal easier than replastering it from scratch. But if the patches are large or extensive it simply is not worth doing—you will never get a surface good enough for an acceptable finish—either paint or wallpaper.

Large-scale DIY jobs present the same problem: if you have hacked the plaster off half a wall it will probably be better to re-plaster the whole of it rather than simply making good the damaged area.

Walls which are intact but have a poor surface because of previous patching could be another candidate. But in this case you need to assess whether it's worth the trouble. Remember too that ready mixed skimming plaster is available for resurfacing sound but uneven plaster. This has good adhesive qualities, so you can apply it to painted plaster—something you can't easily do with ordinary finish plaster.

One of the most common reasons for re-plastering is damp. Plaster which has been badly soaked either disintegrates or 'blows' (comes away from the wall). You can check this by tapping the plaster with a piece of wood; a hollow sound indicates damage.

There are several cures for damp walls, depending on what the cause is. While most of them call for plastering skills, it cannot be stressed too highly that there is no point in replastering until you are certain that the damp has been eliminated and the wall given at least several weeks to dry out.

The other all too common reason for re-plastering is that the existing plaster has failed—a problem that can manifest itself in several ways. Cracking is found in all plaster—especially new plaster—because the material has only limited elasticity. But if the cracks become really severe and the plaster blows in some places, it has been in-correctly applied and should be renewed.

Plaster can also fail if it is the wrong type for the wall. It may simply blow, or it could suck all the moisture out of the wall and produce efflorescence—white salty deposits —on the surface. As replastering is the only solution when faced with this problem make sure, therefore, that the plaster you apply is the correct type for the job in hand.

Alternatives to plastering

Faced with the need to replaster, you have two choices of how to go about the job: con-ventional plastering or drylining. Drylining consists of covering the wall with sheets of plasterboard—usually fixed to a framework of battens. This guarantees you a smooth surface, but it will only be level over the whole wall if the framework is level—and achieving this is no easy task.

Drylining becomes progressively more difficult the more corners, recesses and door and window frames you have to deal with. But there are also times when it is the only choice, for example if you want to plaster a painted brick cellar wall (plaster does not adhere readily to paint). Usually, the deci-sion boils down to whether you feel happier working with wood and boards or a trowel and hawk.

Removing the old plaster

DIY plastering is a major undertaking, so divide it into two stages: removing the old plaster and replastering. It does mean that you'll have to live temporarily with a lot of mess, but this is infinitely preferable to a job that turns into a disaster because it's been completed in haste.

Start by removing as much furniture and as many fittings from the room as possible. Cover what you can't take out with dust sheets, and spread more dust sheets along the route to the nearest exit—either at the front or back of the house.

Next work out where to dump the debris. The plaster rubble from an average size wall

1 *Cut a V-shaped groove in the middle of the wall, then work gradually outwards*

takes up plenty of space: if you haven't got the use of a skip or dump, get some strong plastic bags—such as fertilizer or ballast bags—in which to store the rubble until it can be collected.

The wall itself must be as clear of fixtures and fittings as possible. Have radiators unhooked and folded down (or better, capped and removed) by a plumber. Where possible the same should be done for any other pipework likely to obstruct you later.

To deal with power points and sockets, first turn off the electricity at the fuse board or consumer unit main switch. Then remove the faceplates to reveal the backing boxes. These can be left where they are, to be plastered around later. If you suspect that cables are buried in the plaster, make a note of their approximate locations at this stage and remember to go carefully when you start clearing the wall.

Finally, remove all skirtings, picture rails and coving or cornice moulding by prising them away from the wall with a claw hammer or crowbar held against a block of wood. Don't worry about damaging the wall plaster—you're about to strip it.

2 *Try to push the bolster behind the plaster so you can ease it off the wall in large sheets*

To remove the old plaster, you need a club hammer and a sharp bolster; if the plaster turns out to be a cement-based render, you'll also need a drill and masonry bit to help loosen it. The ideal dress is a pair of overalls—plaster dust gets everywhere. To protect your hands wear heavy work gloves and make sure you wear a pair of plastic safety goggles to protect your eyes from dust and flying chips.

Start your demolition in the middle of the wall by cutting a V-shaped channel in the plaster until you reach solid masonry. (If there are any obvious weak points in the plaster you can start there instead.)

The purpose of cutting a channel is to give you enough room to angle your bolster in behind the plaster coats and prise them away from the wall. Do this, working outwards in all directions, by tapping the bolster gently—there's no need to use great force, even with tough render.

Using this method causes most of the plaster to fall away in large sheets. Continue along and across the wall, packing the rubble as you go, until most of the surface is clear. Then hack off the stubborn patches that are bound to remain in cracks and crevices in the masonry.

If you come across any cables or electrical fittings make sure that they are firmly attached to the wall before continuing.

Preparing the wall: Although the fresh plaster will take up most of the unevenness in your brickwork or blockwork, it's no good for filling large holes. Unsound mortar joints could cause the plaster to fail later, so initial preparation of the wall is important.

Rake out any crumbling mortar joints to a depth of 25mm with your bolster then brush away debris. Dampen them with a little clean water and repoint flush with the surrounding masonry using a mortar mix of one part cement to three of soft sand.

Large holes can be patched with pieces of brick. Brush out and dampen them with water before setting the bricks in place with a 1:3 mortar mix.

Preparing for plastering

Professional plasterers have four important advantages over amateurs: they know what plasters to use on any given wall; they have help—in the form of a plasterer's mate; they instinctively know when the plaster is mixed to the right consistency; and their experience teaches them how to use a trowel—something which can be taught, but perfected only after a lot of practice.

Against this, the do-it-yourselfer has time on his side. If he takes it and uses it well, it is possible to produce an acceptable finish. But if he rushes or tries to imitate the professionals, the result is likely to be a disaster. The preparations described below may seem laborious, but they are necessary all the same if you want perfect results.

Choosing and buying plaster

Selecting the right plaster for the job is part of the plasterer's art: it can make all the difference between a good and bad finish.

Repair plaster of the type sold in small bags at hardware and DIY stores is no good for this job: you need to go to a builder's merchant where you can be sure of getting the right materials—in bulk at a competitive price.

Plasters vary in type, but also from region to region—like sand. To add to the confusion, the terminology is different too. So although the terms below are in general use, always state exactly what you want the plaster for to avoid misunderstandings.

Plaster is nearly always applied in two coats. The undercoat—or *floating coat* as it

Plastering tools: the only tool you really need to buy is a plasterer's laying on trowel—and it's well worth buying a good quality model while you are at it. You may also need one or more angle trowels (see above) to finish off any internal or external corners neatly. All the rest of the tools—the scaffold square, scratcher and hawk—can be home-made using a few odd offcuts of timber

is generally called—makes up the bulk of the job; the usual thickness is about 12mm. On top of this goes the *finishing coat*, with a thickness of around 2mm. Hence the following classifications.

Browning: This is the standard floating coat plaster for semi-porous surfaces such as brick and light aggregate block. It has a good filling capacity and does not suck too much moisture out of the wall.

Bonding: The floating coat plaster to use on less porous surfaces such as concrete and dense concrete block. It has good adhesive qualities, which makes it easier to apply than browning. But if you use it on brickwork which is any way damp—and most external walls are—it will suck the moisture straight out to ruin the surface finish.

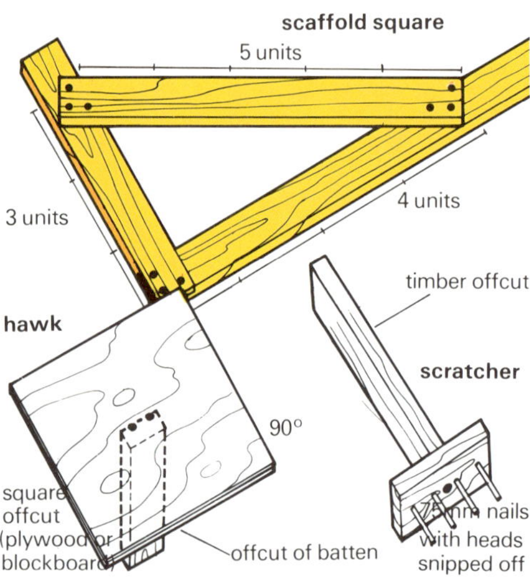

Use the materials and dimensions above as a guide when making your own plastering tools

Finish plaster: Used for the finish coat, it is very fine and hence has good smoothing qualities. But use it to any great thickness and you'll be in trouble. Finish varies in colour from brand to brand and area to area.

Quantities: All plaster comes in bags of varying size, but it's the overall quantities that should concern you. The material is cheap, so always overestimate. As a rough guide, for every 600mm square of wall, allow 3kg of floating coat plaster and 1.3kg of finish.

Cement render: Don't let this confuse you. Render is a mixture of cement and sharp sand, not a type of plaster. Its main use is on external walls, but it is sometimes applied in place of floating coat plaster—usually with waterproofer added—to protect from damp.

Tools and other materials

First and foremost you need a plasterer's *laying on trowel*. Most professionals have at least two: one for the floating coat and one for the finish. Assuming that you won't be doing a lot of plastering you can get by with one, but make sure it is the best quality you can afford—the cheap types found in hardware stores simply aren't any good for proper plastering. Internal and external *corner trowels* are also a good investment: you may be able to scrape by without them, but the extra trouble this causes isn't really worth the saving.

The rest of the equipment should cause no problems. You need a *spotboard* to put the mixed plaster on—a piece of chipboard, plywood or blockboard about a metre square and laid on bricks will do. Make up your own *hawk* for holding the plaster from two offcuts of timber, as shown below.

For scoring the floating coat plaster prior to finishing you need a *scratcher*: knock about six oval nails through the end of an offcut of timber and then snip or saw the heads off.

You need two standard size plastic buckets—one for mixing the plaster and one for carrying water. And a spirit level is a vital piece of equipment—for aligning the setting out battens.

Other materials: Requirements here will vary according to the nature and scope of the job. For the setting out battens, buy lengths of 12mm square sawn softwood to match the height of your wall. You need enough to divide the wall into bays of approximately 1.3m width. To go with the battens, get a 1.5m length of timber to act as a straightedge—a length of planed 75mm × 25mm is suitable. Sight along the piece you choose to make sure that it *is* straight. And if you decide to plaster an external corner the traditional way, you will need a 100mm × 25mm board.

The modern solution is to use galvanized steel corner strips which you pin in place and then plaster around.

If there are window reveals or recesses in the wall, a scaffold square will be needed. You can make your own, as shown left.

Finally, buy masonry nails for securing the setting out guides, boards and strips.

Setting out the wall

If you haven't already done so, prepare the room as you did when stripping the old plaster. Set up your spotboard reasonably near the site so that you don't have to travel too far with the hawk.

Start with the setting out battens. Take the first one and nail it to the top of the wall. Then lay your spirit level against the side, adjust it until it is plumb, and nail it at the foot of the wall.

3 *Begin by fixing each of the vertical battens into mortar joints using masonry nails*

4 *Check that each batten is plumb. Pack out low spots with card and scraps of ply*

5 *Then check that the front face of each batten is level using the timber straightedge*

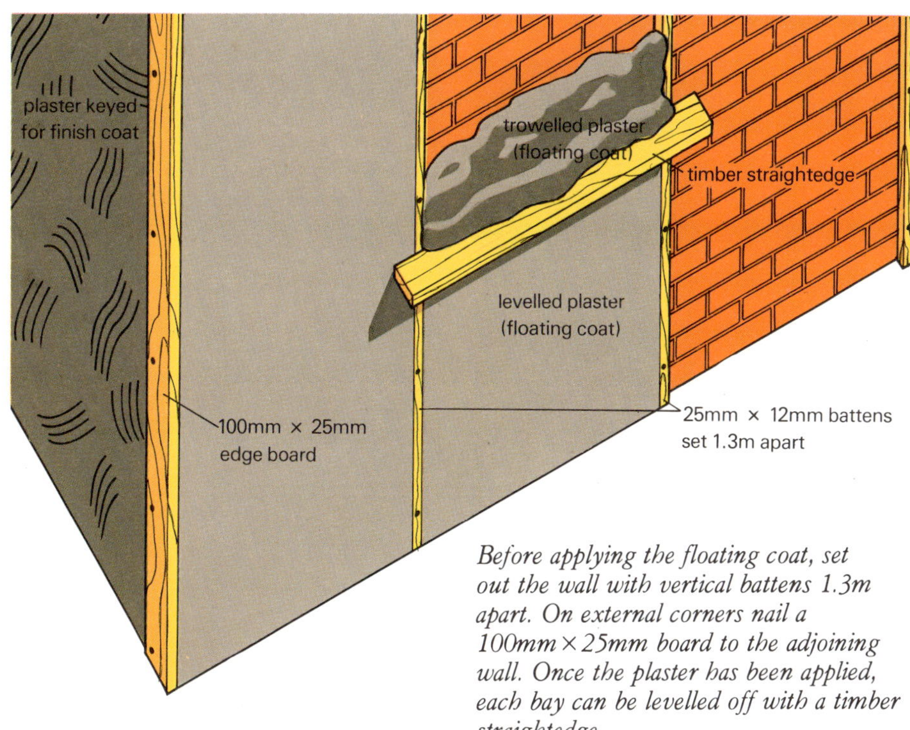

Before applying the floating coat, set out the wall with vertical battens 1.3m apart. On external corners nail a 100mm × 25mm board to the adjoining wall. Once the plaster has been applied, each bay can be levelled off with a timber straightedge

6 *On external corners nail a board to the adjoining wall. Level it off with the battens*

7 *Before you start, dampen the brickwork using water mixed with PVA adhesive*

Now lay your level against the face of the batten and check that it is plumb in this plane; if it isn't, ease it from the wall slightly and pack out the low spots with scraps of card or wood. Refix the batten and recheck that it is plumb along both the side and the face with the level.

Repeat this procedure for all the setting out battens, spacing them at rough 1.3m intervals. When they are all up, take the longest straight edged board you can find and lay it across the battens at the top, the middle and the bottom. If any are conspicuously proud or recessed, pack them as described above and recheck with the board. When all the battens are level, you know you've got a perfectly true framework against which to apply the floating coat.

The next step is to fix any other guide boards or strips. Cut corner strips to size with a hacksaw and nail them in place where needed, checking that they are plumb with your level as you go. If you use an external corner board, nail it to the ad-

Immediately prior to plastering, mix up half a small tin of PVA bonding adhesive in a bucketful of water and use this to dampen—NOT soak—the entire wall. This prevents over-rapid drying of the floating coat and aids adhesion.

joining wall so that it is plumb, with exactly 12mm protruding on the side you are intending to plaster.

Mixing plaster

If you can, get a helper to do the mixing: it's hard work and if you have to do it yourself you're likely to get hot and bothered—which is not conducive to good plastering.

Floating coat and finish plaster are both mixed in the same way—in a bucket—in batches of a third of a bucketful at a time.

Put the water in the bucket first, filling it about a third full. (Do it the other way round and the plaster will clog and go lumpy.) Then add the plaster, a little at a time, stirring quite vigorously as you go.

Continue stirring and adding plaster until the mixture in the bucket reaches the consistency of thick cream—really thick and 'porridge-like' in the case of floating coat plaster; a bit thinner for the finish coat.

When the batch is the right consistency, empty it out onto the spotboard, clean the mixing bucket thoroughly, and start mixing the next. Be warned however: you won't know how much to mix until you know how much you can handle, so start with small amounts only—the most important thing is to avoid the plaster drying before you get a chance to use it. Always reject a batch which looks as if it is 'going off'.

Applying the floating coat

When you are absolutely ready to start, mix up the floating coat plaster and transfer it onto the spotboard. Then scrape a manageable amount off the spotboard onto your hawk with the laying on trowel.

Carry the hawk to the first bay—aim to start in the middle and work outwards. Adopt the following procedure each time you apply plaster to the wall:
• Tilt the hawk slightly towards you.
• Cut into the load on the hawk with the trowel blade, separating an amount which is roughly the size of the trowel.
• Slide this up the hawk with the trowel blade, so that it rolls onto the trowel blade in the process.
• Press the plaster hard against the wall and sweep the trowel upwards in a curving movement. Keep your arm fairly rigid so that you work from the shoulder rather than the wrist. Hold the trowel blade almost parallel to the wall, but with the upper edge slightly tilted towards you so that more plaster is fed onto the wall as you move it.

8 *Work on one bay at a time. Apply plaster and then level off with the straightedge. Start at the bottom and move the straightedge up*

9 *Leave the plaster to dry for one hour, then roughen up the surface with the scratcher. Follow by removing the battens and filling the gaps (inset). Level off neatly*

You will find that the finish plaster spreads and smoothes more easily than the floating coat. Take extra care not to let the edges of the trowel blade dig in and you should get a reasonably flat finish.

Inevitably, though, there will be trowel marks all across the surface. Leave these for the moment, until you have covered the entire section to the correct thickness.

You remove the marks and do the final smoothing with a combination of your trowel and a paintbrush dampened with clean water. The exact method is a matter of personal preference: some people wet the trowel blade then smooth the plaster; others wet the plaster before applying a dry blade.

There are two golden rules about smoothing—or 'polishing' as it's often called. The first is that your trowel must be perfectly clean and flat; the second is that

> ★ WATCH POINT ★
>
> As you flatten the plaster, it will smooth out. But if you keep pressing and spreading, cracks will appear. At this point stop: it is time to reload the trowel.

Continue in this way until the bay is filled just proud of the battens. You now have to level it using your timber straightedge.

Hold the timber hard against the battens, at the foot of the wall. Run it up the wall, shifting the straightedge from side to side in a scissoring motion, so that the high points on the floating coat are cut off.

Once you have levelled the bay, fill any obvious low points with more plaster, clean the trowel, and smooth off any places where the plaster has 'caught'. If necessary, re-check that the bay is level.

Repeat the entire plastering and levelling procedure on each subsequent bay. At internal corners, use the full length of the trowel blade—or your cornering trowel, if

> ★ WATCH POINT ★
>
> Always work upwards to cut off any excess; if you work downwards the plaster is certain to pull and could possibly drop off the wall.

you have one—to cut the new plaster neatly. On external corners scrape the plaster against the corner strip or edging board so that you leave a depression about 2mm deep—to allow for the finish coat.

After about one hour, by which time the plaster should be semi-dry, take up your scratcher and swirl it across the entire surface to leave score marks similar to those in step 9. Take care not to apply too much pressure on the scratcher—start gently and increase it gradually.

When the scratching is completed, dig out the setting out battens by prising them away against the floor and the ceiling. Fill the trenches that are left with fresh floating coat plaster and smooth this off level with the surrounding surface. Take care not to disturb the surrounding floating coat plaster more than is necessary.

Leave the floating coat to dry for at least another four hours before attempting to apply the finish plaster.

Applying the finish plaster

This is applied in the same way—and using the same technique—as the floating coat. But the job is much more difficult, because you don't have any battens to work against.

Aim to make the finish coat about 2mm thick. If you are plastering a large wall, do it in two or more complete sections—you can sand where they join later—rather than risk the plaster drying before smoothing it.

10 *Give the wall a final polish, wetting the surface first*

you must dampen the plaster only enough to remove the ridges and marks—any more, and you will stop it from hardening

You have quite a long time to work on the wall—about half an hour—but don't push your luck. If there are some spots that you just can't get flat, leave them for sanding later rather than risk ruining the newly-plastered surface.

Finishing awkward corners

Window reveals, alcoves and recesses can be plastered in the normal way, but it's very hard to get them level. The answer is to separate them from the main job so that you have an edge to work to. Then, when you apply the floating coat, use a scaffold square to check that the plaster is at right angles to the other surfaces; skim off the excess and smooth corners with a corner trowel.

FLOORING AN ATTIC

Attic space is often ignored—even though it can add half as much again to the floor area of your house. One problem is that the space is usually not floored over, so it is difficult—even dangerous—to move about in. Consequently, most people leave the area unused—except perhaps for a small circle around the loft hatch where odd boxes and suitcases are thrown in. Flooring over an attic space is not difficult, however, provided you plan carefully.

Planning considerations

First, you should decide what you are going to do with your attic once you have floored it. If you intend only to store relatively light-weight items in it—boxes, suitcases, a few spare chairs and the like, then your problems are relatively small.

If you're thinking of using the loft to store heavier items, or if you're flooring it as part of converting a loft into a usable room, you'll probably need to strengthen the existing floor joists. These are unlikely to be strong enough to bear much extra weight once the floor decking has been laid on top of them.

The next consideration is access. If your existing loft hatch is not large enough to manoeuvre sheet flooring through, or needs to be larger to take items for storage, you'll need to enlarge the opening. If you have no loft hatch at all, you will need to create one.

Materials and tools

There are two main choices for the loft flooring—sheet decking (of which flooring-grade chipboard is the most widely available) and softwood boards. Which you choose depends mainly on how easy access to your loft is, and on the shape and size of the floor you are laying. Both types can be bought from any builders' or timber merchants. Because of the size and weight of the timber you're likely to require, its delivery cost should be borne in mind when shopping for a 'best buy'.

Sheet flooring can cover a large area in one go, so potentially it is quicker to lay. But if you have to do a lot of cutting—either to get it into the loft through the hatch, or because your loft is a small or awkward size—then sheet materials lose their advant-

age, and boarding may be easier to lay.

If you decide to use sheet flooring, buy flooring-grade chipboard, tongued and grooved on all edges. This comes in 2440mm × 610mm sheets, and either 18mm thick (for use when the joists are up to 400mm apart) or 22mm thick for joist centres of up to 600mm. Softwood boards are normally 125mm wide, and 16mm thick (for joists at 400mm centres) or 19mm for joists at 600mm.

Chipboard flooring needs supporting beneath board edges, with 100mm × 50mm noggins fixed between the joists. You'll need at least enough of this material to run down both sides of the loft (that is, the direction at right angles to the joists), and probably about the same amount again

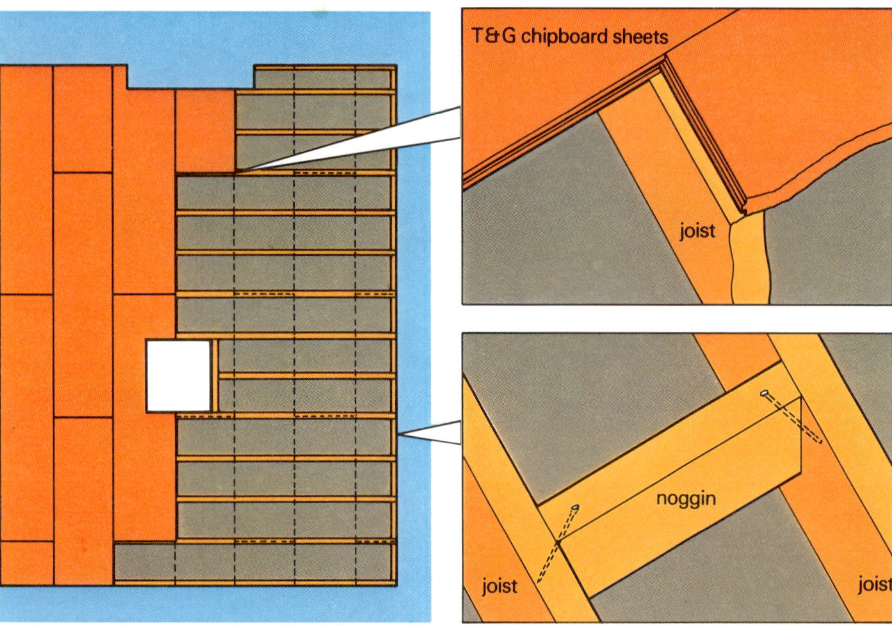

1 *Lay the first sheet up against the eaves or stud wall and secure it to the joists with 50mm annular ring nails*

Careful planning will avoid wasting time and materials. Draw a scale plan of your loft and use pieces of paper, cut to the same scale, to work out the most economical cutting plan

All cut edges must be supported. Try to plan the layout so that the sheets naturally join over a joist (top). Where sheets are left unsupported, fix a noggin (bottom) for additional strength

4 *Wherever you need to have access to the ceiling cavity, measure and mark the appropriate sheet. Then cut out the panel*

<table>
<tr><td>

★ WATCH POINT ★

Before you start cutting, make a rough sketch of your loft, marking in the exact positions of all the joists. Use pieces of paper, cut to the same scale, to represent the size of sheets you can get through your loft hatch. Move these pieces around on your plan until you achieve the most economical cutting plan, taking into account that, as far as possible, cut edges should not run at right angles to joists (to minimize the number of noggins you have to fit in the area).

</td></tr>
</table>

The decking can be cut with any hand or power saw, though chipboard soon blunts ordinary tools and is best cut with a saw or saw blade having hardened teeth.

You need ordinary carpentry tools: hammers, screwdrivers, marking knife or pencil. For boards, hire a flooring clamp or two, or use an old broad-bladed chisel as a lever: both should be used with a waste piece of timber to protect the tongue and groove edge.

You will need a sturdy ladder to get you into the loft. Also, make sure you provide adequate safe lighting up there. Don't just rely on a single bulb: it's worth arranging a few table lamps on an extension lead.

for intermediate supports where required.

You will need plenty of nails, of course. For sheet material, it is preferable to use annular ring nails—50mm long for 18mm sheets, 63mm for 22mm sheets—but ordinary roundheads will do. You need about three nails per metre run of joists. For boards, use lost-head nails—40mm long for 16mm boards; 50mm for 19mm board. And here you will need about 16 per metre run of joist.

Access traps (see Laying sheet flooring) in sheet flooring are usually screwed into place with 8-gauge steel countersunk screws 32mm or 38mm long.

Laying sheet flooring

Sheet floor decking can be laid surprisingly quickly—if you have good access to your loft and large clear spaces to work in.

The first job is to cut up the sheets of chipboard or plywood so that they will go through the loft hatch. Aim to have the sheets as large as possible so that you don't make cuts unnecessarily.

All cut edges will have to be supported, either by the joists or (if the cut edges are at right angles to the joists) by noggins: take this into account when you are deciding how to cut the sheets. Tongued and

grooved edges running at right angles to the joists need no extra support, but those running parallel to joists must be positioned above a joist: this arrangement is likely to be somewhat trickier.

While planning the cutting, remember that you will need access panels so that you can easily get at such things as electrical joint boxes and ceiling fittings for the room below, and all water pipes.

Start laying up against a wall or the eaves, if you are decking the whole attic. Preferably place the board lengthways on to the joists. This edge of the sheet will need securing to noggins where it runs at right angles to the joists—use 100mm×50mm sawn softwood, skew-nailed to the joists.

2 *Where a sheet falls across a joist, mark both sides at the centre of the joist, join the marks then cut the sheet*

3 *When fixing a supporting noggin in place, cut it slightly oversize and hammer it down before skew-nailing it*

5 *Both the access panel and the sheets adjacent to it must have plain edges, so remove the tongues and grooves concerned*

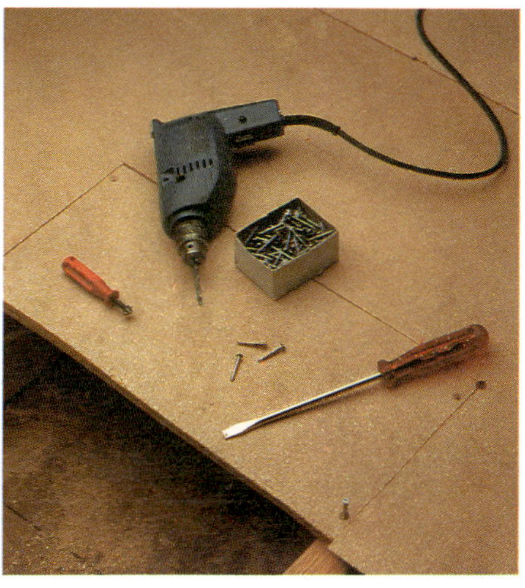

6 *Having drilled and countersunk clearance holes in the access panel, use 32mm steel screws to secure the panel to the joists*

Fixing noggins is a little easier if you cut them slightly too large for the gap between the joists and hammer them into place. Skew-nailing is then less likely to disturb their positioning.

If the sheet has not got cut edges, it can now be nailed in place. Use one nail every 300mm into the joists along the edges of the board; one every 600mm into joists in between. Unless the joists are further apart than the standard 400mm or 600mm, it is not really necessary to nail into the noggins.

Butt the next sheet tightly up to the first, making sure the tongues and grooves interlock properly, and nail as for the first. After you have laid the first row, subsequent sheets should be laid in a 'brick' pattern, so that joints do not coincide.

Whenever you come across a sheet with cut edges, drop it into position first, and mark a line across the joists where the edge falls. Remove the sheet and cut and fit noggins so that they straddle the marked line. Then both the sheet you are laying and the adjacent one will be properly supported.

When you get close to the position of an access panel, remember that all sheets adjacent to it must have plain edges, which may mean removing the tongues and

grooves from some sheets. You can do this with a plane, but an ordinary blade will need frequent sharpening. Add noggins to 'frame' the opening between the joists.

Fix the access panels themselves with countersunk screws at 300mm intervals on all four sides. First, however, drill and countersink clearance holes in the panels at least 20mm from the edges. When you want to remove the trap simply unscrew it.

Laying floorboards

There is little point in doing any pre-planning if you are laying floorboards. Simply haul them into the loft, in long lengths, and nail them down.

Softwood boards, although they are thinner than chipboard sheets, are sturdy enough not to need any noggins. But it is essential that, where you have to join boards

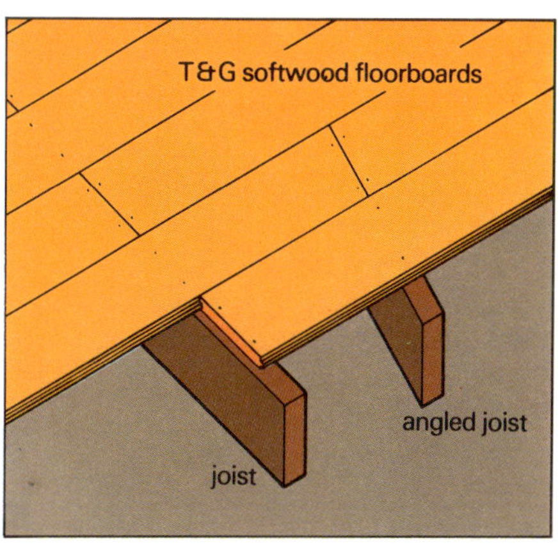

Floorboards must join over a joist. If the joist is, for some reason, angled you must mark and cut the boards at the same angle where they join at the centre of the joist

along their length, these joints fall over a joist so that each board is supported. Most of the boards will probably need to be cut.

Place the first board in position in the loft, and mark on it the centre of the last joist it covers. Cut the board carefully at this point: you may find that the joist does not run at right angles to the board, in which case your cut must run at the same angle too.

Nail this board in position, using two nails, into the centre line of each joist. Nail through the face of the board. Keep the nails 20mm away from the edges of the board.

Subsequent boards should be butted tight up to those already laid, making sure the tongues and grooves interlock properly. To force the boards together, you can use a flooring cramp which is placed over a joist alongside the last board. As you adjust the cramp, it grips the joist tightly and pushes the board tightly against its neighbour.

Alternatively, drive a wide-bladed chisel into the joist right alongside the board, and use this as a lever to force the board against its neighbour. Be careful not to damage the board's tongue when doing this—if necessary, place a narrow offcut of board, which includes a groove, over the tongue before using the chisel.

People rarely bother with access traps in boarded floors—but, especially as you will be using tongued and grooved boards, it will make life easier in the future if you do so. Do this by removing, with a chisel, the lower part of the groove in the length of board forming the trap, and in the section of the adjacent board. (The trap must, of course, start and end over a joist.) Screw the trap down with 30mm or 32mm counter-sunk screws.

Insulation

Most likely, your existing loft will be insulated with material laid between the joists you are about to cover up. There is nothing to stop you leaving the insulation there but the loft will be extremely cold in winter, and any heating in it will be extremely expensive to run. If you are only planning to use the loft in summer, or for storage, this will not matter.

If you do want to use the loft all the year round, it is better to place insulation along the line of the roof rafters. You must be very careful in that you should allow for plenty of

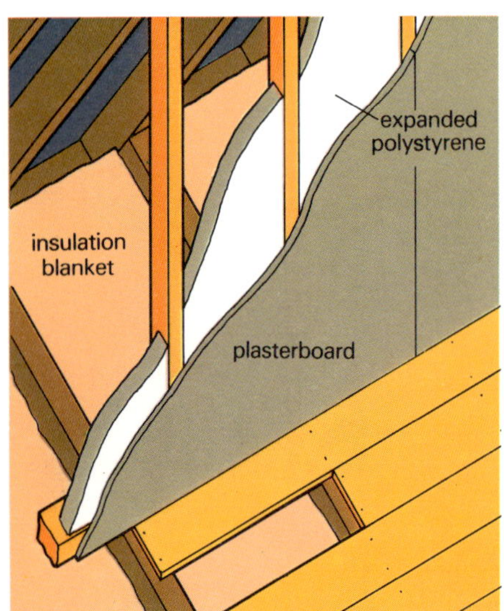

Insulate the eaves area with 100mm thick blanket laid between the joists and expanded polystyrene sheets between the studs of a partition wall

7 *Lay the board in position and mark on it the centre of the last joist that it covers. Then cut the board carefully to length*

9 *Alternatively, if the area being floored is relatively small, you can get by with a broad-bladed chisel. Use this as a lever*

air-flow between the rafters, to prevent any chance of rot starting. You must not simply pack insulation into the gaps between the rafters: instead, use a rigid form of insulation that you can fix to the face of the rafters, leaving a large air-gap between it and the roof covering for ventilation.

In a full-scale loft conversion, the floor is likely to stop short of the eaves at a dwarf stud wall, which rises vertically to meet the rafters. Insulate behind this wall at the floor-joist level, and also insulate the wall itself.

Finishing touches

Provided the joists you have been nailing to are regular in size and present a flat surface, there should be very little finishing off

8 *The boards must be butted up tight before nailing; if you're flooring a large area it's worth hiring a flooring clamp*

10 *To make an access panel in a boarded floor, cut the number of boards then screw two battens to them*

needed. Normally, it is simply a matter of sweeping the surface and cleaning away off-cuts, shavings and so on.

Whatever sort of flooring you then intend to lay, go over the surface carefully to make doubly sure that all nails have been driven well home, and are not standing proud above the surface. Punch in any that are.

Almost any sort of floorcovering can be laid directly on top of a chipboard surface. But, however well you lay a boarded floor, it is unlikely to be flat enough to take vinyl floorings directly: you should cover the boards with sheets of hardboard, laid in a brick pattern, and nail down all over as you would do for laying chipboard sheets from scratch. But, as hardboard is thinner and more flexible, it will be much easier to cut, and less awkward to manoeuvre.

CHAPTER 5

CHIMNEYS AND FIREPLACES

Turn a chimney breast into an attractive feature using brick or stone tiles which look and feel just like the real thing. Or you could reinstate an old fireplace which has been bricked or boarded up for years. And if you've got a fireplace in the wrong place, it is just as easy to seal it up to gain more floor space.

CLAD A CHIMNEY BREAST

which will enhance even the plainest room.

Fixing the cladding is straightforward; you just stick the individual brick or stone tiles onto the chimney breast to imitate a natural finish—it's certainly much easier than exposing the real thing and it will do just as much to enhance your fire surround. With the added benefit of a wide choice of textures, colours and shapes—and your own choice of a pattern to use—there's bound to be something for every room and every taste.

Although you can achieve a similar effect by hacking off all the plaster from the wall, it is a messy and time-consuming job, and there's really no guarantee that the masonry beneath will be worth displaying. Doing the job this way guarantees good looks and solves any problems that might occur at the points where the mantel and surround meets the wall—brick and tile cladding can be fixed directly on top of the plaster surface.

Planning considerations

The only requirement for fixing masonry cladding is a fairly smooth, dry and sound wall, although most types will accommodate slight irregularities.

Strip off any wallcovering and remove the skirting board, picture rail and coving; you may choose to refix these later.

Examine the plasterwork for soundness. Tap the surface with your knuckles and listen for a hollow sound, which could indicate that the plaster has 'blown'—lost its grip with the masonry. In this case, you'd be wise to hack off the loose material back to sound edges, undercut the perimeter of the hole and refill with new plaster—you can buy this in small bags ideal for making minor repairs.

Electrical socket outlets are sometimes fixed on the return wall of a chimney breast, within the alcove; if these are surface-mounted you can easily cut the tiles to fit around them, but if they're flush-mounted you'll have to bring the outlets forward to the finished level of the cladding (see Dealing with socket outlets).

The fire surround shouldn't present too much of a problem, whatever it's made from. As the tiles are only about 15mm thick, they won't encroach on the mantel-shelf unduly, or protrude beyond the sides or side pillars.

Every room needs a focal point to catch the eye and draw together the various decorative elements within it; in many homes it is the fireplace which provides this natural centre of attraction.

Even if the fire's been blocked off in favour of central heating, the chimney breast itself is likely to remain the most prominent structural feature in the room and the most obvious point around which to base a co-ordinated decorative scheme.

You could decorate the chimney breast with paint or a wallcovering to emphasize it as a focal point, but there's a range of textured brick or stone cladding that can help you to create a really spectacular effect

When you're planning the bonding arrangement for the tiles (see below) make sure that a row of whole tiles will coincide with the top of the mantelshelf: don't try to cut them lengthways to run along the top. If there's likely to be a gap at top or bottom that's smaller than a whole tile, conceal the discrepancy with skirting board or coving.

If the fire surround is a rectangular or stepped design, simply cut out the tiles to fit around it. But if it incorporates curves, you'll have to make a template and carefully nibble the tiles to shape using a pair of pincers for the job.

Types of cladding

•**Brick tiles** not only look authentic but also feel real. This is because they're actually genuine brick slips—thin slivers sliced from kiln-produced bricks.

Tiles come in a diverse selection of colours to imitate popular brick types—commonly rich red-browns, pinks, buff and sandy tones, whites, greys and burnt mottled finishes. Textures range from fairly smooth to cracked or heavily ridged faces to mimic bricks both old and new. Some types also have irregular chipped edges like old bricks to add an extra touch of realism.

The tiles are aproximately brick-sized—215mm × 65mm—but are only about 15mm thick. They're sold in boxes typically containing about 30 tiles—enough to cover an area of about 1m × 500mm.

In addition to flat tiles you can also buy angled external corner tiles, which incor-porate a stretcher (long) and a header (short) face. For the same reason, some tiles can even be bent to cope with corners: you just heat the tile with a hair dryer or hot air paint stripper—or dip it in hot water— and then bend it to shape. Check which method is re-commended for the tiles you choose.

•**Stone tiles** are reconstructed from moulds to resemble natural stone blocks and they're actually made from recon-stituted stone. They're either irregularly-shaped for a random effect, or rectangular for a more formal, coursed finish. Various sizes of both types are made, from about 100mm across to about 300mm across. Colour choice is intended to imitate local stone types—with varying degrees of suc-cess—and is typically white, buff or grey, although weathered versions of these are also available.

Bonding patterns

Brick tiles can be laid in a host of different bonding arrangements to give the effect you want. You're not limited by any structural requirements, so you can create a flamboy-ant, dramatic effect that would be impos-sible to build from real bricks—perhaps fix-ing the courses vertically, diagonally or in a parquet design—or just opt for a more con-ventional bond. Remember, complex pat-terns may look striking but they demand a lot of cutting of tiles—which can be wasteful as well as time-consuming, and can create problems at corners. The more dramatic they are, the less realistic they'll look.

Random stone tiles are easier to arrange on the wall: just position them where you want to achieve a pleasing pattern. Aim for a blend of different sizes and shapes for the most realistic-looking effect.

Coursed stone tiles are more suited to a formal, geometric arrangement, but again a good mix of small and large, square and rec-tangular faces gives a more true-to-life finished effect.

It's a good idea to experiment beforehand by laying tiles out on a flat area approxi-mately equivalent to the area of the chimney breast. Rearrange the tiles until you're satisfied, taking corners and obstacles into account, then number the tiles in the order you wish to lay them.

Tools and materials

Fixing brick or stone tiles can be carried out with few tools. You'll need a claw hammer for attaching (and removing) temporary framing battens plus some 25mm masonry nails. Cutting some tiles will be necessary to maintain the bonding pattern at the edges, and this can be done using a club hammer and bolster chisel, or a tile cutter—although some tiles can be cut with a sharp pair of scissors or simply snapped. If you plan to

Bonding arrangements need not be hampered by structural considerations —you can copy common brick bonds or devise your own. With tiles, almost any pattern is possible, though corners need careful planning

Natural weathered brick or stone tiles are available in a range of colours, sizes and textures. The wide choice guarantees endless possibilities for decorating with all the warmth and charm of local materials

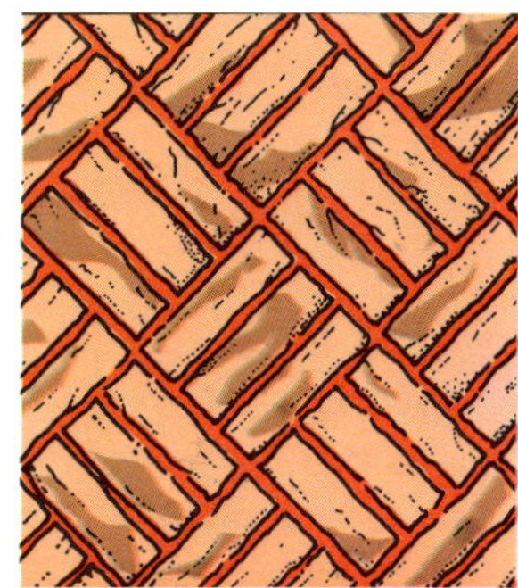

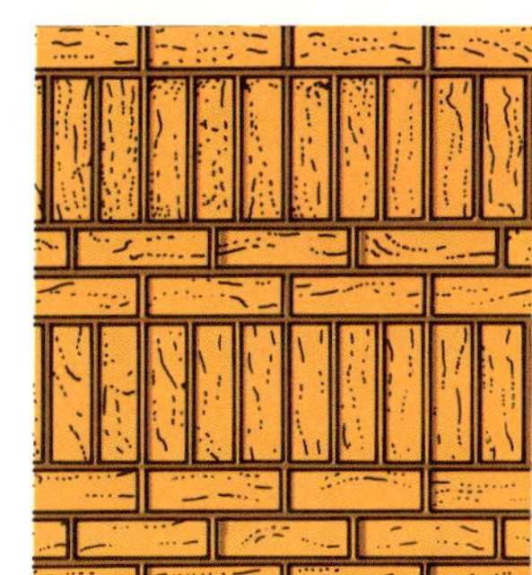

finish off the mortar joints with a decorative profile you'll also need a pointing trowel and some ready-mixed pointing mortar.

In addition to the tiles you'll need to buy sufficient adhesive for fixing them to the wall. This usually comes in 2.5 litre tubs with a notched applicator, although some makers recommend any reputable tiling adhesive for attaching their tiles. You'll need a wide-bladed filling knife for applying adhesive for stone tiles.

Wall preparation may require a number of tools, from stripping knives and chisels to plastering trowels.

Preparing the walls

Imitation brick and stone tiles must be stuck to a clean, sound and dry bare wall. If you're hanging brick faces or coursed stones you'll need to attach temporary battens to the wall as a positioning guide for the cladding, and as a support to help keep it in position while the adhesive sets.

Strip off any wallpaper as far back as the edges of the area you wish to tile. Score through the paper along this border using a trimming knife—strip off to the scored line. You may need to hire a steam stripper if sponging the wallpaper doesn't soften it sufficiently for you to strip it.

You can generally clad on top of painted surfaces as long as the paint is sound. Scrape off the loose parts and lightly abrade the surface as a 'key' for the adhesive.

Wash down the wall with warm water and a little detergent to remove dust and grease, and allow it to dry. Meanwhile, cut lengths of 19mm × 12mm softwood to fit around the chimney breast as a baseline support for the courses of tiles.

Before you fix the battens, measure the wall from the ceiling down to check that a number of whole tiles plus 10mm mortar joints will fit; measure from the top of the mantelshelf to the floor to ensure that a course of whole tiles will run along the top. Position the support battens accordingly.

Drive masonry nails into the battens at

300mm intervals so that they just break through on the other side, then hold each batten in place—with a spirit level on top to ensure it's horizontal. Tap the nails all the way in to secure the battens to the wall.

If the old skirting board is narrow enough, it's easiest to use it as the support batten, then to fix a wider skirting on top.

Irregular-shaped stone faces don't require any support or course battens, but it's important that brick tiles (and stone rectangles) are laid perfectly level to avoid a lopsided effect, so you should mark the course positions on the wall in pencil. Alternatively, set up stringlines tied to nails on vertical battens fixed where the chimney breast meets the wall, and held away by blocks at its external corners. Check that the strings are horizontal with a spirit level. To save having to set up strings for each

1 *Strip off wallpaper back to the bare plaster. Wash the surface to remove dust and grease and allow to dry*

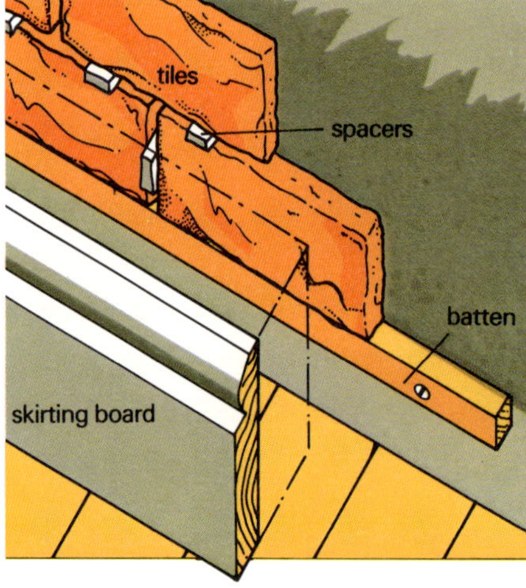

Calculate how many courses you need—remove skirtings to avoid undue cutting and so that you can refix them on top of the tiles later

course, simply move the same string and corner blocks higher after you complete each course.

Stringlines and battens can get in the way when you're cladding a chimney breast with these tiles, so cut a single batten to reach from floor to ceiling and mark it off in increments of brick courses plus mortar joints. Hold it against the rows as you fix them, as a levelling guide.

It's also important to work out where the vertical joints fall—bear in mind that the external corners of the breast must be clad with special corner tiles (or bent tiles) so that any cutting can be done on the less obvious internal corners. Use the tiles—in the pattern of your choice—to mark the positions of the joints of the first few rows. Subsequent rows of tiles will take these as their guide.

Once you've prepared the chimney breast for hanging the tiles, roll back the floorcovering or, if this isn't possible, lay down dust sheets to catch any adhesive or mortar droppings.

Dealing with socket outlets

Surface-mounted sockets can simply be tiled around without you having to reposition them or you can remove them (switch off at the mains first), tile the wall behind, then refix them to the new surface. Flush-mounted types will have to be removed and refixed at the new level.

Turn off the power at the mains—or remove the relevant circuit fuse—then unscrew the socket faceplate and draw it forward. Disconnect the cable cores and set the faceplate aside. Unscrew the mounting box and remove it from the wall.

Cut a piece of 15mm thick chipboard to fit snugly within the recess and drill a hole through which to feed the cable (if necessary). Screw the chipboard into wallplugs set into the masonry.

Cut tiles to fit around the recess, then refix the mounting box within the recess, screwing it to the chipboard fillet. This will set the faceplate forward by the required amount. Feed the cable through the mounting box, making sure it passes through a rubber grommet to prevent chafing, then reconnect the cable cores to the terminal on the back of the faceplate.

Screw the faceplate back on to the box, then restore the power and test the socket.

Attaching brick tiles

Brick tiles are easy to stick to the wall using a thick, mortar-coloured adhesive, which you apply with a notched spreader. First of all you have to prepare and measure the wall, then decide on a bonding pattern.

Unpack the boxes of tiles and lay them near the chimney breast. Clear a space and dry-lay several rows of tiles to experiment with patterns. Mix tiles from different boxes for a more even distribution of colours, as

If you find it difficult to envisage the overall effect of the patterns when the tiles are lying flat on the floor, experiment with various bonds by sticking several rows temporarily to the wall, making use of sticky double-sided foam fixing pads.

batch tones can vary slightly.

The 'joint' spaces between the tiles are set by small 25mm × 20mm pieces of expanded polystyrene, which you cut to size with a trimming knife from a sheet of packing material provided with the tiles. Insert these between the tiles at each corner and vertical joint for a regular spacing.

Starting on one of the chimney breast side walls, spread on adhesive using the notched plastic applicator provided with the adhesive. Cover an easily manageable area of about 1 square metre. Press the first tile onto the adhesive, resting it on the batten. Use a slight wiggling motion to bed the tile into place—make sure it aligns with the vertical joint marks you have made. You may have to cut a tile—using a bolster and hammer—to fit up to the return wall.

Place a polystyrene spacer against the outer edge of the tile, then position the next tile on the batten. Continue in this way to the external corner.

At the corner you can either use a preformed angled corner tile, which you stick on as previously described, or bend a tile to turn the corner.

To bend a tile, first mark on its rear face where you want to bend it, then place it on a

2 *Attach a support batten at the lowest level possible. Apply adhesive to the wall with the notched spreader provided*

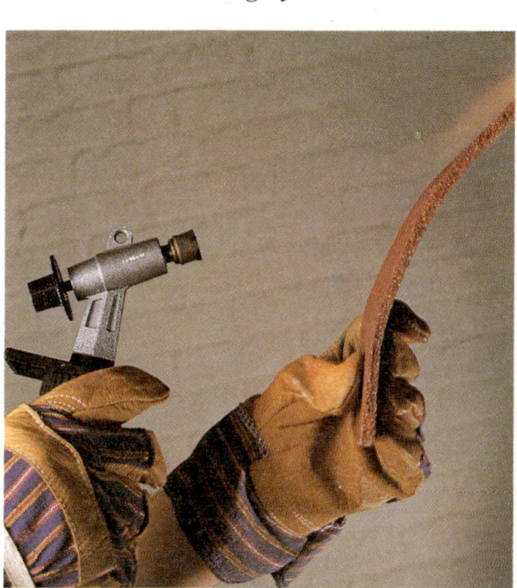

4 *At corners, alternate the long and short faces of the special corner tiles to match the bonding of real brickwork*

3 *Press the tiles into the adhesive and place spacers between each. Check the coursing as you go, especially at corners*

5 *Fit the spacers between the brick tiles throughout to ensure regular vertical and horizontal joint thicknesses*

heat-proof surface (a concrete step, for example). Play the jet of a hot-air paint stripper (or the flame of a blowtorch) over the surface for a few minutes.

Put on some thick gloves, or wrap the tile in thick cloths, then bend it gently into a right angle at your mark. You'll find it easier to bend it around a corner of the wall.

Continue to work up the chimney breast, sticking on tiles with spacers between. Whatever the bond, you'll certainly have to cut some tiles to fit internal corners. Do this using a club hammer and bolster chisel.

First mark the tile by laying it on top of the last whole tile. Place a second dry tile on top, butting up against the wall. Mark the middle tile where the top tile overlaps it. Scribe both faces of the tile using your chisel, then place the tile on a thin bed of sand. Tap the chisel gently on both sides of

6 *Some types of tile can be bent by applying heat from a blowtorch or hot air stripper—useful for some patterns*

the tile until it eventually snaps.

You can also use a conventional tile cutter to cut brick tiles, or a hired tile cutter for thicker ones, though some can be cut with a sharp pair of scissors.

Trimming the tiles to fit round the fire surround can be awkward, especially if the surround is embellished with decorative mouldings, or has complex curves.

Use a profile gauge to judge the shape or make a template from thin paper, by pushing it into the profile of the surround, then cut out the shape. Transfer it to the tile. Score the cutting line with a tile cutter, then nibble away the waste using a pair of pincers. Be careful not to try to break off too large a portion of the tile, or it may snap unevenly and you will not be able to use it.

If the surround is just too fiddly to cut tiles to fit around, fill in the gaps with car body filler. While it's still soft, flick on some dust from ground tiles for an invisible patch.

Fixing stone tiles

Imitation stone tiles are stuck onto the wall in the same way as brick faces, although you can lay them in either a random or coursed pattern. Random tiles are easier to attach, but pointing is more difficult.

If you're using irregularly-shaped stone tiles, you'll have to apply a thin layer of adhesive to the wall to provide a base coat that will conceal the original wall surface and imitate mortar between the stones. Trowel on a thick bed of adhesive using a wide-bladed filling knife and leave to dry for about two hours, or preferably overnight.

To fix the stones, butter the back of each one with a 3mm thick layer of adhesive, applied with the filling knife. Apply a larger amount to the edges of the tile so that it squeezes out and closes any gaps as you attach it to the wall. Trowel dabs of mortar onto the back of the tile, then press it against the wall, starting at the bottom.

Irregularly-shaped stone tiles give you the freedom to place them in whatever pattern you like. For realism, though, avoid grouping together too many small stones; intersperse them with the larger ones and fill in any large gaps with smaller stones or fragments you have cut.

Stones are easy to cut; for a random shape you can simply snap pieces off with your bare hands. If any edges look too harsh, just chip them down until you achieve a more natural-looking shape.

External corners in random stone tiles need special treatment if they are to look authentic. Choose large stones and cut

7 *Spread on a thick bed as a base and allow to dry. This can be the 'pointing' between stones though it's generally too flat*

8 *Butter the back of the tiles with adhesive. Apply it round the edges and in thick dabs in the centre of the tile*

9 *Press the tiles into place in the arrangement of your choice. External corners need a special treatment (see step 4)*

them in half with a coping saw—use one half for one angle and one half for the return. Roughly mitre the inside edges with a planer file for a neat fit, then apply the two sides to the corner. Fill the gaps at the corner with adhesive and disguise them by rubbing stone powder into the adhesive while it is still wet. Use the powder from the mitring process.

Rectangular coursed stone tiles—which have basically flat edges—are available in large block sizes and smaller units, to give a more formal bonding pattern. They're laid in exactly the same way as their irregular counterparts, and can be cut to size with a hacksaw, or snapped along a scored line.

If you're not satisfied with the appearance of the joints—they're often set back too far and appear far more level than the surfaces of the stones—you can always point them in the normal way (see: Pointing the joints). Doing so is likely to be far more difficult than pointing brick tiles because the angles and profiles are more irregular. But if you colour the mortar, it is possible to achieve even more spectacular and authentic results.

Pointing the joints

If you want to give the chimney breast a softer, more decorative finish, you can point the joints. Using a dry mixed pointing compound there are three basic pointing profiles:

•**Weathered joints.** Hold the trowel against a vertical joint and press in about 3mm at the side to form a slight angle. Draw the blade off the edge of the brick to remove excess mortar. Shape the horizontals at the top in the same way.

•**Rounded joints.** Draw a short length of 13mm diameter plastic tube, or a piece of dowel or metal rod, along the vertical and then the horizontal joints to form a gently curved indent.

•**Flush joints.** Rub the surface of the mortar when it's almost dry with a wad of hessian to leave it smooth and level with the faces of the bricks.

To point irregular stonework, it's obviously best to use flush joints shaped to match the profiles of the stone. Much depends on experimentation. Don't overfill the joints—build up the pointing until you're satisfied with the general shape.

It's also a good idea to experiment with a coloured mortar additive to accentuate the variegated tones of the stone faces. Just add the pigment to the mortar mix—experiment with a variety of colours; grey, black, green and yellow are commonly available.

Fires have always been a centre of attraction but, as central heating became more popular, many people blocked off their fireplaces and disposed of the decorative surrounds and mantelpieces. In doing so, they often lost a distinctive visual feature which radiators, efficient though they may be, cannot replace.

Nowadays, real fires are finding favour once more and there are also authentic looking solid fuel-effect gas fires, which offer a 'cleaner' form of direct heating, and which you can install yourself.

If you feel you've been rash in banishing the fireplace from your home's decorative scheme—or you've moved into a house which has suffered this fate—don't despair; reinstating a disused flue and installing a new decorative surround is quite straightforward.

Choosing a fireplace

Whether you search for a discarded original in junk shops, on demolition sites and at house clearances, or buy a brand new or reproduction model from a specialist supplier, you're sure to find a fireplace to suit your style of decor and—equally important—the proportions of your room.

The most basic type consists of a tiled concrete slab, often with a stepped profile, fixed against the wall, complete with a matching hearth. The fireback is usually made out of fireclay and the grate is a separate metal fitting.

Other more decorative fireplaces consist of a timber, marble or metal surround and mantel. These generally have an ornate cast-iron insert incorporating the grate and fireback.

If you opt for the home-made touch, kits are available containing special bricks, blocks or stones, which you can use to construct your own fire surround.

Types of finish vary considerably. Tiled surrounds may be plain or decoratively patterned, timber ones painted or varnished (to enhance the wood grain); metal surrounds are also commonly painted, but may be blacked and burnished.

Cast iron metal inserts were traditionally painted matt black—fireback, grate and all. This type looks particularly elegant when fitted with a surround and mantel featuring mouldings or carvings. You can usually mix and match tiles from the side channels,

and some antique dealers specialize in exchanging (and selling) original fireplace tiles—many of which are quite valuable.

If you want an original cast-iron fireplace and surround, be prepared to have it renovated—it's likely to be fairly rusty after being stored outside in all weathers. Examine it before purchase for missing or badly corroded parts that might affect its looks or performance, and which you might not be able to replace.

Not all fireplaces are the same size: they can measure anything from 300mm across to about 1200mm or more. So it's important that you choose one which will fit in your fireplace recess, and which is not so large that it would completely dominate the room in which it will go.

Measure the overall width of the chimney breast so you can look for a mantel and surround that's not too large or too small. Also, accurately note the height, width and front-to-back dimensions of the recess.

Fireplace formats

Before you start to open up a blocked off fireplace, it's useful to understand how each part fits into place.

Most fireplaces consist of a constructional hearth (**A** in the diagram, overleaf)

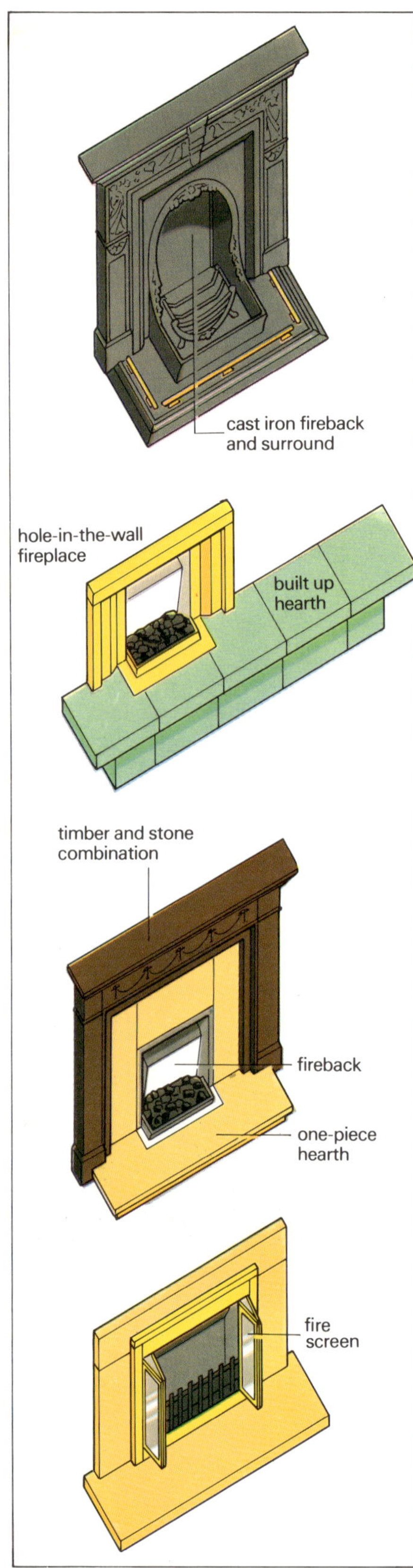

Fireplaces can be bought in all sorts of shapes and sizes and a variety of materials. Apart from looks, the ways in which they are assembled differ too

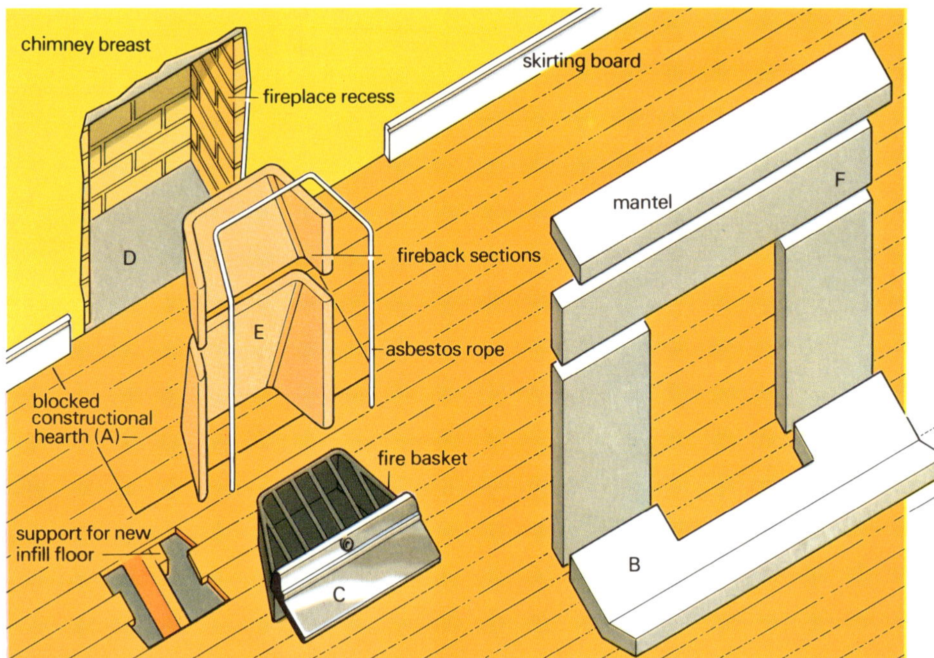

built to a standard size directly on the over-site concrete to prevent the spread of fire. The decorative (or superimposed) hearth (**B**) is set on top of the hearth.

The fire itself—contained in a grate or basket (**C**)—usually sits on a back hearth (**D**) within the recess. An angled fireback (**E**) channels smoke and fumes up the chimney while protecting the masonry of the flue from the heat of the fire. Ventilation needs serious thought—some fires draw air from the room while others are fed from vents built into the fire itself. You may need to reinstate the original ventilation.

The fire surround (**F**) is the decorative part of the fireplace, and usually includes a mantel; the surround may be made of tiled concrete, timber, cast-iron or marble (or an imitation product). It's usually fixed to the chimney breast around the recess with metal lugs and screws, or retained by metal ties; timber types are screwed to a batten framework fixed to the wall.

Some older types of surround include a cast iron insert, which combines grate, fireback and flue throat in one unit.

First steps

To find out how your fireplace was blocked off, tap the wall around the ventilation grille with your knuckles.

Roll back the floorcovering: on a timber floor, the hearth may have been broken up and new floorboards laid to continue the existing run, or the hearth may have been screeded level with the boards. With luck,

Common fireplace formats include integral front hearths—you may have to rebuild the constructional hearth as well as the fireback

the original hearth may be intact. On a solid floor, screed cement may have been used to level off the hearth with the surroundings.

The rest of the structure is more difficult to analyse from the outside. You may be able to remove the vent and peer inside the recess using a torch and mirror but most likely you'll have to break through the infill (see Opening up the recess).

Remove a small portion of the infill at the top of the blocked off opening to check on the condition of the lintel supporting the span: you may find a concrete beam, a metal bar or even a timber lintel has been used, and in some cases the opening will be supported by a brick soldier arch.

Remember, the full weight of the chimney breast for all the floors above will bear down on this point if it's left unsupported. Seek expert advice if you're not sure what to do.

The requirements for recommissioning a fireplace are simply that the flue and chimney breast are in serviceable condition (see Checking the flue) and that adequate ventilation is reinstated for the flue to 'draw'.

In addition to the fireplace, surround and fireback or firebricks you'll need fire cement and asbestos rope (for sealing gaps or bedding down firebricks or backs), gypsum plaster (for making good) and plenty of tough polythene sacks for disposing of the inevitable debris.

Opening up the recess

Start to open up the fireplace recess at a top corner, so you can examine the condition of the lintel or arch supporting the masonry above, plus its side bearers. First of all you have to locate the perimeter of the opening.

Roll back any carpeting from around the chimney breast and spread polythene dust sheets over the floor. Strip off any wall-covering from the area of the fireplace opening and look for a telltale ridge or variation in plaster colour. If you can't readily spot the perimeter, tapping with your knuckles may enlighten you. Score through the wallpaper around the perimeter to avoid tearing it back further than necessary.

Chop into the plaster at one of the top corners, using a club hammer and cold chisel until you reach the brick, block or plasterboard infill. Chop away more plaster to expose about a 600mm section of lintel, then chop down about 300mm to reveal the condition of the lintel bearers.

You should then be able to see how the infill is attached to the sides of the opening. If bricks have been used, and they're toothed into the side walls, seek professional advice before continuing.

So long as the lintel or arch bears down on at least a half brick at each side, you can go ahead and remove the infill. Hack off the rest of the plaster within the perimeter using a bolster chisel and club hammer, then start to chop out the individual bricks or blocks.

If you're certain the structure of the fireplace is sound, you'll find it far easier to chop out the bricks or blocks from the ventilation grill, working outwards.

Where plasterboard has been used, the job's much simpler—just expose the edges of the panel and lever it from its timber frame (set within the opening) using a crowbar. Prise away the timber frame from within the opening, after first checking that it isn't helping to support the bricks and masonry above.

Bag up the debris straight away—but save whole bricks for re-use elsewhere—and dispose of it. Clear any debris from the recess and if the fireback is still in place, examine it for damage. If it's badly deteriorated, or your replacement fireplace has its

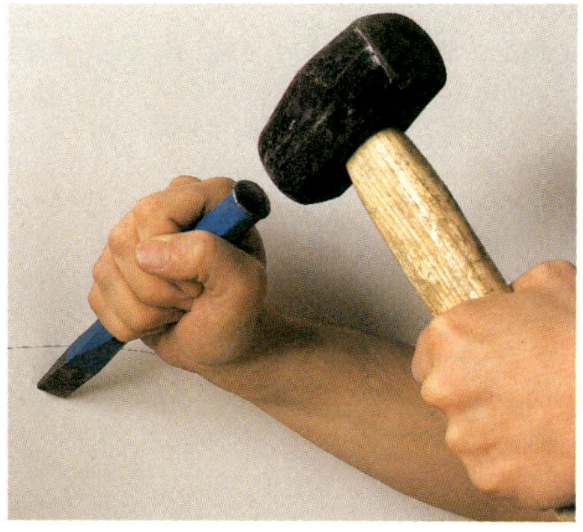

1 Drive a cold chisel into the corner of the new plaster to reveal the type of blocking and the lintel over the opening

2 Fully remove the blocking to reveal the exact size of the fireplace recess. Roll back carpets to expose the hearth

own (sizes do vary), hack it out and lever it away with a crowbar. Clean up the recess.

Examine the flue for suitability (see Checking the flue), then measure up the opening for the new fireplace. The vital statistics you'll need to take include the height of the opening, its width and the front-to-back depth. Also note the overall width of the chimney breast so you can obtain a suitable mantel and matching decorative surround.

Checking the flue

If you intend to install an open fire (or a gas solid fuel-effect type) you must ensure that both the fireplace and flue are sound.

Examine the brickwork around the opening, then peer up the chimney to look for blockages or faults in the masonry. Check the flue lining at the same time—it will probably be a layer of fire cement.

If any airbricks have been let into the

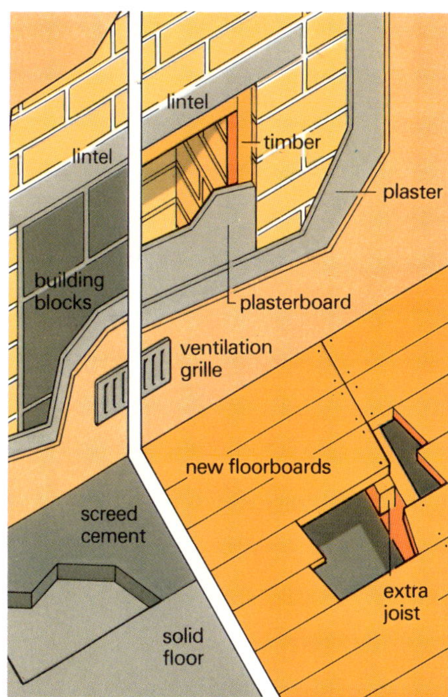

The recess blocking may have been made with plasterboard or with bricks or blocks. Floorboards or screed may cover the hearth

structure of the chimney for ventilation these must be replaced with solid bricks.

Now go outside and look up at the chimney stack. Check that the masonry is in good repair, that it isn't leaning and that the pot is undamaged.

The pot may have been fitted with a metal or ceramic cap, which is intended to

Simply looking up the chimney (armed with a torch) is the best way to examine the structure, but if the flue is too small, use a mirror to reflect the inside of the chimney.

seal off the flue from rain yet keep it ventilated. You'll have to remove this before you can re-use the fire.

In some cases, the pot may have been removed and the stack sealed with a concrete slab, with airbricks fitted around the sides for airflow; the stack may even have been cut down in size to a mere stub when the fireplace was blocked off.

Reinstating the chimney in this case will mean substantial rebuilding of the stack and the fitting of a new pot—not a job to be undertaken lightly or without adequate access to the roof.

Remaking the hearth

How you fit your new decorative hearth depends on the way the original one was removed. It may simply be a matter of cutting back the surface and bedding tiles in mortar—or you may have to rebuild the constructional slab and back hearth.

If the original fireplace had a decorative hearth of tiles set flush with the floorboards, and these are still fixed and in good order, you may be able to retain them.

Sometimes, however, they're set at an angle at the back to fit along the line of the original surround. Your new surround will probably not match this profile exactly, so you may prefer to replace them with new ceramic or quarry tiles.

Break up the tiles and remove them using a bolster chisel and club hammer.

Fireplace tiles commonly measure about 110mm × 52mm, although versions about

3 *Most hearths need rebuilding to provide a fireback at the new hearth level. Remove boards and erect formwork*

50mm square are also available, so you shouldn't have any trouble refitting new ones on the hearth.

Remove all traces of old mortar (or tiling adhesive if this has been used) and clean up the base of the hearth.

Brush out any dust and debris, then wet the concrete surface to improve the adhesion of the mortar and prevent it from drying out too rapidly. Mix up a bucketful of fairly dry ready-mixed bricklaying mortar and spread this on the hearth to a depth of approximately 6mm.

Bed each tile in place, starting at the outer corners and working inwards to fill the hearth. Laying hearth tiles is exactly like laying quarry tiles.

If the original hearth has been cut back so that floorboards could be continued up to the chimney breast, prise these up with a club hammer and bolster chisel and remove the extra joists that will have been fitted to support them.

Clean up the hacked-back surface of the constructional hearth, removing loose debris and dust. You'll need to rig up a timber formwork box to mould and retain a new concrete mix while it sets. Measure the dimensions of the hearth—average size hearths are about 980mm × 360mm—and cut out panels of thin plywood or hardboard.

Wedge the panels between what's left of the slab and the walls surrounding it—nailing them to the timber plate on top if possible. Pin together the corners or fix them with battens so the concrete can't seep out.

Prepare a concrete mix of 1 part cement, 2 parts sharp sand, and 3 parts aggregate so it's stiff but workable. Wet the top of the original slab, then tip in the wet concrete.

Level off the concrete about 50mm below

Grease the framework with release agent or old engine oil in order to prevent the concrete sticking to it.

the finished surface of the hearth to allow for a mortar screed plus tiling. Use a straight-edged length of timber cut to fit between the formwork to compact the mix using a chopping action. Draw the timber across the concrete to smooth it, and check that it's level. Leave the concrete for about 48 hours to set before adding a screed.

Add a mortar mix of 1 part cement to 4 parts sand, and smooth it off level with the floor surface if you're fitting a raised hearth, or bed tiles in the top for a recessed hearth. Take the screed into the fireplace recess itself, if the back hearth is damaged.

If your fireplace includes an integral hearth, like the one shown, there's no need to rebuild the constructional hearth as long as the back hearth is rebuilt to the new height and the gap between the two is sealed with asbestos rope and fire cement.

If you're laying a new back hearth, set a length of asbestos rope (available from builders' merchants) in the mortar, between it and the front decorative hearth. This allows for any expansion caused by the heat (which could crack the surface) and provides a non-combustible barrier.

Rebuilding the fireback

The fireback protects the masonry of the chimney from the intense heat of the fire, channels smoke and fumes up the flue via its angled throat, and throws heat out into the room. Firebacks are either a single unit or separate bricks, which you cement into place. The type you'll need depends on the fire you've chosen.

If you're fitting a tiled slab fire surround, or the type without an integral flue and fireback, you'll probably have to install a completely new fireback. The type you'll need is probably the single unit.

Firebacks are sold in standard widths—commonly 406mm and 457mm, although larger sizes are available. If the original one is still there, measure the inside front open-

4 *Rebuild the old constructional hearth to the level you need to match the fireback and the new hearth—use a stiff concrete mix*

5 *Continue the concrete into the base of the recess. Place asbestos rope between the hearth and the fireback concrete*

6 *With many firebacks, you need to cut the unit into two pieces along a pre-formed line. Use a bolster and hammer to do so*

7 *Use fire cement and asbestos rope to site and level the fireback. Place corrugated card behind—it chars away later and forms a gap*

8 *Trowel a layer of fire cement on to the top of the lower section. Make sure you cover the asbestos rope at the sides with fire cement, too*

9 *Bed the top section on the lower one and continue the rope and fire cement around the joint between the wall and fireback*

10 *Fill the gap behind with hardcore and weak mortar. Build up flaunching at the top to match the shape of the fireback throat*

back—must be sealed with asbestos rope to provide a non-combustible buffer to prevent cracking due to expansion. You may need to test fit the fireback and build out the sides of the recess for a tight fit. Cut the rope to length and tack it in place with masonry nails at the top.

Lift the lower fireback section into place and tap it down evenly on the mortar, using the handle of your club hammer. Check with a spirit level that it's horizontal at the top and vertical within the opening. Pull it forward against the asbestos rope, so it compresses it slightly against the top and sides.

The space behind the fireback—back and sides—must be filled with a weak mortar mix of one part cement to nine parts sand.

Tip in the mix and add some rubble to bulk it out—old bricks or pieces of the damaged original fireback will do. Compact the mix lightly behind the fireback—make

> **★ WATCH POINT ★**
>
> Before you add the mortar, tuck one or two sheets of corrugated cardboard behind the fireback. This chars away later and provides an expansion gap.

sure you don't dislodge the lower section and that it remains flush at the front.

Trowel a 19mm thick layer of fire cement—it's available in tins from builders' merchants—along the top of the lower fireback section, and lift the top section into place, pressed against the asbestos rope attached at the sides and top.

Point in the sides over the rope with fire cement then run a wet paintbrush over it to leave a smooth finish.

Tip more weak mortar mix and rubble into the gap behind the fireback, then build up mortar flaunching over it at the back so that its slope matches that of the fireback's angled throat. Smooth the mortar flaunching with a damp trowel.

Cast-iron fireplaces with integral flue throats usually have firebricks cemented in at the base, around the grate, where the fire sits. Often these bricks—flat or U-shaped—are intact on old fires, but new ones are readily available from builders' merchants and hardware stores. Simply measure the size you need across the front opening, then check it for fit against the fire, before you fit the metal insert in the opening.

Clean up the rim of the opening where the brick fits and trowel new fire cement onto the brick. Press it against the metal rim. Point in the front joint for neatness.

ing to give you the size for the replacement. Otherwise, measure the width of the recess and order the size that corresponds.

Some one-piece firebacks must be split in two along a pre-formed weakness line, then cemented back together again when fitted; this joint allows for expansion to prevent cracking. Make sure you know which sort you're buying. To split the fireback, tap along the break line very gently (it will take quite some time) using a club hammer and bolster chisel, until it splits in two. You'll then have two parts: a bottom section and a top section.

Mix up a little mortar and trowel a 19mm thick screed along the bottom of the recess on which to bed the lower section of the fireback. The top and sides of the opening—between the walls and the fire-

Fitting the surround and mantel

Whether you're installing a tiled slab surround, a brick or stone frontage, or a cast-
iron insert with separate side pillars and
mantel, the procedure is virtually the same:
the components must be held against the
wall with integral lugs. Timber and marble
surrounds are the exception. The former
are sometimes fixed with screws to battens;
the latter need special metal ties to hold
them in place.

To fix a tiled slab surround, measure the
height and width, transfer these dimensions
to the wall and cut back the plaster with a
25mm margin all round, using a club hammer and bolster chisel.

Lift the surround into place and rest it
against the wall. Check that it's central on
the chimney breast, then drill holes through
the integral lugs (usually about 75mm
from the top; sometimes at the bottom) to
take the fixing screws. Secure the surround
to the wall in the appropriate manner.

Set the tiled hearth slab on the constructional slab using a bed of 3:1 sand/cement
mortar, about 20mm thick.

Cast-iron surrounds with separate pillars
and mantel are more complicated. Sometimes the metal inserts have to be bolted to
the wall, and details depend on the exact
type. More usually, the unit simply rests
against the wall without the need to attach it.

When you're measuring up for the metal
insert, the vital statistics are the height and
width of the projecting fireback/flue throat
section: this must fit within the recess easily
so that the insert's flat front panel rests
against the front of the chimney breast.
Check the dimensions before you buy. The
unit usually incorporates a throat closure
plate: make sure there's room to open this.

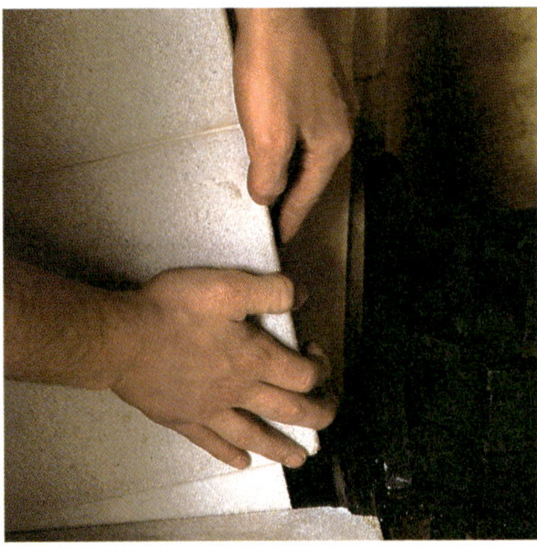

11 *Level or attach the hearth with fire
cement before adding the side
pillars (these are fixed in a number of
ways, shown below)*

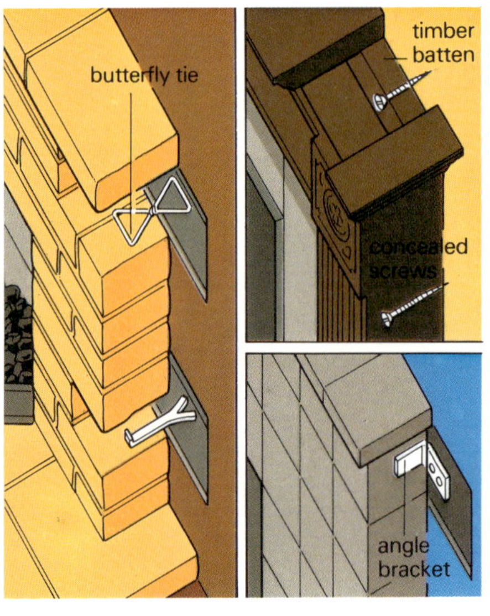

*Fixing methods for pillars may be any of
those shown—make sure the pillars are
vertical and the correct distance apart*

Prepare the fireplace opening for the
insert by hacking back the plaster all round,
then lift it into position.

Types of surround to fit round metal
inserts vary considerably: they may be a

single unit or separate components such as
side pillars, mantel and front cross panel
(which fits under the mantel).

If your surround has integral lugs, simply
offer it up to the wall and mark how much
plaster you'll have to remove around the
perimeter. Chop away the plaster, then
screw the surround to the wall.

Marble surrounds (or those made from
simulated materials) probably won't have
any lugs so you'll have to attach the components with metal ties. You can use wire
butterfly ties, as used in cavity wall construction, or right-angled strips of galvanized metal with screw holes on the up-
standing part of the fixing.

Side pillars usually incorporate a recess at
the top, into which you can mortar the tie.

Prop the pillars upright with long timber
battens, then check them for level and make
sure they are plumb. Adjust the props to set
the pillars vertically.

To use butterfly ties, chop out the mortar
joint between two bricks, level with the
pillar recesses. Slot one wing of the tie into
the joint and rest the other in the pillar
recess. Mix up some mortar and trowel it
into the recess, covering the tie. Fill in the
mortar joint.

Galvanized strips are fixed similarly.
They're screwed to the wall, saving you
from having to rake out the mortar joints.

Fit the cross panel when the mortar holding the pillars has set. The panel rests on a
ledge formed in the side pillars, usually on
small corbels. You don't need to stick these
in place, although you can bed them in a
little fire cement.

Centre the mantel within the width of the
chimney breast and mark the wall to indicate how much plaster you'll have to cut
back so it can fit flush against the masonry.
Remove the mantel, chop out the plaster,
then trowel some fire cement around the
top rim of each pillar. Return the mantel to
the pillars and tap it down gently but firmly.
Scoop off any excess cement that's squeezed
out, then check the shelf for level—across
its width and from front to back. Adjust the
thickness of the cement bed if necessary.

To complete the fireplace—whichever
type of surround you've fitted—make good
the channel around the perimeter with a
one-coat plaster application.

Timber surrounds often require slightly
different treatment: they may be screwed
directly to the wall, the screw heads concealed by mouldings or wood pellets, or
they may include fixing lugs. Alternatively,
you might have to nail timber battening to
the wall first, then screw the surround to
this length of battening.

REMOVING A FIREPLACE

A disused or unsightly fireplace can be an annoying waste of space and spoil the general scheme of your decor by serving as an obsolete centre of attention. Removing the fireplace itself—but leaving the chimney breast intact—leads to a better use of space and also helps to prevent expensive heat loss at the same time.

The job itself isn't difficult but it is messy, disruptive and can involve some heavy lifting. It's best to work with an assistant to remove the bulk of the debris.

The necessary sequence of steps will largely depend on the construction of your fireplace—the materials used, method of fixing, type of fireback, and how the surround is attached to the hearth at the base.

After the job's done, it's a matter of repairing the damage to walls and floors caused by the removal, redecorating and arranging for the chimney pot to be capped.

Planning considerations

Before you begin any detailed planning, examine the fireplace—get the chimney swept first and you'll minimize any mess.

Try to familiarize yourself with how the fireplace is constructed and how it's likely to be fixed to the chimney breast or wall (see diagram on page 101).

Consider what to use for blocking the opening. Lightweight concrete building blocks and mortar are best because they provide comparable stability but if your fireplace is made of brick you can save money by using those you take out (as long as you clean them before re-using them). On the other hand, using plasterboard nailed to a timber framework would allow you to decorate more quickly—although you still need to 'skim' the surface with plaster to disguise the false front.

The removal itself will be messy, so protect furnishings or furniture and remove curtains. Make sure you have dust sheets, plastic sheets or something similar to cover those items you can't take out of the room.

You'll also need a large plastic sheet (heavy duty) to cover the carpet from the point where you fold it back round the hearth area.

Debris: Getting rid of the debris is worth some advance thought. Some of the concrete can be taken out in one piece but much will have to be broken up, so make

sure that you have a supply of heavy duty plastic bags at hand—they're available from builder's merchants. A wheelbarrow is useful for carrying out the bags and smaller debris. Clear a path to the nearest outside door and protect the carpet.

Materials and tools

You only need a few tools; long cold chisel, crowbar or nailbar, club hammer, bolster, screwdriver, hacksaw, plane or planer file, drill and assortment of bits, bricklayer's trowel, plasterer's trowel and spirit level.

Materials will depend on the method you use. For blocking with building blocks or bricks, you need to re-use the old bricks from the fireback or surround or buy new lightweight building blocks. Various sizes of aerated blocks are available but the one most commonly available measures 440mm × 215mm × 100mm. Measure the area to be filled and work out how many you need—you may not be able to do so ac-

curately until you've removed the fire surround. You also need a three-brick high airbrick, a medium size bag of ready mixed bricklaying mortar (about 2kg should be sufficient), browning and finishing plaster (a 50kg bag of each is more than enough though you could use modern one-coat plaster too), steel mesh plastering strips to cover the join between the old and the new, 19mm flat topped galvanized nails and an adjustable ventilator cover to fit on the room side of the fireplace.

For panelling you'll have to measure up and see what size of plasterboard is required. You'll also need 50mm × 25mm battens for a framework, 50mm countersunk screws, wall-plugs, scrim mesh to cover the joins between panel and fireplace, galvanized nails to secure the plasterboard to the frame and finishing plaster only.

Whichever method you use to block the opening, order extra matching skirting board to fill the gap created by the removal of the fireplace—it's easiest to remove the boards from either side and install a completely new run of skirting rather than patching in.

If the floor is solid you'll need extra sand and cement to fill the holes left by the hearth. If it's made of timber, you'll need extra floorboards.

Removing the fireplace

Protect your eyes against flying fragments—wear goggles, gloves and protective clothing. First clear a space and protect furnishings against dust and damage. Provide a clear route to the outside. Work in the order surround, fireback, hearth.

Begin by removing any skirting boards on either side of the fireplace—gently lever off with a bolster or claw hammer to avoid damage to the surrounding plasterwork. How you remove the rest of the surround depends upon how it's constructed and fixed to the wall (see diagrams opposite).

Tiles on a concrete slab: Metal lugs with securing screws are usually located about 75mm from the top of the surround on either side of the fireplace. To release the fixings some damage to the surrounding plaster is inevitable. Minimize it by cutting into the plaster with a bolster and hammer all the way round appoximately 25mm from the edge of the surround. Chunks of plaster will then be less likely to fall off later or as you prise away the surround—this can happen if you remove plaster from around the fixings only.

Different fixing methods

When you have exposed the fixings, remove the screws. If they are tight—and penetrating oil doesn't do the trick—try inserting the blade of an old screwdriver into the screw slot and tap firmly—the vibration may dislodge the screw's hold. If not, drill out the screw head with a high speed steel (HSS) drill bit of the appropriate size.

If you find nails securing the fixings instead of screws, prise them out. The end of a crowbar may come in useful here—a sharp blow with a bolster and hammer will probably be needed to start the nail off.

With the screws or nails removed, the surround will be ready to come out. In general, surrounds come out in one piece so get an assistant to take the weight.

What you find when the surround comes away depends on the age and quality of the original installation. You may be deluged by dust and rubble from the bricks that supported the fireback or you may find this brickwork intact—the latter is more convenient but have sacks handy anyway.

Place a crowbar between the surround and the wall and lever gently. Prise at a number of points to loosen the whole surround at once—it should release itself fairly easily. Make sure you have an assistant to take the weight as it moves away from the wall. Then lower the surround gently to the ground until you are ready to dispose of it.

If the surround won't come away in one piece, break it up with a cold chisel and club hammer. Cut through any reinforcing bars with a hacksaw and put the debris into bags or straight into your wheelbarrow.

Cast iron fireplaces: Fixings for these types are likely to be lugs and screws buried behind the plaster at the edges—perhaps four instead of two. If there is a separate section of cast iron framing the opening, you'll have to loosen the nuts and bolts securing it or cut through them with a hacksaw. Move the surround in one piece if you can. Remember that attractive fire surrounds may well have considerable second-hand value. Check locally to see if there is an architectural salvage merchant in your area—they might be interested in your surround.

Timber surround fireplaces: Any separate mantle section must be loosened with a club hammer and lifted out first—it may be plastered into the wall or just fixed to the top of the surround. The main surround will be screwed to battens—the screws may be countersunk and filled or plugged with wood. Tap the surface until

1 *Prise away the skirting board carefully from both sides. You'll fit a new section later*

2 *Chip off plaster to expose lugs. Unscrew these or drill out the screws if rusted in*

3 *Prise away the surround—take care as it is heavy and may move surprisingly easily*

4 *Remove the fireback. One-piece backs may need breaking up to get them out. Built-up backs come apart easily*

Built-up surrounds have lugs mortared into the wall. Dismantle bit-by-bit.
Tiled or iron surrounds have lugs at the side buried in plaster and fixed with screws.
Timber surrounds may be screwed directly to the wall or fixed with side lugs

you hear a change of sound, scrape off the filler and undo the screws. Lift the surround away from the wall.

If you can't find the screws it may be that the surround is fixed to side lugs similar to those already described, so remove them in the same way. But if neither of these fixings seem obvious, use a crowbar to level the surround away. You may need to chip off any tiled inner sections to reveal any concealed fixings on the inside.

Brick or stone fireplaces: Dismantle this type bit by bit and clean the bricks if you intend to re-use them. Start by forcing the bolster into the top course of mortar. Tap free each brick in turn and take it out. Continue working downwards. If you come across metal ties between brick and wall, release them by knocking out the mortar and working the ties loose by pushing them backwards and forwards until they pull free.

Just above the fire opening, you may find a steel plate acting as a lintel for the material of the surround itself (don't confuse it with the lintel for the chimney breast which you **must** leave in place). Take out the surround's lintel, then continue work.

Removing the fireback

The fireback is the portion of the fireplace behind the opening—it contains fire-resistant material to support the fuel and reflect heat. It's wise to remove the fireback so that you can provide the necessary space for blocking the opening.

There are different types of fireback (depending on the age of the fireplace and the builder) so the dismantling process will vary slightly from one case to another.
Fireproof clay shell: This is in one piece and you will have to chip away at the mortar holding it to pull it away from the chimney breast. It may not pull out easily so your only alternative is to break it into sections and remove it in pieces.

Once it's out there will be rubble, infill and soot, so carefully clean this out.
Firebrick backs: Some fireplaces—even fairly modern ones—have a construction of individual firebricks rather than a one piece shell. Start chipping away from a cold chisel and club hammer or a small crowbar until you get all the bricks out. Once you manage to break up the first two bricks you should be able to lever away the others without too much difficulty. Clear away the rubble in the same way.
Solid steel castings: These are to be found in older fireplaces (especially cast iron ones) and are in three pieces—back wall, sides and surround. Prise each part away from the

chimney breast. If one won't move try another—they may be interdependent. If they still won't move, search around for fixings and remove them before continuing—use one of the variety of methods suggested earlier.

Back boilers

A living room or kitchen fireplace may have a back boiler built into it (see diagram).

If you block up the fireplace, the boiler must be removed otherwise there's a risk of water in it freezing in cold weather and causing bursts and leaks that will be almost impossible to repair.

Don't be tempted to leave the feed pipes connected to the hot water cylinder by cutting them at the boiler end and blanking them off—you must disconnect them at the cylinder end to prevent all possibility of potential leaks and bursts.
Boiler removal: The boiler is linked to the hot water cylinder by two pipes—the flow and return pipes. You must drain the

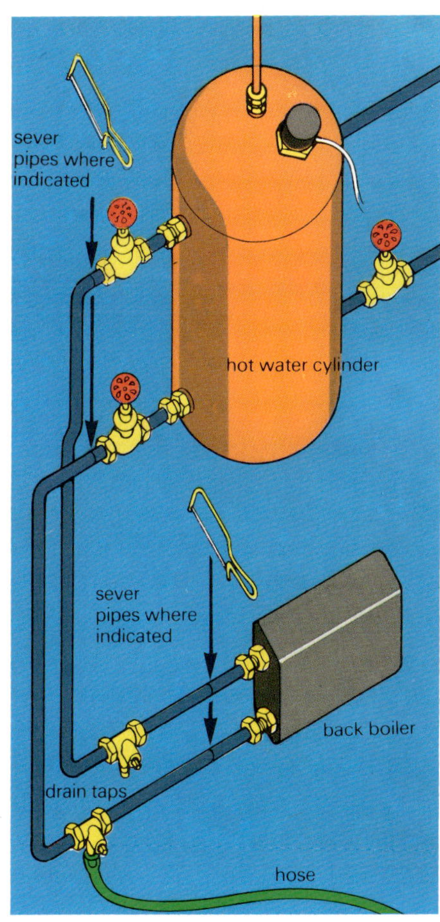

If there's a back boiler, turn off the supply and drain the pipes. Then cut the pipes at boiler and cylinder and cap off

system to remove the water then cut the pipes at the cylinder end and blank them off.

First empty the hot water system—turn off the mains water stop tap and open all the basin and bath taps to drain the water and allow air in. The boiler drain taps are generally in the wall next to the fire surround—attach hoses to these, run them outside and then open the taps.

When the system is empty, disconnect the feed pipes from cylinder to boiler at the point where they leave the cylinder. Joints may be compression joints or capillary joints. In either case, use a hacksaw to cut through the pipes about 50mm from the joint. Blank off the pipe ends from the cylinder with compression-type pipe blank caps of a matching size—use PTFE tape for a fully watertight fit. Refill the hot water system by turning on the mains stop tap and adjusting the basin and bath taps to give only a steady trickle. When the trickle is fluent and has stopped spluttering, turn the taps on and allow the system to fill up. Check the pipe blanking caps for leaks.

Remove any firebricks around the boiler and lift out. You don't need to remove the feed pipes from the wall—as long as they are empty. Remove any boiler accessories—like the flue—at the same time.

5 *Lever up the hearth. On wooden floors there's a concrete or brick shelf beneath the mortar bedding of the hearth itself*

leave the base alone. Fill any holes or cracks in the mortar with a 3:1 mix of sand and cement to the level of the surrounding floor. Add a little waterproofing agent to the screed to prevent damp penetration from below. Finish off with a steel float.

Blocking the opening

You can close the opening left by the removal of the fireplace with building blocks or with plasterboard—but before you do so you must arrange for enough ventilation inside the chimney.

Adequate ventilation is important if you are to avoid condensation and stale air—both of which can cause external staining and expensive rot.

There is a further consideration, too. At some stage—preferably when you're working on the roof—you should either remove the redundant chimney pot and block off the stack so that water won't seep downwards, or simply cap the pot. In neither case should you seal the chimney breast totally—some air must be allowed to circulate freely.

With or without this measure, the free flow of air may cause an uncomfortable draught and a corresponding heat loss. You must decide at this stage—before you block the chimney—whether you can make a compromise between the vital ventilation and the possible discomfort of the heat loss. The ideal situation is to install an adjustable ventilator grille at the fireplace and to allow controllable ventilation inside the chimney. Block the opening with your ventilator

Levelling the hearth

On a solid floor, the hearth itself is bedded with a thin layer of mortar—you need to remove it to make the floor level with the rest of the room. On timber floors there may be something different—the hearth may sit on a 'shelf' of concrete projecting from the chimney breast or on a brickwork projection.

You should be able to lift out the concrete bedding in one piece. Drive a cold chisel under the hearth and break the bond. When a good size gap has opened, push in your crowbar and lever the whole thing away from the floor. You'll need help to lift the hearth out.

If the hearth is recessed and has a layer of tiles flush with the floor, all you need do is take them off with a hammer and chisel and

Fill solid floors with concrete. Fill the opening with lightweight blocks or panel in with plasterboard—always include a vent. Fill a wood floor with extra boards

grille in mind—place an airbrick in the blockwork as you proceed.

Aerated blocks: Measure the opening to find how many blocks you need to use— you'll probably need to cut at least one. Spread a 10mm layer of ready mixed brick-laying mortar across the opening. Insert a layer of heavy duty polythene as a damp proof course, then spread a further layer of mortar on top. Start building up your block-work, remembering that approximately 100mm from the bottom you must install an airbrick—later to be covered with the ventilator grille.

Mark and cut a block at the appropriate place to accept the larger sort of airbrick (three bricks in height). Use a bolster and hammer or a masonry saw to cut the block.

As you add subsequent courses, check that blocks or bricks are aligned by holding a straightedge or a spirit level against the face of the blockwork.

When the work is complete, make a final check with your straightedge or spirit level that the blocks are flush and then leave the mortar to dry.

Plasterboard and framework: Measure the perimeter of the opening and cut 50mm × 25mm battens to make a simple frame. Fix in the battens, recessing them to take account of the thickness of the board—the frame must be set back from the face of the wall so that the plasterboard finishes flush. Use 50mm No. 8 screws and wallplugs. Cut the plasterboard to fit the opening then cut a hole 100mm from the bottom of the board to accept the ventilator grille—use the grille itself to mark the size of cut. Drill holes at the corners of your marked area and insert a padsaw to join them and remove the waste. Screw or nail the board to the frame.

simpler to use but it is more expensive.

In the case of block or brickwork, you can plaster 12 hours after the mortar is dry. First clean up the brickwork around the opening. Before you begin plastering, spray some water over the surface with a plant spray container or brush on some water.

Traditional plaster: Rake out the mortar between the new brick or blockwork to a depth of about 10mm to ensure a good key. Apply a first coat of plaster (browning) with a plastering trowel—don't cover the ventilation area. Next apply a skim of finishing plaster, making quite sure the new plaster is flush with the existing wall.

When the plaster is thoroughly dry, fit a ventilation grille over the airbrick.

For plasterboard, either use jointing tape and compound or 'skim' the surface with a thin layer of finishing plaster.

DIY one coat plaster: For a small job like this, you can use a ready mixed plaster such as Polyplasta, in place of both kinds of traditional plaster and for laying the blocks. It takes four hours to set, so there is plenty of time to get a really smooth finish for decorating right away. If in any doubt about the finish, try bringing the first coat of plaster

Use a ready-mix bag of fine mortar, or make your own with one part of cement to three parts of sharp concreting sand.

Trowel the mix onto the base and work it roughly into position. Use the surround to give you the level by working a straightedge across from side to side with a sawing action. After establishing a level, finish off with a wood or metal float.

The important thing to avoid is over-trowelling. This brings the cement to the surface which will tend to be dusty and crumbly as a result. After a few hours, the water will have risen to the surface by itself. This is the moment for a few finishing strokes with the float. If the weather is hot or the house is well heated, cover the screed with polythene or wet sacking for twenty-four hours to cure properly. A final coat of dilute PVA will reduce the tendency to dust even further.

After about 24 hours (less for ready-mixed plaster) you should be able to replace skirting boards and other fixed woodwork but a fully plastered wall will take a considerable time to dry out enough to decorate. In the meantime, apply a coat of emulsion paint.

6 *Arrange a layer of polythene over the first course to act as a DPC*

7 *Position the airbrick flush with the surrounding plaster—not the blockwork*

8 *To improve the adhesion of the plaster, rake out the mortar joints*

9 *Bring the browning coat of plaster close up to the final level. Skim when hard*

Cover the join of the frame and existing wall with fibre scrim if you intend to finish with a thin skim of finishing plaster. If you don't want to finish in this way, screw a timber moulding through the board and into the frame battens behind. Tidy up by restoring the surrounding plaster.

Finishing off

When finishing off, you have a choice of plasters. You can either mix your own or buy a DIY one coat type—available ready-mixed in various sizes of tub. The latter is

up almost to level, and then putting on either a final coat of ready-mixed skimming plaster, or a thin coat of the general purpose variety that you can work until you have a smooth finish.

Screeding a hearth: The final work is screeding over the hearth to bring it up to level, if you are not going to sand the floor.

Clean off all dust and rubble from the surface of the concrete underfloor and remove all loose material. Damp down with plenty of water and prime the surface with some PVA adhesive.

In either case, add some more PVA to the mix that you prepare for the screeding.

Timber floors: If your floor is stripped and sanded you'll want to match the exposed hearth area to the surrounding floor. Break up the concrete base, take it up and remove any rubble and infill underneath. Fix a new joist close to the wall between the joists on either side; this will enable you to nail a batten to the existing joists and nail the new joist to the battens.

Cut back the existing floorboards to the nearest joists and nail a 100mm × 50mm timber to the existing joists to support the ends of the new floorboards. Trim them to size and fit. Treat the new timbers with preservative.

INDEX